Mass Affluence

Mass Affluence

Seven New Rules

of Marketing to

Today's Consumer

PAUL NUNES

BRIAN JOHNSON

Harvard Business School Press

Boston, Massachusetts

Library of Congress Cataloging-in-Publication Data

Nunes, Paul, 1963–
    Mass affluence: seven new rules of marketing to today's consumer / Paul Nunes,
Brian Johnson.
        p.   cm.
    Includes index.
    ISBN 1-59139-196-2
    1. Marketing—United States. 2. Affluent consumers—United States.
3. Consumers—United States. 4. Consumer behavior—United States. 5. Product
management—United States. 6. Consumer satisfaction—United States. I. Johnson,
Brian, 1960– II. Title.
    HF5415.1.N86   2004
    658.8—dc22

                                                                        2004002471

The paper used in this publication meets the minimum requirements of the American
National Standard for Information Sciences—Permanence of Paper for Printed Library
Materials, ANSI Z39.48-1992.

To Joan, Jonathan, Charlotte, and Michael

To Joni, Becky, Adam, and Bruce

Contents

Preface and Acknowledgments

For years now, marketers have been infatuated with notions of relationship marketing. It seems that every store, every manufacturer, and even every casino today offers its customers the chance to be recognized personally through the use of a loyalty card or another affinity program. And most marketing mail now comes written in terms so familiar it might as well be a letter from a personal friend.

Some of this rush to communicate with individual customers has happened because marketers have heard the siren song of technology, promising them enormous benefits from infinite segmentation. As a result, they worship one-to-one marketing as its ne plus ultra. And there's no doubt that at least a few companies have increased their profitability dramatically as a result of their efforts along those lines.

But many marketers are starting to recognize that embracing microsegmentation strategies without reservation can lead to trouble. The costs of acquiring data and creating knowledge on individual customers, for example, often swamp the financial benefits to companies. And many times, targeted customers simply don't have more to give (in terms of increased spending and margin), even when companies do know their needs and desires perfectly. On top of that, microsegmentation can give marketers a sort of customer-focus myopia, causing them to lose of sight of big-picture trends and market-level opportunities.

So it is no surprise that a growing number of marketers are eagerly awaiting the pendulum's swing back to mass-marketing approaches.

They look forward to the simplicity that comes from making media buys that blanket every possible consumer. They anticipate the clarity of mind and purpose that comes from defining new products for broad swathes of customers—products based on engineering excellence, designer creativity, and brand management's confidence and experience, not the tyranny of the wants of individual customer kings.[1]

The problem is, yesterday's rules of mass marketing are not the promise of success they once were. Many companies that currently sell to the mass market are falling short of their potential. This is true even if they are profitable and can claim that their organizations are stable. Why? Because the mass market that so many companies sell to is not what most marketers think it is. It has nuances that most marketers are missing (who can blame them; they're in the thick of things). In fact, the very term *mass market* is founded on an outdated theory of wealth distribution. Born of the industrial revolution, the mass market saw its real growth spurt in the United States in the postwar 1950s—in the intersection of mass communication, mass transportation (thanks in part to the new interstate highway system), and the pent-up mass savings of a fully employed work force deprived of spending by war rationing. Today, however, the term *mass market* is misleading. When marketers plan strategy, the old mass market that many of them have in mind no longer exists and is therefore no longer relevant. What's more, the terms that have been used, loosely, to describe how that market has moved and morphed since the 1950s are, at best, imprecise and, more often than not, genuinely misleading. To a company attempting to position and price its offerings, that kind of fuzziness is dangerous.

Consider *mass affluence*—the core subject of this book. The term has been bandied about in marketing and economic circles at least since 1958, when John Kenneth Galbraith published his seminal work, *The Affluent Society*. In recent years, the term has often been used, narrowly, as a synonym for those who found wealth in the late 1990s boom era. But does it have a single definition that everyone understands? No. And more importantly, do marketers—even marketing colleagues in the same company—agree on what it means and share a common understanding of the term when they're planning strategy? More often than not, the answer is, again, no. In fact, for all the discussion of the phenomenon and all the attention that the term *mass affluence* has received, we have been unable to find a single doctrine of marketing advice that serves business executives looking to understand how this broad-based increase in wealth has and should inform marketing decisions. As a research and literary theme, mass affluence has been given its due from journalists, with a continuous progression of popular books like *Bobos in Paradise, Luxury Fever, Living It Up: Our Love Affair with Luxury,* and *Affluenza.* Further back, we had *The Millionaire Next Door,* which was preceded in the early 1980s by *The Preppy Handbook,* among others. The list could go on.

The topic has also been well considered from a sociopolitical perspective, with modern writers like Pierre Bourdieu in *La Distinction,* and Kevin Phillips in *Wealth and Democracy.* Before them, there was Galbraith, as we mentioned, explaining in the 1950s America's need to keep up with the Joneses. And Thorstein Veblen gave us conspicuous consumption long before there were Yuppies, in his *Theory of the Leisure Class,* first published in 1899. But we are unaware of any book that has isolated and studied mass affluence from a *marketing strategy* perspective, specifically, how this new affluence affects marketing strategy fundamentals.

Marketers struggle today to understand how marketing, and in particular mass marketing, has changed because of mass affluence. And while there has always been a market for luxury goods, and the rich have always been the core customer segment for targeted, microsegmented services, the topic of successfully selling to the affluent en masse has not been well explored.

Put simply, the elite rich niche is still there. But increasingly, there is another broad market level just below that elite segment but well above the radar of most mass marketers.

What's needed is an approach that considers the facts about mass affluence and delivers a comprehensive view of how companies can change their marketing strategies to capture the value created from greater consumer affluence. That is why we wrote this book; that's what we're attempting to provide.

We see executives seeking to take greater advantage of the mass-affluence phenomena—the increasingly deeper but not bottomless pockets of the market in general—but uncertain as to whether there really are any new principles to apply. We believe there are. The affluent marketplace poses significant challenges, with consumers more empowered, discerning, and, sometimes, just unwilling to spend what they are truly capable of spending. But it is also a marketplace of great opportunity, born of ever increasing discretionary spending capability.

A few progressive companies have nailed these new strategies; we'll reveal the ways in which they're aligning their marketing game plans with the new realities of U.S. income distribution. More companies have not, and we'll suggest approaches that can be tailored to fit various organizations' needs.

This book is primarily for marketers in companies that have served the mass market for a long time and are now hoping for new approaches to doing so better, by accelerating growth and boosting profitability. We ask the fundamental question that established companies must face: "Have my offerings grown, both in price and value, commensurate with the growth in wealth of the marketplace?" The strategies we outline are intended to provide guidance to those for whom the answer is no.

We write also for intra- and entrepreneurs looking for ways to enter the market with high-end or otherwise expensive offerings that may start as niche offerings, but who are expecting those offerings to achieve their full potential when they one day serve a mass market. Product developers charged with spearheading top-line growth, we expect, will also find our work useful, because we define new approaches to gaining customers and increasing not just share of wallet (the amount of consumer spending in a category) but share of pay stub (the amount a consumer could or should be spending in a category).

It is our fervent hope, of course, that all executives who have seen mass affluence arise in their markets and have struggled with what it could mean for their business will find inspiration and form innovative ideas in these pages about how to improve their business performance.

About the Research

In our experience as consultants, researchers, teachers, and authors, we are no strangers to the quest to better understand customers and their behavior. Paul has led research in marketing strategy for Accenture since 1997, as an executive research fellow and director of research in the Accenture Institute for High Performance Business, where he has also worked closely with the company's consulting practice. His interest in marketing strategy flourished in his days as a graduate student at the Kellogg Graduate School of Management, and continued throughout his years as director of research for Accenture's Technology Assessment Group. It became clear in assessing the future of emerging technologies such as the Internet in the 1990s, that many of them would have a decisive impact on all aspects of marketing. In addition to helping drive Accenture's practice, Paul's research has been published and featured in a wide range of popular publications and academic journals.

Brian's former role as global managing partner for Accenture's marketing strategy practice led him to a deep understanding of how the goals and processes of marketing are changing. In 2003, Brian moved to Wall Street, where he is applying his marketing insights as the senior research analyst covering the U.S. automotive sector for Sanford C. Bernstein. Brian has also taught customer relationship management strategy as an adjunct professor of marketing at the Kellogg School of Management.

Though we have both been immersed in customer management and marketing strategy issues since the early 1990s, the turning point in our consideration of mass-affluence issues came after one of us took a simple trip to a baseball game with a few colleagues. None of us was a regular attendee, so we bought the best box seats available, using the opportunity to splurge a bit. We expected to find ourselves seated with corporate types and dot-com millionaires (it was the height of the Internet boom at the time) or at least in the middle of a crowd that was clearly well heeled. We were surprised to discover instead that the seats were filled mostly with average sports fans, many with children, and most of these fans were there as if spending two or three hundred dollars to see a baseball game were the most normal thing in the world.

We might have thought it a curious anomaly (theater and ballpark seats have always been sold at differentiated prices), but later, in speaking with John Harrington, the former owner and CEO of the Red Sox, we learned that this middle-class occupation of box seats was to be expected. The vast majority of the franchise's customers, he told us, were regularly requesting the most expensive seats available, settling for the cheaper seats only when no others were available. And not just to see the best teams.

This piqued our curiosity because we had also seen attempts to differentiate one-size-fits-all offerings at places like amusement parks and ski slopes, and we had seen no end to the building of premium seating facilities at sports arenas in our respective cities. This change was fundamentally different to us than the rise of new luxury brands, like Lexus automobiles. It was an invasion of wealth into areas that were once relatively sacred bastions of customer equality. In seeking to understand what would drive such a change and what it could mean for society, we researched the topic and wrote the *Harvard Business Review* case "Are Some Customers More Equal Than Others?"

This case seemed to strike a chord in managers and executives, creating some of the best and most heated discussions we have had in recent years on the purposes and goals of marketing strategy. It spurred us to delve more deeply into customer income and spending. We extensively analyzed the publicly available data on household and individual income and expenditure, including data from the U.S. Census Bureau, Internal Revenue Service, and Bureau of Labor Statistics (whose Consumer Expenditure Survey is the most comprehensive annual survey of household consumer spending we found). While conducting this research, we discovered that household spending was not keeping pace with its income growth for households whose incomes were growing the most. A few of the findings from this research were published in a June 2002 *Harvard Business Review* article, "Target the Almost Rich." Many more of the research findings are highlighted in this book.

While conducting this research, we also began to form an understanding of how income demographics affect business strategy. It wasn't enough simply to know that spending was not keeping up with income growth; it was important to us to know why. In September 2002, we conducted the Accenture Consumer Attitudes Toward Innovation Survey, the results of which we have presented throughout the book. More than 3,500 consumers participated, across the United States and Europe (France, Germany, Spain, and the United Kingdom).

The survey was multiple-choice and was conducted online, with the assistance of a global survey company. The study used weighting to correct for known biases from online surveying. For the purposes of the survey, *innovation* was defined for respondents as "entirely new products and services, or substantial improvements to products and services, which make them more valuable to consumers." We learned a great deal from this survey about what consumers do, and do not, value in innovation. We also learned how consumer attitudes about recent and expected future innovation in market offerings often, but not always, vary by income level.

In forming our views on how mass affluence is driving a sea change in marketing, we have also drawn extensively on our own experiences and those of our colleagues, in working with clients. As we advise these clients, we also learn from them what works best in serving a wide range of disposable incomes in today's consumer environment. These experiences were supplemented by countless hours of secondary research, conducted across literally hundreds of sources, from academic journals to books to the popular press. But no research is complete without in-person discussions with those who are leading the way, so we again express our deep appreciation to the executives we interviewed for this book. Their stories, as you will see, are the real story of this book.

Acknowledgments

It has been in writing this book that we discovered the real meaning of affluence: the fortune of having treasured friends and associates willing to give so much of their time and energy to help make our project successful. We owe a great deal to many, and it is more than can be expressed in a few short pages. We thank everyone involved for making us so truly rich.

Our immediate thanks go to the executives, both named and unnamed in this book, who gave so generously of their time in discussing these ideas with us and who gave us the insights we are privileged to share with our readers. We give very special thanks to Julia Kirby, the wonderful instigator of this adventure and its constant muse, and to Melinda Merino, our editor at HBS Press, for her infinite patience, confidence and guidance. Joseph Sawyer and Vikram Mahidar, our research team, were invaluable, working tirelessly to create not only this book, but the three others that were eventually edited out (sorry, guys); we could not have done it without them. We thank H. James Wilson, more collaborator than editor, without whom we would never have arrived, and Regina Maruca, who brilliantly helped us with our prose.

We wish to thank the fellows of Accenture's Institute for High Performance: Bob Thomas, Jane Linder, Jeanne Harris, Jeff Brooks, Meredith Vey, and especially Susan Cantrell for her generous contribution in reading early drafts of the book. We give special thanks to Tom Davenport, who has provided more inspiration and guidance than he can know, and to Ajit Kambil for his years of support and friendship.

It gives us great pleasure to thank all of our colleagues at Accenture, whose constant support and extensive experience serving clients made this book at all possible, especially Mike May, Global Managing Partner—Strategy, for his continuous sponsorship of this effort, Tim Breene, Chief Strategy Officer, for his steadfast backing and encouragement, and Bill Copacino, Group Chief Executive—Business Consulting, for his generous gift of time in discussing aspects of the book and for his support. We also are grateful to John Staton, Jeffrey Merrihue, Stephen Dull, and Susan Gurewitsch for their exceptional contributions.

Certainly, no research on affluence can be accomplished without engaging affluent people in long discussions about matters related to affluence. For this we enlisted some of our dearest friends and colleagues, Kris Mastronardi, Vikas Krishan, Steve Schultz, Eric Clemons, Bill Lenihan, Michael Cavanaugh and Gong Li, Jim and Lucy Hospodarsky, Elan Bair, Laurent Petizon, Trevor and Cecelia Mundt, Robert Harper, Bill Jacobs, and Adam Sciortino. We thank them for their keen insights, and some for their exemplary mass affluent lifestyles as well. We could hardly avoid discussing the topic at the holiday dinner table, either, so for their time and patience in listening to our stories, and for the stories of their own they so generously shared, we thank Wendy Heimann-Nunes, Julie and Kevin Mullen, Jane Cummings, Jennifer Cummings, Jack Cummings, Mrs. Cummings, Amy Nunes, Marc Nunes, Katie Nunes, and Alex Nunes.

Others who helped considerably in researching, editing, and marketing the book mustn't be forgotten, and include Christina Lapointe, Margaret Stergios, Alex Beal, Amanda Himlan, Patrick Lynch, Alice Hartley, and Bernie Thiel. We thank them for their dedication to the cause.

The past always creates a lasting influence on the present, and in this case we feel it has been an especially positive one. A partial list of those we wish to thank who inspired and guided us along the way includes Bob Roll, Mike Davis, Rick Stuckey, Mary Etherington, Marie Weirich, Gene Lavengood, Martin Borowczyk, William "Doc" Napiwocki, and Mary and Dennis Loken. We also remember Diane Wilson, who was both mentor and friend.

The most special thanks are of course reserved for family. Paul wishes to express his deepest thanks to his wife Joan, his cheeseburger, whose love and kindness have been a blessing he scarcely deserves (especially throughout the process of writing this book), and to his children, Jonathan, Charlotte, and Michael, who constantly fill his life with joy; to his mother, Hilda Nunes, his longest and greatest supporter, who has always known the truly valuable things in life are not really things; and to his brothers, Marcus Nunes and Joseph Nunes, two finer of which no one has ever had.

Brian is deeply grateful for the unceasing support from his wife, Joni, who is still the best writer in the family, and to his children, Bruce, Adam, and Rebecca, who have put up with nights and weekends on the book on top of other commitments.

1

The New Mass Market

While most companies have been busy trying to build one-on-one relationships with their customers (with varying degrees of success), a surprising thing has occurred. A number of businesses have been making startling amounts of money from offerings that don't "know" their individual buyers very well at all. These products and services are based on the interpretation of widely held needs and are not particularly concerned with their buyers' specific characteristics. In short, they are mass market offerings.

Take Procter & Gamble (P&G), a cornerstone of mass marketing from its earliest days. It stumbled for a time at the most recent turn of the century, but under new leadership, it has come back strong in the early 2000s, largely on the strength of a few new products. The company's July 2003 earnings report cited three examples of mass-market innovations instrumental in its return to success:

- Crest-branded whitening products, including Whitestrips and NightEffects, which helped grow a $50 million niche business in tooth whitening into a $750 million industry in just two years, with P&G grabbing 60 percent of that market

- Swiffer mop, which pioneered the $900 million global surface-cleaning-system category, a category that virtually didn't exist as recently as 1997, and of which P&G now owns 60 percent

- Olay skin care products, including Regenerist, a product that captured nearly a tenth of the facial moisturizer market in its first three months, and which, combined with Total Effects, gave P&G a twelve-share gain in the category in a single year

Contrast P&G's performance with that of a direct competitor. Although it too has a portfolio of consumer products, some of which are very successful, new introductions launching new billion-dollar categories have been notably absent in the period we're referencing. This deficiency has caused concern about the company's ability to sustain its earnings projections; noted analysts have blamed the categories the company is in. But consider this: Before P&G invigorated them, were oral care, household cleaning products, and facial cream the categories that anyone had singled out for explosive growth?

Not that the phenomenon of producing successful new offerings with mass appeal is limited to consumer products. Purchase categories from housing (Toll Brothers builders) to restaurants (Panera Bread) to clothing retailers (Talbots) to lifestyle purveyors (Tommy Bahama) have all seen their fortunes grow over the years by serving millions of diverse consumers with essentially the same product. New mass-market categories are emerging as well; they're poised to grow quickly and their range includes everything from car sharing (Zipcar) to shared personal chefs.

Why should some companies do better than others at selling to the mass market? The answer is straightforward: The companies that are meeting with success have altered their strategies to serve *today's* mass market—a market very different from the one that inspired the first mass-marketing movement. These companies understand that the principles of mass marketing as they knew them (for decades!) no longer apply. They know this because they recognize three major changes that have occurred since those principles were first created—changes that dramatically affect the way in which today's customer must be courted.

First, today's consumers, en masse, are far more affluent in terms of wealth and income (and, critically, discretionary income) than their predecessors. This is particularly true for a certain segment of upper-income, but not extravagantly rich, households. Not only are averages up, but income is more widely dispersed than before; in fact, a new shape of income distribution has emerged, with powerful implications for strategy.[1]

Second, consumer spending patterns have changed, despite the increase in affluence. One change is a drastic reduction in per-dollar-of-income spending in the households that have the most. This pullback represents a tremendous challenge for marketers, but also an unprecedented opportunity for those with the right offerings.

Finally, consumers now want more options for spending their growing affluence, beyond traditional luxury offerings. In many cases, offerings perceived as lavish or luxury goods are being rejected outright. Affluent spending is no longer synonymous with luxury spending, and while some companies may achieve a measure of immediate success by shifting to a luxury-goods mentality, that success is unlikely to be broad based or long-lived.

Those are the broad strokes. As we go through this chapter, and in the chapters that follow, we will explore in detail how the mass market has changed and continues to change, and why the rules of marketing must also change if they are to successfully capture today's mass market. Drawing on our own consumer research and on conversations we've had with executives at leading companies, we will articulate the seven new rules of mass marketing, and we will illustrate the kinds of strategies that those new rules call for.

Where Is the New Mass Market?

When notorious criminal Willie Sutton was asked why he robbed banks, he allegedly replied, "Because that's where the money is."[2] He later denied ever saying the line, claiming it was the invention of an aggressive reporter on deadline. But he quickly added, "If anybody had asked me, I'd have probably said it. That's what almost anybody would say . . . it couldn't be more obvious."[3]

Maybe Willie Sutton knew where the money was. But do the members of today's society at large, and marketing executives in particular, know where it is? The three critical differences we just identified regarding today's consumers are all about "where the money is," and yet when we asked a diverse group of people to describe the distribution of income in the United States, we received an astonishingly wide range of responses. The majority of respondents speculated that income distribution in the United States, depicted graphically, looked like a bell curve—a thick center of middle-class earners, with thinning tails on either side.

That majority was wrong. And that misconception—the prevalent belief that where the money is in the United States is a bell curve—has dangerous implications for companies whose marketing strategy focuses on the mass market as the middle class.

Of course, it's not easy to get an accurate picture of income distribution these days. Depending on how you crunch the numbers and plot your graph, you can create almost any kind of picture of income distribution you choose. The popularity of charts that display income earners in a nonlinear fashion (i.e., without equal-sized data points on the axes), for example, is a partial explanation for the bell-curve theory of household income distribution that supports the strong belief in a middle class. The U.S. Census Bureau's chosen graphical representation, for example, yields a plausible bell curve that has come to be somewhat of a standard in the way income distribution is represented in the United States. But on that chart, and on many others, each data point corresponds to a different size of income range, anywhere from a span of $5,000 to $50,000. The picture is accordingly misshapen and therefore misleading—for consumers, for policy makers, and for businesses.

We believe we've crunched the numbers in a way that presents the results with as little distortion as possible, which is critical for marketers. We were strict about data point definition, insisting that each point represent the same size of income range (in this case, $5,000—which required us to perform a small amount of interpolation and smoothing). As we calculate it, the shape of the curve in fact shows a ski slope, not a bell curve.[4] Starting with a large mass at the left-hand side, which represents lower-income households, the curve slopes downward until it eventually (and somewhat quickly) flattens out, forming a very thin tail of higher-income households (figure 1-1).

Where is the traditional mass market—the middle class—in this picture? Is it even there? Our graph indicates a significant number of

FIGURE 1-1

U.S. Household Income Distribution

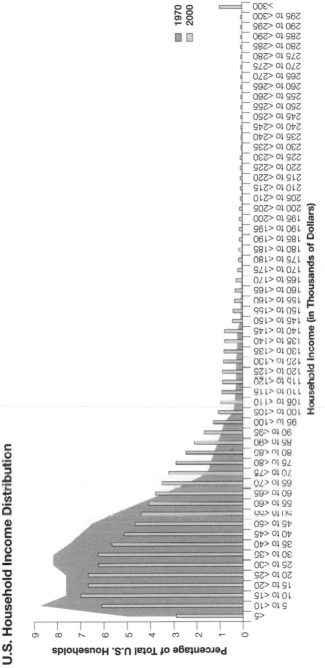

The shape of income distribution in the United States has changed dramatically since 1970, changing the nature of average earners and the middle class.

Data source: U.S. Department of Commerce, Bureau of the Census, "Money Income in the United States: 2000," <www.census.gov/prod/2001pubs/p60-213.pdf> (accessed 5 November 2003).

Household income expressed in 2000 CPI-U-RS dollars: incremental values interpolated from larger increments when not available.

low-income households, but it does not show a huge middle-class mass market of consumers. What it shows, instead, when viewed over time, is a mass market that has shifted significantly upscale.

Who Moved My Income?

The current shape of income distribution, and how it has evolved since the 1970s, is extremely relevant to marketers. In 1970, only 3.7 percent of the population made more than $100,000 a year in (roughly) today's dollars.[5] By the year 2001, that percentage had grown to 13.8! Put another way, where once one out of every twenty-seven households was well off in terms of income (having the equivalent of a six-figure income) in 1970, the ratio is now closer to one out of every seven households. In the same period, the percentage of households with real incomes between $75,000 and $100,000 more than doubled, from 4.4 percent to 10.8 percent. Combined, the two changes have made the total number of households earning over $75,000 in 2000 nearly one in four. Paraphrasing Walt Kelly's Pogo, we have met the affluent, and they are us.

Where did these new higher earners come from? Though one would hope they would have come from the lowest earners, somewhat predictably these additional households came mostly from those in the $35,000 to $49,999 annual income range. This group saw its percentage of households drop from 22.1 to 15.4 percent of total earners between 1967 and 2001. With poverty bounded at zero and incomes being near limitless (consider for example Michael Eisner's annual compensation at Disney—which has *averaged* more than $121 million since 1997— and you get the idea), the result is not terribly surprising.[6] There has been a nearly predictable stretching out and leveling, with the pivot point lying around $65,000, as the intersection of the statistical trends demonstrates.[7] This chart reveals a shift in household income levels that is far broader in its base, and more structurally important, than many have imagined.

But it is not the income growth of the newly affluent middle of the diagram's curve alone that is important (though this growth has been great). Equally important are the relative shifts on both the left- and right-hand sides of the curve that complete the picture. Though these differences are plainly significant in terms of distribution of incomes, they become even more significant when viewed in terms of the shift in buying power. The proportions of total income have always been highly skewed, but the dramatic change since the 1970s is a phenomenon marketers ignore at their peril. The top 1 percent of earners has seen its share of income explode—growing from less than 10 percent of the nation's total income in 1979 to roughly 18 percent of the total by 1997, and nearly 21 percent in 2000.[8] For those below the median income, *share* of total income has steadily declined, making them a gradually less substantive part of total income.

Together these trends create a mass market that is substantively different in terms of spending power than existed immediately after World War II, when mass-marketing precepts first emerged. This change presents three important take-aways for marketers. First, households in the "fat tail" of the income distribution curve are now far more important to marketers than they ever were before, as both a source of spending and as the influencers of other consumers. Second, every possible mass-market product (from milk to board games to laundry detergent) is now being sold across a wider range of abilities to pay, causing mass marketers to face a broader range of consumer expectations, demands, and propensity to spend. Third, the change in the locus of spending power among consumers, toward the fewer households that have greater incomes, is likely to have dramatic, if hard-to-quantify, implications for consumer behavior. Marketers must carefully evaluate the implications of this change in spending power, which range from how consumption is linked to personal identity creation, all the way to consumer attitudes about the Joneses, and what, if anything, consumers intend to do to keep up with them. (For example, our consumer survey uncovered that nearly two-thirds of consumers believe it is getting harder to tell what a person earns by his or her purchasing.)[9]

These differences render today's mass market fundamentally different from the original mass market of the past. To distinguish this new market from its predecessor, highlighting in particular its new, broad-based income wealth, we call it the *moneyed masses*. We have used the term throughout the book to stand for not any particular range of income, but for the majority of households affected by a substantial rise in wealth and income and possessing an unprecedented level of discretionary spending power. We leave it to individual marketers to set the lower (and upper) limits of income range for the relevant mass market to be targeted in their industry, but the characterization is true for all industries in most industrialized countries. Mass affluence has had a pronounced effect in the United Kingdom as well, for example. Studies conducted for the United Kingdom's financial services industry were some of the first to use to that term. The idea of mass affluence is also well recognized in other European countries, including France and Spain. Identified by some observers as the well-off middle class (as opposed to the ultrarich), this category of earner, which must be defined relative to an individual economy, is exploding in numbers in countries like China, India, Costa Rica, and the Philippines.

Much of the global phenomenon comes from an increasing sharing of the wealth. *BusinessWeek* has documented the trend of exporting service and knowledge work, including roles as complex as architecture and engineering, from the United States to countries like Hungary.[10] The global market for business process outsourcing (BPO) is estimated to grow to $226 billion by 2005.[11] These trends have already begun, and will continue, to drive the development of a perhaps smaller, but not insignificant, market of newly affluent consumers in a number of other nations. The collective outcome is a world filled with countries whose mass market is no longer uniform or universally strapped for cash. Companies need no longer search national markets for pockets of consumers who can afford innovation. Instead, there is a startling amount of business opportunity to be captured in global gross domestic product (GDP) growth, despite temporary economic setbacks.

The Underspent American

We live in an age of unprecedented riches, a situation affecting households of all income levels, not just because of income growth and wealth increases, but because of what our spending buys us. Owing to the deflationary pressure on so many of the goods we consume—from food to clothing to home electronics—many of America's poorest households are doing substantially better than their incomes would suggest. Poorer homes possess in great numbers the products once reserved for the middle class, including such items as washing machines, clothes dryers, dishwashers, color televisions, and personal computers.[12] Even Robert Frank, author of *Luxury Fever,* a jeremiad against wasteful consumption spending led by the rich, concedes, "The bottom twenty percent of earners now spend just 47 percent of their incomes on food, clothing and shelter, down from 70 percent as recently as 1920. For most families, the current economic challenge is to acquire not the goods they need but the goods they want."[13]

As consumers' absolute needs continue to shrink as a portion of total income, even those with modest incomes are finding that a greater amount of their spending is discretionary. For those with even higher incomes, the growth in the buying power of money, as well as the growth in their incomes, means they receive just that much more gravy, with dominant portions of their income now being completely discretionary. This unspoken-for portion of affluent consumers' paychecks is a bounty to be won by marketers.

But just as people believe (incorrectly) that the shape of income distribution in the United States resembles a bell curve, many also believe (equally incorrectly) that high-income households greedily consume this bounty and that the rich will even go so far as to leverage their income to achieve an ever grander lifestyle. From Aristophanes' play *Wealth* in 388 B.C., to the endless versions of the TV show *Lifestyles of the Rich and Famous,* including the most recent, MTV's hit show *Cribs,* the media delight in exhibiting the wealthy immersed in the bounty of their lavish expenditure. But if applied beyond movie stars, professional athletes, and rap artists, the idea of disproportionate levels of expenditure among the affluent is another dangerous misconception, particularly if you're a marketer. Because nothing, it appears, could be further from the truth.

Though many marketers drove their companies to scale up production of luxury offerings during the boom 1990s, these same companies now face significant overcapacity in such high-end goods as million-dollar condos, exotic automobiles, and country-club golf courses. All these offerings have experienced a glut in the marketplace that experts expect will take years to come into line with real demand. Though it is easy to blame Internet mania for marketers' overconfidence in affluent spending, there were signs of broader buyer hesitance for some time before the bubble burst, for those with the ability to see them.

Let's take a closer look at how the majority of Americans have really been spending their money. To better understand the consumption habits of U.S. households, we researched the data gathered by the Consumer Expenditure Survey of the U.S. Department of Labor, Bureau of Labor Statistics. We paid particular attention to how spending and income have changed over time, above all for the more affluent households.

What we found in the data flouted conventional wisdom. While more households were earning more than ever, those making the most (the top 20 percent) made up only 37 percent of total expenditures in 2002, though their income constituted nearly 50 percent of total income that year (figure 1-2).

On top of this pattern, the households in this quintile spent on average *less* over time, when spending was measured as a percentage of before-tax income.[14] Expenditure as a percentage of total income has been on a downward slide for these folks, dropping from an average of 74.6 percent between 1984 and 1986 to an average of 68.6 percent between 1998 and 2000 (figure 1-3).[15]

When we calculated the difference between what they actually spent and what they would have spent had they kept their proportion of spending the same, and when we multiplied the difference over the 21.8 million households in this quintile, it translated to a loss of more than $100 billion in consumption spending in 2000 alone. The number of dollars in lost consumption is even greater when one considers that the fastest-growing spending category for the top quintile is insurance and pensions, a disbursement that is more like an investment than real consumption. Consequently, the top quintile's actual consumption spending was lower still.

This decrease in real consumption was, in some ways, to be expected. Many households have been concerned with their retirement prospects and the future of Social Security in the United States, which might have left them feeling vulnerable and in need of greater savings. But outside those causes, households with higher lifetime incomes have

FIGURE 1-2

Quintiles of Income Before Taxes

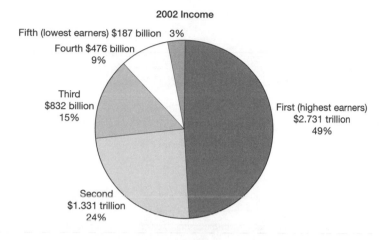

2002 Income

Fifth (lowest earners) $187 billion 3%

Fourth $476 billion 9%

Third $832 billion 15%

First (highest earners) $2.731 trillion 49%

Second $1.331 trillion 24%

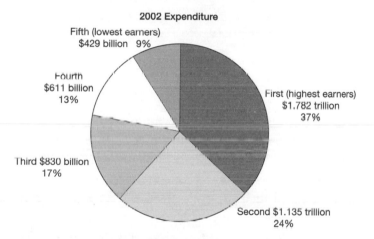

2002 Expenditure

Fifth (lowest earners) $429 billion 9%

Fourth $611 billion 13%

First (highest earners) $1.782 trillion 37%

Third $830 billion 17%

Second $1.135 trillion 24%

While the top 20 percent of households took home 49 percent of total income in 2002, they expended only 37 percent of total spending.

Data source: U.S. Department of Labor, Bureau of Labor Statistics, Consumer Expenditures Survey 2002, <http://www.bls.gov/cex/csxstnd.htm> (accessed 5 November 2003)

well-documented higher lifetime savings rates.[16] The question is why, and what level of threat does this increased savings pose to consumer spending in an increasingly affluent society? Though many reasons have been suggested for the increase in savings—from people's wanting to create a lasting dynasty of wealth and power to their simply saving for a

FIGURE 1-3

Average Expenditure of Top Quintile, as a Percentage of Income Before Taxes

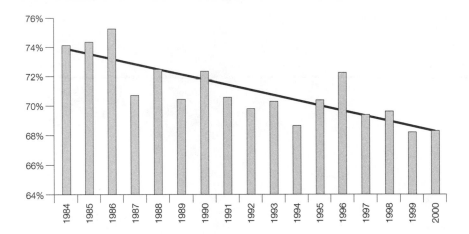

Though the top 20 percent of earners saw their income grow dramatically in the 1990s, their spending as a percentage of total income saw a steady decline.

Data source: U.S. Department of Labor, Bureau of Labor Statistics, Consumer Expenditure Surveys 1984 to 2000, <http://www.bls.gov/cex/csxstnd.htm> (accessed 5 November 2003).

rainy day—none seems to be *the* answer.[17] What does emerge is that wealth appears to be a consumer good as much as any other good, something consumers choose to buy more of as they are better able to afford it.

So while America's income rich certainly live well, they do not in general live beyond their means. In fact, while the top quintile saw its average after-tax income grow 48 percent in the years between 1990 and 2000, its average total expenditure grew only 38 percent. This growth rate was nearly identical to (just 0.3 percent higher than) the spending growth of the poorest quintile—a surprising fact since the poorest quintile's income grew by only 30 percent in this period, 8 percent *less* than its spending did in the same period.

What, then, makes marketers and the public persist in believing that the top earners spend in proportion to their income? A few observations support the notion, though they are misleading when one looks at the whole ball of wax. For example, the lion's share of consumption *is* done by top earners. The top 20 percent of households by income still constitute 38 percent of total consumption expenditure. Such a disparity can hardly go unnoticed by the average consumer. Also partly to blame is the relative amount of media coverage that focuses on affluent spending. We are bombarded not just with the attention to Donald Trump's properties in New York or Palm Beach, or J. Lo's rings, but the misleadingly affluent lifestyles television portrays, especially in situation comedies. Ever notice the furnishings on these shows and wonder, "How can they afford that?"[18]

Focusing on past spending behavior also serves to confuse companies today. Examining total spending in nominal dollars reveals significant growth in all quintiles, especially the top quintile during this period. But when total expenditures are converted to real dollars (i.e., they are adjusted for inflation), the malaise in spending becomes more apparent. And it is not until expenditure is expressed as a percentage of total income that the real downward trend in spending appears and the top quintile's dramatic decline becomes readily apparent.

This downward trend in spending has been far more severe in some industries than in others, elevating its importance to companies and marketers in these industries in particular. In our study of spending trends over time—by category of the offering and by income—we found that, since the 1980s, certain expenditures, like food and apparel, were especially hard hit in terms of real dollar spending. Others, like health, education, and pensions, saw increases in spending, particularly among the affluent. Throughout the book, we will explore in more detail the lessons to be learned from both sets of industries.[19]

The disparity between spending and earnings is partly a result of the failure of wealth effects to catch up with consumers' spending habits. Other causes are factors like low-cost offshore sourcing and technology obsolescence—two factors that conspire to keep prices low. But this lack of spending must also be seen, at least in part, as a failure on the part of companies to innovate their way to increased consumer spending in the categories that lost spending as a share of income. After all, almost every consumer we surveyed told us they would be willing to spend more for their purchases in many categories, if they could only find ones that better fit their needs. Such statements came from 68 percent of respondents earning less than $50,000 and rose to 87 percent (!) of those earning more than $150,000.

When asked about the number of *personally valuable* innovations they had seen in the last couple of years, upward of 50 percent of consumers we surveyed said they saw *none*, and up to 70 percent saw either none or only one or two in each category tested. This was especially true for those with household incomes over $100,000. These consumers saw significantly less valuable innovation in nearly every category.[20] Overall, however, disappointment with innovation can be considered so high that there is clear opportunity for creative companies to succeed wildly in every industry, even in those considered stagnant, as P&G has done in consumer products. The remaining chapters focus on how a new set of mass-marketing rules for today's moneyed mass market can lead companies to better, more customer-valued innovation.

Longing for Luxury . . . Whatever That Is

This brings us to a final popular misconception shared by many companies: that selling to affluent consumers, past and present, old and new, is all about selling luxury. Some marketers may be inclined to think that because there is a long history of companies catering to the rich, the traditional marketing approach of creating luxury offerings to satisfy wealthier customers, though it may need some accelerated innovation, is otherwise an adequate solution for serving the moneyed masses. But selling luxury to the few is not the business opportunity many people believe it to be, for reasons we will soon see. And if selling luxury to the few is a dicey proposition, then creating luxury for the masses, as some have advised, is likely to be equally perilous.

To understand why luxury is no longer the answer for capturing the spending potential in the moneyed masses, it is critically important to understand what luxury is—and isn't.

But defining luxury is an extremely difficult task, and therein lies at least part of the problem in attempting to successfully create luxury for the masses. For example, for marketing purposes, luxury is most often classified as some percentage of the most expensive goods in a category, or those priced above a certain threshold. While this definition is easy to understand, it fails to provide much insight. By this measure, most everything the wealthy consume is a luxury, whether they intend it to be or not. And many of America's richest do not intend to buy luxury. In *The Millionaire Next Door,* Thomas Stanley and William Danko clearly document the disconnect between wealth and the purchasing of expensive items, reporting on how these millionaires drive very ordinary cars and consume mostly other pedestrian products. According to their survey, more than half of American millionaires report never spending more than $399 on a suit of clothing, $140 on a pair of shoes, or $235 on a wristwatch.[21] So while being expensive can produce high-income buyers when the offering is attractive, it is rarely reason enough to induce purchasing from the moneyed masses.

Luxury is also often defined by its built-in attribute of being trivial, or having few or no functional benefits over lower-priced competitors. Triviality has been understood as a fundamental part of luxury since Thorstein Veblen talked of waste as a core element of conspicuous consumption in his *Theory of the Leisure Class.* But waste is not only out of fashion; it is absolutely frowned upon. Gone are the potlatches that would bankrupt the chieftains of our day, and any trip to a Wal-Mart or an outlet mall would confirm that even among the rich, value is in.

Another marketing approach to defining luxury is by brand status. With this approach, certain high-status brands become luxury brands, and the companies that produce them, luxury goods makers. Examples are companies like Louis Vuitton Moet Hennessy (LVMH), Tiffany, Burberry, Hermes, Gucci, and other brands that are frequently researched by investment analysts together, under the category of luxury makers, and are even put into sector mutual funds, as did UBS Global Asset Management with its UBS (Lux) Focused Fund—Top Luxury. This measure of luxury leads to a luxury market, worth an estimated $75 billion worldwide. Though large, this number is not a significant portion of the total spending of the wealthy. This luxury market ignores many items, however, such as luxury cars and yachts, because they may not be on the list of high-status brands. Thus one can see the difficulty in using a brand-based understanding of luxury as a way of targeting consumers by income.

While this brand-based definition may align with most consumers' understanding of luxury, it is again not consistent with the buying behavior of the income rich. In their research on the consumption of luxury, Bernard Dubois and Patrick Duquesne found that while income is a strong predictor of luxury purchasing—a sensible conclusion, since larger incomes facilitate the purchase of luxury at any level of underlying desire—culture is a more powerful predictor.[22] Specifically, they found that persons who were "on trend," that is, more receptive to risk taking, more positive and proactive in their lives, and less accepting of formal or traditional structures, were more likely to purchase luxury. The researchers also found that this trait was evenly split between the income rich and income poor. So while a good income enables luxury spending, more important is a certain personal and cultural predisposition to it.

Dubois and Duquesne also measured luxury consumption against two types of luxury, defined as "accessible" and "exceptional," based on the relative prices. This delineation allowed them to capture a wider range of behaviors, but again, the preconceived notions embedded in the researchers' particular choices highlight the subjective nature of luxury. Neither is luxury branding a guarantee of business success. Though it bears the tag line "Prestige is never passé," UBS's top luxury-focused fund declined roughly 40 percent (in Euros) between its inception in 2000 and early 2003, failing to outperform the market in any significant way. This performance should not be surprising. Maintaining these luxury brands' images often requires margin-destroying levels of investment. For example, advertising costs regularly represent 10 percent of sales in the luxury goods industry, versus the 2, 3, or sometimes 5 percent spent in most other industries.[23] Premiere luxury goods makers have been driven into bankruptcy trying to maintain and extract the value of their brands, from Lamborghini (in the 1980s) to Gucci (in 1993) to Chaumet (the jewelry maker, in the 1980s). Selling true branded luxury is, as Gian Luigi Longinotti-Buitoni describes it in *Selling Dreams,* a highly speculative, and expensive, proposition.[24]

Economists define luxury goods as those whose consumption goes up as income increases. This can be a little hard to conceptualize, but may be the most practical of all definitions for the design of real luxury offerings. The definition articulates that luxury is not what one buys, but what one continues to buy ever more of as income increases, forgoing replacing a product with a more attractive substitute. If we think this through, many products, like cellular phones and $6 sandwiches, are briefly luxuries, but are then quickly sated and cease to be luxury items. So selling *real* luxury is a design principle every maker can aspire to: an offering that not only is attractive, but also creates a need that is never fully satisfied.

Overcoming Mass Parsimony

Where does all of this leave us? How can a company begin to address the opportunity that exists in the unspent portion of the moneyed masses' income, if not through luxury offerings? The answer to those questions, in detail, is the focus of the rest of the book. But for broad purposes here, suffice it to emphasize that traditional mass-marketing strategies won't serve.

Traditional mass-marketing strategies for growing category spending, for example, focus solely on increasing consumption. They require driving greater frequency or quantity of use, or the discovery or creation of new uses. These are time-tested approaches, but they won't lead marketers to "where the money is" any better than before. The pent-up disposable income created by mass parsimony will not be captured by incremental growth and the introduction of new uses for yesterday's offerings. To grow category spending dramatically, companies must consciously break out of this marketing tradition, recognizing and responding to a bigger picture of consumption.

This kind of change starts when marketers recognize that savings is discretionary—it is a choice consumers are making against alternatives. Today, the best paid of the moneyed masses are finding it their most attractive choice. At the core, all successful sales growth strategies lead consumers to different choices. Nontraditional strategies must now grow spending through meaningful innovation targeted directly at today's new mass market.

The Seven New Rules of Mass Marketing

To achieve the kind of growth we've just described, which companies desire today—both in terms of margins and in terms of market share— companies must ask themselves whether their best chances lie not in increased microsegmentation, but in a better, more finely tuned form of

FIGURE 1-4

The Seven New Rules of Marketing to Today's Consumers

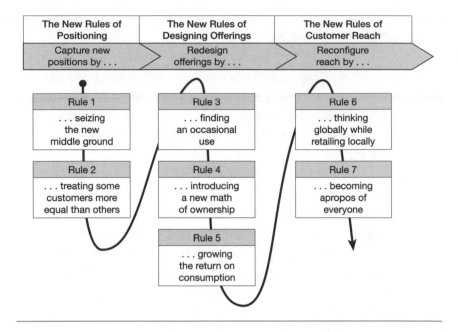

mass marketing. Not traditional mass marketing per se, but a new approach designed for the new shape of today's mass market, a strategy for moneyed-mass marketing. We call these recommended changes the seven new rules of marketing to today's mass market. Companies both large and small are achieving substantial growth using this new approach to serving today's mass market. To apply the new rules, companies need to undertake a three-step process of marketing reinvention. They must capture new market positions, redesign their offerings to satisfy those positions, and then reconfigure the channels and promotion of these offerings (figure 1-4). This book is organized broadly around those three marketing steps.

The New Rules of Positioning

Part 1 of this book is designed to aid marketers in taking the first step toward selling to today's mass market: repositioning offerings. In chapter 2, "Seize the New Middle Ground," we exhort marketers to find new positions between the real luxury goods in the market and the best of products that are strictly mass market. These positions entail volume selling, but at price points considerably higher than previously thought possible, as Kraft has done with its DiGiorno brand in the frozen-pizza market. While the price point must remain low enough to support broad, everyday consumption, it must also exist well above the conventional price paid for the best traditional solution.

Our primary research confirms that such an opportunity exists. The majority of consumers reported they often must choose between offerings that are too expensive and that deliver more than they need, and offerings that are priced below what they would be willing to pay and that do not fulfill their requirements.

Not all companies, however, come to moneyed-mass marketing with a clean slate. Chapter 3, "Treat Some Customers More Equal Than Others," lays out how leading companies are overcoming the challenges involved in repositioning existing offerings despite heavy sunk costs in infrastructure, or cultural and regulatory constraints against selling a broader range of differentiated offerings. Despite the challenges, we see winners at repositioning. For example, both the Deer Valley ski resort and the theme park operator Universal Studios have cautiously grown their offerings to capture different levels of profit from different levels of value provided, while remaining committed to their existing assets and customer base. We also see winners in companies like MDVIP, which overcame an initial adverse reaction from parts of society to make higher levels of general medical care accessible to the mass market at a higher price.

The New Rules of Designing Offerings

In part 2 of this book, we lay out three fundamental approaches marketers can take to modifying offerings and to defining new ones that are better suited to the moneyed masses. Each approach corresponds to a reinvention of one of the three core attributes of an offering: its context (in terms of the intended buyer's current possessions and subscriptions), the nature of its ownership, and the nature of the value it delivers (the customer's perceived return on the price paid).

In chapter 4, "Find an Occasional Use," we explore the first of these approaches: changing the offering's context within the world of what a consumer already owns or subscribes to. Most consumers, and especially the more affluent ones, have already acquired lots of "stuff." Selling to those who have much is harder than to those with little. We therefore explore how companies creatively define "new" products that the moneyed masses simply must have and, as importantly, are willing to make room for in their figuratively and literally crowded lives. Examples are surprisingly plentiful: everything from Nike's Aqua Sock, designed specifically for water sports, to Williams-Sonoma's steamer made just for asparagus. These products may not experience daily wear or use, but are highly valued for how well they fit the occasion.

In chapter 5, "Introduce a New Math of Ownership," we explore how companies are redefining the nature of possession to convert the unaffordable to the affordable. Companies like IKEA are making their offerings more attainable by altering deeply held beliefs about the appropriate length of ownership for goods in their industry. Other companies are redefining the number of consumers that normally share ownership, and the means by which payment is made. In sum, these marketers are reinventing possession's key components—duration, payment, and property rights—to create offerings that are better suited to the real-life circumstances of the affluent. In addition, successful companies are rethinking their offerings in terms of the real costs they pose to their consumers, including acquisition, maintenance, storage, and, eventually, disposal.

The third important aspect of any offering is its value proposition, specifically the return a consumer can expect from his or her purchase investment. In chapter 6, "Grow the Return on Consumption," we reveal how companies are tying their offerings in to the very nature of investments. Some companies, like Talbots, are paying dividends, not just to their shareholders but to their customers. Others, like shoe company Allen-Edmonds, are focusing on delivering undiminished use over time. Together, these different approaches are moving traditional goods, clothing in these examples, out of the world of consumption into the more attractive world of durable investments.

The New Rules of Customer Reach

Part 3 of the book addresses the changes successful marketers are making to their channel and promotion strategies to better serve the new shape of household income distribution, while also focusing more on those consumers and households with the greatest discretionary spending. Many of the biggest trends in business since the 1990s have focused on cutting costs, which has left many companies badly positioned to create and deliver the kind of channels and promotions needed to capture greater spending and margins from those who have it to give.

In chapter 7, "Think Global, Retail Local," we observe how the most successful companies are evolving channels for better serving the moneyed masses. Rather than focusing on customers and existing offerings, these companies are becoming more market-centric and informed. This new centricity is set in motion through creative and informed decisions about product mix, decor, amenities, and locations that serve both local markets and the larger goals of the retailer's brand. While the retail mall business has languished in recent years, innovators like real estate developer Poag & McEwen have redefined the landscape, quite literally, to create shopping environments better suited to today's mass market. Other companies, including leaders like Walgreens, and Dell in partnership with Sears, have turned to technology to reinvent their channels for today's more affluent consumer behavior.

A big part of managing profitable investment in customers, that is, improving the return on investment (ROI) of customer care, is managing the costs of acquiring them. In chapter 8, "Become Apropos of Everyone," we look at the new approaches companies are using to better and more cost-effectively target, attract, and retain well-heeled customers—approaches that make dramatic improvements in relevance to a mass audience. Today's moneyed masses are better informed than ever, thanks to Web sites like e-pinions and cable channels like House and Garden TV, and are ever more proactive in their shopping behavior. They are also more marketing savvy than ever, aging baby boomers being the first generation exposed to professional marketing all their lives.

Consumers' increasing knowledge of the wiles of marketers makes today's mass-market advertising and promotion as much a question of influencing the influencers as selling directly to the market. In chapter 8, we take you inside the world of events marketing targeted at the affluent, where for the price of drink, literally, companies like Scotch distiller Johnnie Walker are getting an hour or more of prosperous consumers' undivided attention. We also look at how traditional advertising and promotions are changing in response to mass affluence, making product placement for even exotic offerings like James Bond's movie BMW a more critical, everyday component of the brand development marketing mix.

What Next?

In part 4, the final section of the book, we conclude with a look into the future of the mass market and how it might be served. In chapter 9, "Tomorrow's Mass Market," we examine where the mass market is heading and why the new market, and the rules that shape its demands, will be relevant for quite some time. We also added an epilogue, Reenvisioning an Industry, to close the book with an exercise that brings all of our rules and recommendations into clearer focus, applying the concepts and methods presented in this book to the world of jewelry and watches. Applying the rules to a specific industry, segment, or subsegment is not really the end, however. We feel strongly it will be just the beginning.

The Continuing Evolution of Mass Marketing

In *New and Improved: The History of Mass Marketing in America,* Harvard business historian Richard Tedlow saw three phases of mass marketing.[25] The first phase was the fragmented selling that companies were forced to do before the end of the nineteenth century—individual stores in individual cities, without national distribution or brands. The railroads and telegraphs ushered in a second phase, which unified the nation into a single mass market and which lasted roughly until the mid-1900s. This was the golden age of consumer products and retailer brands like GM and Ford, Coke and Pepsi, Sears and A&P.

The third phase Tedlow identified was one of segmentation. Starting as early as the General Motors price pyramid in the 1920s (intended to compete with Ford's mass-market offerings), segmentation gained speed in the late 1960s as the generation gap demanded different offerings for young and old. Segmentation at the end of the twentieth century evolved to include relationship marketing, one-to-one marketing, and highly targeted and sophisticated direct marketing.

Tedlow was dead-on right in his analysis. But the pendulum is swinging again. The fourth phase of marketing, as we see it, keeps the best of relationship marketing, but clearly sets its sights on capturing the potential returns from selling to the broadest range of customers possible (figure 1-5).

FIGURE 1-5

The Cycle of Marketing Approaches

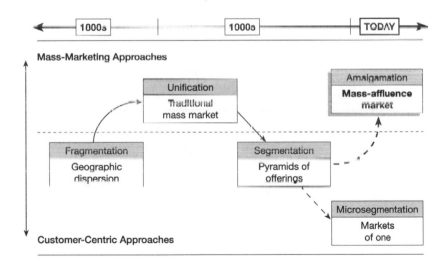

Although the history of marketing strategy has appeared to be a steady march to customer-centricity, it can also be viewed as a wave that cycles between customer and market focus.

Adapted from Richard S. Tedlow, *New and Improved: The Story of Mass Marketing in America* (New York: Basic Books, 1990), 4.

This new phase doesn't invalidate the emphasis companies are placing on customer relationship management or technologies focused on customer insight; instead, this fourth phase helps balance that emphasis with a leaning toward profitability and market growth. The most successful implementations of these technologies, in other words, seek not to limit the customers served and to serve them better, but rather to enable the largest number of customers that can be served profitably to be served, to the limits of their potential profitability. Exploiting this new strategic focus requires a new marketing approach that is unique to its era (table 1-1). Such an approach might be called density marketing because of its concern for the aggregate spending power of a customer mass, and not just its member count.

TABLE 1-1

Core Marketing Components Across Eras

	Individualized Selling (Up to Late 1800s)	Mass Marketing (1870 to 1975)	Relationship Marketing (1975 to 2000)	Mass-Affluence Marketing (2000 to . . .)
Position	Seller-defined by offering	Either mass market or luxury	Endless niches, leading to markets of one	(1) In the new middle ground
Price	Set high, through regional monopoly power or collusion	Set low and clearly marked, to drive volume	Discriminatory, to capture consumer surplus from most beholden customers	(2) Treat some customers more equal than others
Product	Local-market-defined, based on geography and demand	Mass-produced, to satisfy supplier-created international markets	Targeted, through niche products and mass customization	Designed for (3) Occasional use (4) New ownership models (5) Return on consumption
Placement	Independent retailing establishments and sales forces	Mass merchandisers and department stores, piling it high and selling it low	Chain specialty stores and boutiques offering "high-touch" levels of customer service	(6) Global store chains acting through local market-tailored stores
Promotion	Interpersonal sales pitch and negotiation	Mass communications and promotions	Targeted direct marketing	(7) Highly relevant mass communications and promotions

Marketers and executives who step back from microsegmentation and rethink mass marketing along the lines we're discussing will gain a new perspective from which to view their businesses. A fresh outlook is important because, as Tedlow pointed out in his book, the original mass market was not happened upon, but was created by business leaders of vision who invested in new infrastructures and brands and then enjoyed the advantages their early movement conferred upon them. George Eastman "didn't just produce an affordable camera. He also propagated the notion that everybody ought to take pictures."[26]

As we've said, the mass market of today is not the same one that companies faced in the 1940s and 1950s. But companies that recognize the increasing numbers of today's affluent consumers have an opportunity to shape this new mass market, as many celebrated business leaders did for the mass market of an era past. For those who embrace the challenge, the rewards stand to be equally remarkable.

PART ONE

The New Rules of Positioning

2

Seize the New Middle Ground

Old Rule
Avoid middle-market positions between low-cost and premium.

New Rule
Seize the new-middle-ground position, above the best of the conventional offerings and below ultrapremium solutions.

Now that more than 26 million Americans play golf, it is hard to imagine that the sport was once enjoyed by only the wealthiest handful of individuals.[1] But until the mid-1800s, golf was prohibitively expensive, and not just because of club membership dues or greens fees. It was also partly due to the staggering cost of golf balls.

A single golf ball, hand-fashioned in rawhide and stuffed with boiled feathers, was an indulgence that cost the equivalent of $150 to $400. Yet, one ball was hardly enough. A serious wager match required that each golfer's caddie bring at least six balls onto the course, at a potential cost of thousands of dollars.[2] Adding to the expense of golf balls was their frequent tendency, then as now, to become lost. Players had to be rich enough not just to buy golf balls, but also to watch their purchase of several hundred dollars disappear into the woods or a pond without betraying the unseemly impulse to recover it.

Nowadays, of course, losing golf balls hurts egos more than wallets. Ball prices have fallen precipitously, thanks to the rise of mass production serving a new class of affluent with both the time and the inclination to embrace the sport. One can now pay as little as a dollar for a brand new, name-brand golf ball at Wal-Mart or even less for an "experienced" one at a pro shop.[3]

Interestingly, though, this 150-year downward trend is reversing—at least for some brands of golf balls. Certain brands in the golf ball industry have convinced consumers to multiply their spending for golf balls. How did they do it? Shrewd manufacturers created new premium offerings that fulfilled the unmet needs of golfers, while moving the selling price not by just a few cents, but to nearly double the previous high-end selling price. In other words, these manufacturers staked out a lucrative product position between ultimate luxury, in this case, handmade balls, and the recent high end of mass-market outlays. We call this opening in offering possibilities the *new middle ground*.

The Masters of Golf Balls

Let's examine what happened. A few years ago, many sporting-goods manufacturers sensed that a growing number of golfers found top-of-the-line balls inadequate. Certain consumers instead coveted the enhanced capabilities and leading-edge technology that professionals enjoyed. They also wanted a wider array of choices, such as balls with increased spin for better performance around the greens and balls designed for greater distance.

These desires framed a previously unrecognized market for super-premium offerings. And several top manufacturers acted on their newfound knowledge by developing entirely new offerings for the professional market and then rolling those offerings out to amateur golfers at a superpremium price. Nike, for example, a relatively new entrant to golf, introduced its Tour Accuracy ball. Long-time maker Titleist came out with its Pro V1. Both balls featured solid-core technology that increased performance so dramatically; nearly the entire Professional Golfers' Association(PGA) tour adopted them within months. And soon after, casual golfers proved willing to spend more than twice as much to have these golf balls for their weekend rounds. The very popular Pro V1, for example, has a suggested retail price of about $50 per dozen, which represents a substantially higher price than the company's previous high-end offering.

This new price tier has dramatically raised consumers' spending levels and brought the industry back from the brink of commoditization. In the two years since the Pro V1 was introduced in the commercial market, golf balls selling for more than $35 per dozen increased their share of the market by 60 percent, nearly four times the growth rate of those selling for less than $25 per dozen.[4] Although the trend does not necessarily presage the return of the $400 golf ball, it does suggest that golf balls might reach the $10 level in the near future.

This shift in price points also puts tremendous pressure on those that came late to the game. One company that missed the trend, with disastrous results, was Top-Flite Golf Company, which filed for bankruptcy in June 2003 and whose assets were sold to Callaway Golf. Though Top-Flite had launched the most expensive golf ball ever in its time, the Ben Hogan Apex Tour brand, which once retailed for $58 per dozen, it was too late to save the world's largest manufacturer of golf balls from what then CEO Jim Craigie called a market too competitive for the company's level of debt burden.[5]

Staking Out the New Middle Ground

So a select group of golf ball manufacturers successfully penetrated and exploited a new middle ground of market positioning. Was the opportunity industry-specific? We think not. In fact, we believe that the success these manufacturers have enjoyed can be duplicated in many other sectors. Our own consumer research illustrates strong pent-up demand among consumers of all income levels for better-quality offerings sold at a premium but not pure-luxury price. Our findings include these two observations:

Neither existing luxury nor mass-market offerings alone satisfy both the needs and the budgets of the moneyed masses. A full 44 percent of households with over $100,000 in income agree that they often must choose between buying a product that meets their needs but is too expensive, and one that costs less than they would be willing to pay but is not really what they are looking for. This dilemma of unsatisfying choices is especially common for product categories like automobiles, housing, and personal care and services categories like investing and entertainment.[6] Though the very affluent face this dilemma less often than do lower-income segments in some categories, it is shocking that they should face it at all, and especially shocking that so many do. The gap between desirable and affordable offerings, experienced by all consumers, should serve as a marker of significant opportunity and a clarion call to action for marketers and executives in every industry.

Consumers would spend more to have their needs better fulfilled. Our research found that even in difficult economic times, more than three-quarters of households with incomes over $150,000, and roughly 70 percent of all consumers, say that they would spend more on their purchases if they could find better products and services that still fit their budget. So, while parsimony may rule their overall spending, consumers admit considerable spending flexibility when it comes to their individual purchases.

The problem is that even though clear demand exists for a new middle ground between pure luxury and mass-market positions, many companies have failed to see and act on the opportunity. One likely reason is that they have drawn their product position maps too small. In this case, a golf ball maker is likely to see premium brands existing side by side with discount brands and view the market as fully served. Likewise, a toothpaste maker might consider all the positions in its market saturated. Seeing scores of varieties available, ranging from Rembrandt and Tom's of Maine in premium positions (one Tom's variety even features the biblically famous myrrh) to store brands occupying the saver/value positions, a manufacturer could easily conclude that the range of possibilities is covered.

FIGURE 2-1

The New Middle Ground of Positioning

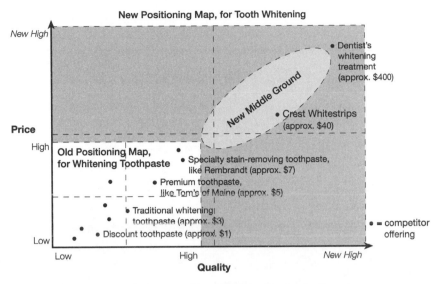

Expanded positioning map for tooth whitening from whitening toothpaste.

The rise of the moneyed masses, with the accompanying broad increases in income across top-earning households, however, obliges executives to widen their maps. For example, if we consider not just the product called toothpaste but the goal of teeth whitening, we now see professional dental whitening treatments anchoring the upper end of superpremium offerings at the top of the map's spectrum. This widening of the product positioning map creates a newly visible gap—the new middle ground—between real performance and the status quo (figure 2-1). The widening creates a sense of new possibilities and a new awareness of the real limits of consumer spending in the market. In this case, it highlighted the opportunity for Procter & Gamble to enter the market with a $40 home whitening product called Crest Whitestrips (we will explore the development of this market-defining new product in more depth later).

These new opportunities shouldn't be confused with *affordable luxury* or the strategy of breaking compromises, both of which call for creating a cheaper version of the premium offerings at hand on an old-style version of the product positioning map. What we are recommending is finding a slot for offerings in the gap between today's real luxury offerings and the best of existing offerings in yesterday's product positioning map.

It is important to consider and expand product positioning maps frequently—at least every few years—because too often, marketers neglect to consider that yesterday's luxury has become today's necessity. For example, where once a European vacation would have counted as the trip of a lifetime, it is now but a weekend getaway for a whole class of New Yorkers. The bar has thus been raised on luxury in the travel category.

But we recognize that at least two chestnuts of conventional wisdom keep many executives from creating such expansive positioning maps for their products, much less from relying on them. The first, which comes straight out of many marketing textbooks, is what is referred to as the heart of strategic marketing: STP, which stands for *segment* the customers first, *target* the attractive segments, and then *position* the offerings. We do not recommend throwing out this approach entirely, but it can be a deterrent to finding new middle ground and serving large masses of customers. Defining fine slices of customer segments as a first step to positioning can lead to very narrow definitions of what qualifies as a premium or luxury offering and can make it harder to expand the map. More importantly, segmenting customers as a first step can make opportunities in the new middle ground seem less significant than they are—even when recognized—because they have not been imagined as potentially attractive across a broad enough range of potential buyers. Executives focused on—and responsible for—their own particular customer segments are not likely to consider whether potential new middle ground offerings would fill similar recognizable gaps in other customer segments. As a result, these marketers may fail to see the larger pan-segment opportunity in a new-middle-ground solution.

There are two additional benefits to be had in starting with a more expansive market view than STP marketing entails. Aiming at an all-encompassing market can help marketers capture greater numbers of low probability buyers—those who for many reasons cannot be relied on to purchase, but may do so. In many cases these are the majority of all buyers. The second benefit is that it helps marketers to capture greater numbers of occasional buyers: those who will purchase to increase the variety in their consumption, but may not be reliable or loyal users. These customers are also often a significant portion of total demand, and with growing affluence, many new middle ground purchases may start as an occasional splurge and develop into a regular habit.

To overcome positioning inertia and to find the new middle ground, we recommend that executives experiment with first thinking only about positioning for the moneyed masses. Executives should pick a substantially higher price point than their category's current average (anywhere from two to ten times higher is a good start) and then imagine what they could possibly offer, given the freedom to spend—on development as well as delivery—that those sorts of price points would give them. What unmet customer needs could be addressed, and what innovative approaches could be considered, if the company were expecting to make that kind of money from each sale? This exercise should lead to ideas like creating a $6 disposable spinning toothbrush—positioned well below $60 rechargeable ones, but well above the $4 or so upper limit for manual toothbrushes—as opposed to looking for another way to angle bristles on a $2 toothbrush.

Only after the ideas and offerings begin to form should marketers consider how the ideas might be tailored and positioned for particular customer segments. At this point, executives may even find that significant tailoring isn't necessary. Products like Chrysler's PT Cruiser automobile and Vans skateboarding shoes, for example, have found their success in having buyers across segments, in every age and income category.

The second chestnut of conventional wisdom—also touted in many basic marketing texts—is the advice to avoid the middle in a position map. This teaching comes from the belief that such offerings are not likely to be sufficiently differentiated. Such a belief arises from defining markets too narrowly and using the common heuristic of defining any market as having mainly mass market and luxury positions. But as our golf ball example demonstrates, the new middle position is often very attractive; sometimes it's even the only viable slot. In the rest of this chapter, we will see how companies are creating tremendous business success by opening their minds to the new middle of the map, once that map is sufficiently broadly defined.

Minding the New-Middle-Ground Gap

Our research reveals three generalized strategies for conquering the middle ground. Which of the three strategies (outlined below) could be right for your product or brand? It depends on your current market position—that is, mass market, luxury brand, or a new entrant—as well as your unique capabilities.

Dominate the new middle. Make the new-middle-ground position the company's core and only focus and raison d'être. This move requires relinquishing any existing positions a company may have in the mass or luxury markets.

Elevate mass-market goods for affluent appeal. Companies can implement this strategy by launching distinctive, higher-quality versions of current offerings. This move may be couched as a brand extension, but must involve real benefit enhancement to be successful.

Open the door to luxury. Carefully introduce more affordable versions of an existing luxury good and brand.

Marketing executives will rightly fear that introducing a new offering tier, from whichever direction, brings added complexity and business risk. A successful introduction requires preserving brand equity, protecting margins, and maintaining operational consistency as new offerings are brought to market. Yet, taking such risks is an imperative for better price realization and business performance.

Dominate the New Middle

In board games like chess and checkers and in field sports like football and soccer, success almost always lies in controlling the center of the playing field. Yet many businesses have moved to the ends of theirs. In some sectors, however, the opportunity presented by consumers in the new middle is so great that business executives must seriously evaluate launching entirely new businesses, or brands and subbrands, dedicated explicitly to the new middle. This step may require abandoning current businesses that are underperforming, for the sake of improving strategic focus and eliminating customer confusion. Which industries merit such a concerted effort? Three characteristics mark those with the greatest potential. First, a substantial gap should exist between how the current mass market and luxury offerings are produced and sold, and there should be a commensurate gap in the relative value they deliver. Second, consumers should have problems or needs not addressed by the mass-market offerings. Finally, a unique approach should be newly available (usually through the creative use of technology) that entrenched players have rejected or missed and that can meet those needs and support economies of scale while producing higher-margin, better-quality offerings.

Housing construction, one such industry, has already produced one of the most successful new-middle-ground "pure plays" in any sector: national home builder Toll Brothers. Founded in 1967, Toll Brothers has evolved from building move-up homes in suburban Philadelphia into the nation's leading provider of affluent residences. The company now enjoys having 39,000 constructed homes under its belt and active projects in twenty-two states. Despite the recent economic slowdown, the company grew to $2.3 billion in revenues in 2002 and reported record income, contracts, order backlog, and revenues in the first quarter of 2003.

Toll Brothers has achieved its success, thanks to a laser focus on the unmet needs of newly affluent home buyers. The company realized that these consumers' needs were not being satisfied by either existing mass-market builders or those dedicated to building luxury homes. What's more—and just as important—the customers' needs weren't being met by the home-building process. Fred Cooper, vice president of finance at Toll Brothers, told us, "We have always targeted a specific niche of sophisticated home buyers. That niche is between completely custom, architect-designed residences and more traditional subdivisions. Our customers want to live in a community of fine homes, yet do not have the time or inclination to do everything themselves—choosing a builder, an architect, and a lot, then navigating the permit and approval process."[7]

Fulfilling this market need and translating it into a successful business has compelled Toll Brothers to build homes that can be delivered leveraging economies of scale from volume production, yet which feature significant levels of customization. While all Toll Brothers homes share common luxury appointments, the company provides customers with thousands of prepriced upgrades and enhancements, from conservatories to four-car garages and specialized landscaping. As Kira McCarron, Toll Brothers vice president of marketing, explains, "Our customers have more desires and wishes than other groups. They want every possible amenity and improvement, and have the financial resources to enjoy them."[8] With its awareness of the moneyed masses' lifestyles, Toll Brothers has even pioneered innovative new home features. Consider its trademarked Spacement, a built-out living area that replaces the dank, unfinished basements that few busy modern professional families would use.

Yet, premium add-ons are more than a way to customize an offering for the middle ground. They also create substantial profit opportunities by enabling companies to capture higher prices at a relatively low cost to deliver. For example, the average Toll Brothers customer now spends about $90,000 on lot premiums and custom options, bringing the entire home tab to $515,000—almost $200,000 more than what other national home builders charge.[9]

Toll Brothers avoided two business risks in securing the new-middle-ground position. The first risk is offering a product that is customized to the point that the company can no longer fully leverage its scale. Toll Brothers has wisely conducted research to understand where this threshold lies. According to Cooper, "We have built homes up to about $1.5 million. Above that level, we perceive two challenges. One is that when you move above a certain range of incomes, the number of target customers rapidly tapers off. As importantly, project management becomes more challenging. Timelines can easily get out of whack on a pure custom project. So, we know where the limits of our model are."[10]

The second risk is that customers will have a negative perception of the mass production that supports affordable new-middle-ground offerings. Affluent consumers want to feel that their purchases are more distinctive and prestigious than mass-market goods, even if their purchases share some of the same components or manufacturing processes. Toll Brothers has tackled this challenge—and differentiated itself from other builders—by offering custom-builder-like customer service, including spending significant time with customers to explore options and resolve issues. To support this level of service, the company is distributing significant control to the level of communities under construction and is staffing projects with responsive, highly skilled professionals. McCarron describes the staffing strategies: "Our construction teams operate like small, independent builders and retain an entrepreneurial spirit. We deliberately staff these groups with well-rounded generalists—such as MBAs, engineers, architects, and land planning experts—so they can provide the better, more personalized service that our customers expect."[11]

Looking ahead, Toll Brothers is confident that its early and consistent focus on the new middle ground has given it a first-mover advantage and has positioned the company to thrive despite emerging industry challenges. The appeal of its homes has already buoyed the company through uncertain economic times—it had an enviable $1.89 billion backlog of contracts in 2003. Yet, the entire home-building industry is beginning to grapple with increasingly restrictive construction regulations and a rise in antidevelopment sentiment. McCarron believes that Toll Brothers is well positioned: "As communities become more vigilant about new development, we benefit from being a known entity that has already built quality homes and attracted desirable new residents. If a community is to accept any development, we think that we are the most likely to be accepted."[12]

Know What You Don't Know About the Moneyed Masses

Although from the very start—even before it went national—Toll Brothers has maintained a sharp focus on the new middle ground, other companies have come to focus successfully on the space between luxury and mass-market positions without such a clear long-term vision or intention. These companies may start in the new middle and have some amount of success, but can lose sight of their customers or their own position in the market. Some companies may have offerings in the luxury and mass markets as well as the middle, but eventually realize that simply having a middle-ground offering is not the same as taking a new-middle-ground position and therefore is no guarantee of success. Without a commitment to the specific desires and needs of the moneyed masses, brands risk attracting a fragmented customer base and becoming the last, desperate choice for two groups: wealthy consumers who are reaching down to save money and mass-market consumers who are compromising while moving up. In either case, the brands miss becoming a worthy goal all their own.

Firms such as Coach and Lacoste have overcome such inertia by initiating programs to generate superior customer knowledge, using the findings to position offerings specifically for the targeted moneyed masses. Doing so has enabled these companies to thrive, despite the recent economic pull-back that has caused many luxury makers to suffer.

Consider how Coach overcame a brand identity crisis in the mid-1990s. Although the company had built its reputation selling high-quality handbags at prices a step below those of haute couture designers, rivals like Kate Spade sapped its momentum by releasing more stylish options at an affordable price point in the high end. Other makers nipped at Coach's heels by improving quality at the lower end. Corporate revenues stalled at around a half billion dollars. Industry analysts feared that the company was drifting into the doldrums.

Coach's turnaround came from a number of changes, not the least of which was the appointment of industry visionary Lew Frankfort as CEO. But the new management team was able to bring the business back to life by relying on—and investing heavily in—customer research. By 2003, the company was spending $2 million per year on customer surveys alone. It has a seven-million-household database that it mines for insight, and over one million e-mail addresses that the company uses to communicate with customers.[13]

Of equal importance, the company uses the results of its consumer research in every step of the product development process, creating linkages from insight to action that ensure it produces exactly what new-middle-ground consumers desire. For example, product launch milestones are now synchronized with customer feedback checkpoints. One year before an impending product launches, Coach invites hundreds of consumers to critique the item and compare it with existing offerings. Products that pass this initial customer screen are then piloted in a selection of stores nationwide six months before their planned companywide rollout, giving Coach the time and flexibility to evaluate sales and customer responses and to make adjustments.[14]

The company's focus on an increased understanding of the needs and desires of new-middle-ground consumers, which it then ties closely to production, has helped Coach release a series of successful bags. Attention to the middle ground has also supported the company's expansion into complementary lines such as men's apparel and luggage.

Coach's commitment to serving the new-middle-ground customer has paid off. In the 2002 fiscal year, Coach's revenues increased 20 percent, to $719 million, while its operating income grew 30 percent, to $137 million.[15] New-middle-ground customers, meanwhile, are enthusiastic about the brand. A 2002 *Women's Wear Daily* survey found that upper-income American women rank Coach's products ahead of those by Ralph Lauren, Fendi, and Hermes. Through market-leading customer insight, Coach successfully moved from being a default brand wedged between higher- and lower-end competitors to a company that serves the middle ground so effectively, some observers believe that it now stimulates entirely new sales.[16]

Sometimes, dominating the new middle ground is a matter of reclaiming your original place. In the case of Lacoste, purveyor of apparel with the famous crocodile logo, the brand spent almost the entire 1990s in an effort to regain its new-middle-ground turf, a position it lost under the ownership of General Mills, which let the brand slide into the mass market.[17] After buying the rights to the brand in the early 1990s, French apparel maker Devanlay has since set about upgrading Lacoste styles, materials, and distribution channels to appeal to consumers in the new middle ground. The shirts, which General Mills had downgraded to a cotton-polyester blend, are now made of Swiss yarn with mother-of-pearl buttons.

With an average price point of $70, the shirts appeal to a new-middle-ground customer who does not want a decidedly mass-market polo shirt for $50 (which is more likely $30 or less at the nearest outlet mall), but who is not willing to exceed the $100-plus price point into the offerings of luxury designers such as Burberry, Brioni, or Zegna. After many years, the Lacoste brand has finally regained its former luster. Lacoste sales grew by 10 to 15 percent every year between 1997 and 2002, reaching $900 million.[18]

Seizing the new middle ground is not a strategy without risks or challenges. Companies must usually overcome a lack of brand recognition while attempting to quickly reach breakeven in an untested position with an often untested business model. Yet, companies must overcome these challenges if they are to create markets instead of simply serving them.

Elevate the Masses' . . . Offerings

Moving from mass-market offerings to new-middle-market offerings is no easy task. Companies accustomed to working on small margins must recoup the entry costs associated with developing higher-quality offerings while sustaining existing economies of scale. And they must ensure that core mass-market customers do not feel abandoned by a brand that has become too hoity-toity for their tastes.

Fortunately, companies can maximize the success of their move upmarket by concentrating on improving and increasing the innovation in their offerings in three distinct ways. First, companies can raise product performance through improved technology. Second, they can infuse items with professional or near-professional capabilities. Finally, they can focus on offerings that radically increase customer convenience.

Better Living Through Technology

One of the most direct ways of gaining higher ground in the new middle is to significantly enhance performance by vastly improving the core technology of an existing offering. This works not only for traditional high-tech goods, but for everyday products as well. One consumer item costing only a couple of dollars and used by millions of Americans every morning is covered by no fewer than thirty-five patents. The product is Gillette's Mach3 razor, and shortly after its introduction in 1998, it became the best-selling razor in America. The creation of the patented technologies demanded a large expenditure for research, development, and marketing (*Fortune* magazine estimates the firm spent one billion dollars to bring the razor to market). The result, however, was an improvement so compelling to consumers that Gillette quickly recouped its initial investment and went on to earn quite a bit more.[19]

When Gillette launched the Mach3 in 1998, the company had already pioneered the market for double-bladed razors. The new model featured a triple-blade technology that the company boasted would provide men a closer shave than would any other razor. But for consumers, this kind of shaving performance would come at a price. The Mach3 retailed for an average price 35 percent higher than that of any other razor in the Gillette line.[20] Expensive, sure, but Gillette's offerings have remained a far cry from the traditional luxury position: a $50 straight razor with mock ivory handle from Caswell-Massey, for example (ideally wielded each morning by one's personal valet or perhaps a local barber).

The value proposition of the new razor proved compelling. It garnered the brand 28 percent of the men's razor market shortly after its introduction. The leap in performance persuaded many consumers to increase their spending on a single pack of razors by over 60 percent. Gillette won this increase despite the decades-long fall in the percentage of income spent on personal care among consumers in the top quintiles of income. And while much has been made of consumer willingness to splurge on personal indulgences—natural soaps, spa treatments, and the like—Gillette's Mach3 had only its shaving performance, not emotion, on its side.

Early in 2002, Gillette raised the price bar again with the launch of its Mach3 Turbo, which included additional technical innovations and a price tag 20 percent higher than even the Mach3.[21] And in January of 2004, Gillette raised the bar again by announcing the M3 Power razor; a battery operated version of the Mach3 Turbo that is protected by 62 patents of its own and which the company says, "outperformed the Mach3 Turbo in consumer tests on 68 measures, including closeness, smoothness and comfort."[22] Though slated to go on sale after the writing of this book, the razor is expected to retail for $14.99, a dramatic 66 percent increase over the $8.99 price of the Mach3 Turbo, with a similar increase in the price of the blades. If the past is any indication, this new product could take Gillette to new level of not just shaving, but business performance. Gillette's success provides a blueprint companies can use for taking technologically better versions of other mass-market goods into the new middle ground. In just a few years, the company transformed with better technologies one of the most mundane of daily items and moved its leading offerings into a dramatically higher price point.

Companies that want to make a similar leap could also learn from Gillette's marketing strategy. The firm took a wise approach to ensuring that its higher-priced offerings did not make any of its more frugal customers feel abandoned—by de-emphasizing, but not abruptly replacing, earlier product lines. Other firms might have been tempted to phase out the former flagship razor, the less expensive SensorExcel, thereby forcing consumers to trade up. But Gillette continued to sell the SensorExcel side by side with the Mach3, even though it focused its marketing dollars on the newer model. In other words, Gillette has managed its product portfolio in an accretive way, continuing to support lower tiers with proven mass-market appeal and avoiding the perception that the company has forsaken core customers in favor of those willing to spend several dollars more for a pack of razors.

Gillette has sustained this kind of success through technology for years, but its fortune hasn't gone unnoticed. Companies must be prepared to defend their patent rights if they think they are being infringed, and Gillette has done just that by litigating against Schick's recently introduced Quattro four-bladed razor. Such a defense can easily cost millions, but winning the battle could mean an even bigger victory. In a similar battle, the courts found that Kodak had infringed on Polaroid's instant photography technology. After a fourteen-year battle, Kodak was eventually forced to pay nearly a billion dollars in restitution to Polaroid, destroy remaining inventory, and give customers refunds. Kodak's failed attempt was estimated to have cost the company a total of nearly $3 billion.[23]

Provide Professional or Near-Professional Capabilities

Another strategy that helps move offerings into the middle ground is emulating offerings used by professionals, but delivering them in a more affordable, if feature-limited, way. For example, consumers are very interested in using at home some of the same products and technologies that they are accustomed to seeing in their doctor's or dentist's office. Perhaps no mass-market product category has exploited this potential as effectively as the oral-care industry. After years of launching innovative new products at premium price points, the category has achieved an enviable milestone: household expenditures on toothbrushes and oral hygiene appliances now increase proportionately with income.

How have oral-care companies reached this milestone? The answer lies in giving consumers access to professional levels of quality—the tools and ingredients once reserved exclusively for dentists. Procter & Gamble, for example, has brought dentist-office-like tooth whitening into the home, with the introduction of Whitestrips. Previously, consumers who wanted to brighten their smile could only choose between a $4 tube of Crest Whitening Toothpaste or $400 professional whitening.

Though fast-following competitors are driving price competition, consumers still regularly pay $40 or more—ten times the cost of a tube of toothpaste—for over-the-counter Whitestrips, a product that packaged the same whitening power that the dentist had for convenient consumer use. Though entry costs were probably steep, the payoff has been tremendous. In their first full year on the market, Whitestrips generated sales of $200 million and became the most profitable item offered by many drugstore chains.[24] Procter & Gamble now vows that it can grow Whitestrips into a $1 billion brand.[25]

Another coup for oral-care firms has been the explosive growth in sales of battery-operated toothbrushes. These items feature motorized heads similar to those used in professional tooth cleaning. Although power toothbrushes have been on the market for many years, they remained mostly at a price point—around $100—apparently too high for broad uptake. New products such as Crest SpinBrush retail for far less, often in the $5 to $7 range.

The new brushes are not luxury replacements or truly luxurious. Their technology lags behind that of the $100 models, and their construction quality is, expectedly, that of a disposable. Instead of trying to imitate the top, companies are using these brushes to "up-sell" the buyers of manual toothbrushes, who have proven willing to spend more for a better experience. These companies thus strategically filled the void between \$3 brushes and \$100 near-dental tools. The success of their efforts has been impressive. Americans bought 22.8 million new powered brushes between July 2001 and July 2002, a 721 percent increase in unit sales over the same period two years earlier. The category as a whole grew by about 48 percent, to \$230 million, according to ACNielsen. Presented with a meaningful, easy-to-understand improvement in product performance—consumers already knew the brushes from years of dentist visits—consumers upgraded their spending and bought the new offerings in record numbers.

Procter & Gamble's success with this strategy is no accident, and the company plans to continue using it. As CEO A. G. Lafley told analysts in 2003, "One of the things we focus on when we try to grow a new category or create a new category, and this is what we did with whitening, is we try to bring things out of the professional area, and I'm not talking about brands, but I'm talking about habits and practices that you can do at home with less risk, more ease and all the rest of it. We will try to make the home hair coloring process a much easier, much simpler experience and that's a big opportunity."[26]

Offer Convenience (at a Price)

Marketers can also support a move into a distinctly higher selling price by reassembling their existing offerings into more convenient packaging and portions. This approach not only exploits the desire of the moneyed masses to spend more on convenience items, but also provides companies several operational advantages. For example, research and development costs for repackaging a product are relatively low, allowing companies to limit their expenses to the development of effective packaging and marketing. What's more, the approach can provide companies new occasions to sell raw materials already at their disposal.

This success at repackaging has certainly been the case in bag salads, which Dole Foods and other firms have created using existing lettuce suppliers. Back in the early 1990s, few food companies might have expected that anyone could build a \$1.6 billion business out of lettuce pieces that looked so unappealing, laborers routinely left them in the field. After some scrubbing, cutting, and packaging, these leftovers look tasty and have found new life in the form of bag salads.

These companies have succeeded by packaging existing ingredients in a way that creates a far more convenient customer experience. Consumers like bag salads because they provide prewashed, premixed, fresh food that can last twice as long in the refrigerator as the same vegetables off the supermarket shelf. In return, shoppers pay twice as much as they would for head lettuce, though few consumers seem to mind.[27] Dole Foods claims that the average consumer buys twelve bags of salad per year, and 74 percent of households have purchased it at least once.[28] The appeal of bag salad is so strong that it can now withstand fluctuations in the price of lettuce. During a 2002 market glut in California, head lettuce prices hit twelve-year lows, yet the price of bag salad did not budge.

Other companies are also adding value by reassembling familiar items in innovative ways that increase consumer convenience. For example, Kraft Foods sells nearly $500 million of its Lunchables, children's meals that provide everything from bologna to pizza, chips, and drinks in a single shrink-wrapped tray. Although parents could buy an entire pound of bologna for as little as $2.50, many will shell out between $2 and $3 for a single, preparation-free box of Lunchables that they can drop into a lunch bag.

A similar approach is helping other firms to profit by taking some of the tedium out of housecleaning. The fast-growing category of cleaning wipes, including products ranging from P&G's Swiffers to Clorox Disinfecting Wipes, is expected to reach nearly $2 billion in sales. The wipes let marketers combine the strength of the household solvents they already manufacture and the convenience of a disposable cleaning cloth. The result is a single, easy-to-use, disposable item that helps the company capture a premium. A package of Clorox wipes costs about $2.75 for thirty sheets, compared with the pennies a consumer would spend simply to dilute a few capfuls of bleach in a basin of water and then apply the mixture with a paper towel.

Cleaning supplies, bag salad, and bologna may seem a bit too ordinary to be the makings of affluent fair. But unlike the megawealthy, the moneyed masses commute, prepare meals, clean their own homes, and do laundry. The products we described, and others, strike at the heart of the busy affluent. These consumers are not prepared financially or spiritually to give up the routines of an ordinary life, but will jump at the chance to perform these activities with less effort, almost regardless of price.

Are there any downsides to this approach for entrenched players? Some customers may feel a sense of brand abandonment, if the new brands and offerings seem too highbrow for their modest lifestyles. And the costs of innovative technologies can be staggering, creating a barrier to entry for many companies concerned about short-term profitability. But as the mass market goes, so too must go those that desire to serve them.

Give Them a Taste of Heaven

"Affordable luxury" cannot help sounding a bit déclassé. After all, luxury is traditionally about distinction and the creation of boundaries that the hoi palloi cannot, and do not, cross. But as many luxury makers have discovered, upholding strict boundaries can be bad for business. A customer base that is too narrow becomes vulnerable to spending volatility, threatening business performance in uncertain economic times. It can also relegate a firm to obsolescence if core customers age without being replaced by younger ones.

Creating entry-level or near-luxury offerings tackles both of these challenges head-on. By selectively reaching down, luxury firms can improve their financial position while grooming their customer base for future growth. And they can count on strong support for this strategy from consumers. Our research found that a majority of consumers at every income level say that they would like to see more lower-priced offerings from luxury brands. Yet extending a luxury brand is an inherently risky proposition. Precious brand images can be quickly tarnished, and the lower margins on down-market offerings can be tough to handle until offsetting high sales volumes are achieved. Others will find moving down-market simply too much of a stretch for their upscale brands. The short life of Grey Poupon Yellow mustard serves as just one example of a premium brand's trying to go too far, too fast. Nonetheless, the latent value of today's best brands—value that comes from the opportunity in the moneyed masses—cannot be captured without careful forays down into the new middle ground.

Three critical tactics successfully exploit this pent-up demand for a taste of the best while managing the three biggest risks that companies face in such a move: First, retain the most important characteristics of the luxury brand while sacrificing other costly components. Second, avoid compromising quality while attempting to maximize sales and control costs. And third, use real and perceived scarcity as a hedge against brand dilution.

Ain't Nothing Like the Real Thing

When creating an entry point to a luxury brand, marketers must be careful not to sacrifice the features and attributes that attract consumers in the first place. Consumers show little interest in what some industry observers call "democratized luxury," which conjures up images of the low-end Gucci accessories that appeared in popular department stores in the 1980s. Consider that a full 72 percent of consumers say that they prefer buying one superior product to multiple lesser goods. The vast majority of consumers want access to the higher quality and performance that gives luxury makers their cachet, but require it at prices they can afford.

To understand how marketers can strike the right balance, consider the recent experiences of high-end automakers. Standard-bearers such as Mercedes, BMW, and Volvo have all pioneered new territory for their brands by launching lower-priced models that sell in the $30,000 range. While many of these vehicles are relatively small sedans, they carry the unmistakable design characteristics of their more expensive counterparts. These makers insist that their affordable luxury models uphold the high standards of quality, safety, and reliability that consumers expect from them. For example, various publications, from *Car and Driver* to *Automobile Magazine,* have showered BMW's 3 Series with quality awards. And Volvo's new XC90 sport utility vehicle (SUV), for a sticker price of just over $33,000, comes equipped with four safety systems that not even a $100,000 Hummer offers.[29] In this way, these brands have moved down-market without compromising the core attributes that make them famous.

As a result, affluent consumers have embraced cars in the entry-level luxury segment with enthusiasm, despite a challenging automotive market. In 2002, automakers sold 600,000 of these models, an increase of 20 percent over the previous year.[30] This type of entry-level demand growth serves luxury makers well as a hedge against volatile demand for their more limited production, top-of-the-line products. While sales of Lexus's entry-level ES300 increased by 86 percent in the first seven months of 2002, its flagship LS430 suffered a 22 percent drop.[31]

Keep Quality Job One

Luxury makers that want to reach down into the middle must plan to address two operational challenges, which if left unchecked can tarnish the brand across all their offerings. The first is to manage effectively the strain on operating capabilities, from the production line to the supply chain to the call center, created by the deliberate increase in sales volumes. While some automakers we just described have successfully made the transition, others have found the downward move more challenging. After Mercedes ramped up production for its new entry-level SUV and A Class lines, the subsequent rise in vehicle problems caused Mercedes to rate a surprisingly low thirteenth among all brands rated in J. D. Power's 2002 survey of new vehicle quality, a rating tied with definitely mass-market Chevrolet.[32] At Jaguar, a similar spate of glitches in its affordable X-Type cars contributed to an overall drop from second to nineteenth place in the same ranking in just one year. This bad news was compounded when X-Type sales fell by 42 percent during the first two months of 2003.[33]

Likewise, firms must not attempt to compensate for the lower margins on entry-level offerings through cost-cutting opportunities that undermine the value to the consumer. In some cases, the efforts to make luxury affordable through production efficiencies can go too far. For example, some industry critics and auto aficionados were disturbed to learn that Ford had decided to build Jaguar's entry-level X-Type on the chassis of its inexpensive Mondeo compact sedan—a rather pedestrian brand association. Christopher W. Cedergren, the managing director of automobile industry consultants Nextrend, told *BusinessWeek,*

"Component-sharing is fine, but it can be trouble if it gets to the point that people start thinking, 'Gee, this is just a gussied-up Ford.'"[34] Even if the customers don't notice at first, competitors might. Stolichnaya grew its sales significantly when it proudly informed the world through an advertising campaign that it was still being produced in Russia, the home of great vodka, whereas its competitors had moved to less qualified places to lower costs—like Smirnoff, which had moved production from Poland to Hartford, Connecticut.

Sometimes the sources of discontent can be quite subtle, and a company may require effective dialogue with consumers to tease out the causes. An extreme but important example comes from the auto industry. One automaker's customers told the company (through customer surveys) that they didn't like the plastic covers used in the dashboard to hide where the components used in the pricier models were supposed to be. The customers saw the covers as a constant reminder that they had bought an entry-level model rather than a true luxury vehicle.

The need to mitigate production-related problems may at first seem like an operational issue—one that falls outside the focus of this book. We nevertheless believe that marketers have a particular role in effectively communicating consumer tolerances and attitudes throughout the organization, and in managing demand planning and sales forecasting. While the pressure to recoup investments quickly in new middle ground offerings is great, overly aggressive short-term sales goals must not be allowed to set the stage for production problems that will hurt long-term brand confidence.

Manage Brand Access

Groucho Marx famously surmised that he'd never want to join a club that would have him as a member. Likewise, near-luxury providers must manage access to their brand if they hope to remain desirable. The key question here, one several automakers have already faced, is just how to retain that all-important aura of exclusiveness while substantially growing the customer base.

One important solution is to create scarcity, even at lower price points. For example, Mercedes has wisely capped target sales of its entry-model C230 Kompressor Sports Coupe (base price near $30,000) at just 18,000 per year, thereby avoiding flooding the market. Dave Schembri, vice president of marketing for Mercedes-Benz in North America, explained to *Automotive News,* "If we stay true to our core values and maintain our objective as an aspirational brand, we can enter any segment."[35]

BMW has achieved the same goal by gradually ramping up production of its popular $18,000 Mini Cooper compact. Helmut Panke, BMW's management board chairman, explains the company's rationale: "It's our philosophy to do expansions step by step. In the ideal case, we should always be one car short in capacity. That means there's always one more customer out there who wants a BMW, and he or she might have to wait one extra period to get it."[36] Panke's words eloquently sum up the goal of any affordable-luxury provider—ensuring that customers feel they have bought into a coveted brand experience, regardless of the price point. This out-of-stock strategy can be applied far beyond offerings as expensive as automobiles. In 2003, the *Wall Street Journal* reported on the trend to "mass-market" waiting lists being created among new middle ground players, to increase the allure for everything from $85 trucker caps from Von Dutch to leather bomber jackets intentionally underproduced at Banana Republic.[37]

For some high end providers, particularly traditional luxury goods makers that rely on fashion as much as functional excellence to sell their products, creating artificial scarcity may not be enough to overcome the risk of brand dilution. But mass affluence creates important opportunities for these companies in their customary markets. The dramatic growth of a new plutocracy in the United States—households earning over $300,000 as indicated on Figure 1-1—represents a windfall of opportunity for sales growth (for some makers signifying a return to targeting customers by income rather than aspiration or desired symbolic use). In addition, the growth of new middle ground offerings can leave many consumers wanting an even better solution once they have had a taste of what's possible; a desire luxury makers must be ready to act on. For example, many dentists are finding demand for their whitening services is being driven by those disappointed, or excited, by the results they have already achieved using new middle ground solutions such as Crest White Strips.

The threat to the traditional luxury position from mass affluence comes from price and spending creep. With the number of cars priced between $100,000 and $200,000 jumping to 17 from 9 between 2003 and 2004—with new offerings from BMW, Audi, and even Volkswagen—a $150,000 Bentley can start to look pretty middle of the road. Diageo responded to mass affluence driven price and spending creep in the spirits market by creating its Reserve Brands Group of luxury drinks in 2003, which includes Johnnie Walker Gold and Blue and Tanqueray No. 10. This was on top of its already premium offerings. So for some luxury goods makers, the challenge of mass affluence is as much to ensure that part of the business stays ahead of mass consumption, and out of the new middle ground, as it is to find ways to move down into it.

From Filling a Gap to Building a Ladder

As companies converge on the new middle ground to serve new affluence—moving up-market, down-market, and directly into the space—marketers should expect the shape of entire markets to change. Offerings once structured into clear tiers will evolve into a blurry continuum of products and services that mirror the increasing diversity of consumer income distribution.

The restaurant industry provides an early glimpse of how such changes are likely to play out in other sectors. In just a few short years, it has spawned no fewer than four new market positions.

At the high end, the most exclusive restaurants have sought to leverage their brand value by moving into the new middle with lower-priced concept restaurants that still uphold the chef's commitment to quality dining. In France, Michelin-starred chefs initially raised eyebrows by opening more casual brasseries and bistros not far from the haute-cuisine establishments that built their reputations—a trend that has spread to U.S. metropolitan areas. Among the most coveted restaurant reservations in New York City, for example, is an evening at Chef Daniel

Boulud's top-rated restaurant, Daniel, where diners can expect to pay top dollar for some of the finest food in the world. But those on a more limited budget or wishing to splurge more often can now enjoy his talents in the more affordable, if more understated, sister restaurants Café Boulud and DB Bistro Moderne.

Meanwhile, one step below, several new restaurants have launched to serve the moneyed masses' dining needs on a daily basis. Consider the Cheesecake Factory. Its format combines the convenience and service of mass-market eateries such as Applebee's with the refined menu choices found at up-market specialty restaurants. As a result, customers now often wait more than two hours to get a table among the Egyptian-tomb-meets-Roman-bath decor at locations in mass-affluent havens such as Beverly Hills, California (the restaurant's first location), Chestnut Hill, Massachusetts, and Woodlands, Texas.[38]

For affluent consumers on the go, upstarts such as Panera Bread and Pret A Manger have made waves by creating a third tier that provides a more refined alternative to fast food—the so-called fast-casual segment. At Panera, each location offers bread freshly baked on the premises, as well as sandwiches, soups, and salads in the $6 price range. Some industry observers believe that this niche, currently just under $5 billion in annual revenues and comprising 2 percent of the market, could overtake the $50 billion casual-dining sector by around 2012.[39]

The fast-casual segment is a certainly a significant opportunity space, but its existence and emergence should not shock anyone. Some credit Panera as being the archetypal luxury for the masses, but surprisingly, the brand occupies essentially the same cost position McDonald's once held when it first started out (calculating sandwich costs by the amount of work time required at the average wage, then and now). Since 1970, McDonald's hamburgers are down 20 percent in terms of the number of minutes a person must work to buy one. During the same period, the famous Big Mac—itself an example of a move to a higher price point by an increased portion size with its now famous two all-beef patties—has declined by 13 percent.[40] The turning point that opened the door to the higher-quality fast-casual position probably came in 1997, when "McDonald's stunned the burger world by announcing a deep discount on its signature sandwich, the Big Mac."[41] Some scholars believe the decision resulted in more than a downward pricing move, but a downward positioning of the entire category, particularly after McDonald's failed to capture higher price points with new sandwiches like the premium-priced Arch Deluxe. As Gene Cameron, vice president of marketing at fast-casual eatery Baja Fresh, told *Brandweek,* "We didn't outgrow fast food. Fast food didn't grow with us."[42]

It is no surprise, then, that even the lowest tier of eateries, quick-service restaurants, or "fast food," is now reaching back up to capture a more moneyed crowd. Taco Bell, for example, has found a successful new product line with its Border Bowls line, which uses fresher and higher-quality ingredients. While the price points are hardly exclusive at $3 to $3.50 per bowl, Taco Bell president Emil Boleck explains that the company is trying to create a new tier between the fast-food giants and fast-casual eateries.[43] The company asserts that the meals have already helped the chain to attract new customer segments and increase same-store sales by nearly 10 percent.[44]

Brand New

Many of the same production efficiencies that enable companies to expand the range of their targeted customers apply across the entire range of consumer spending potential, leading companies to build what are known as brand pyramids. Production efficiencies are one leading driver, but channel access or power, and even shared accounting or customer care capabilities can drive multitiered brand management in companies. Most recently, this approach has focused, appropriately, on increasing the brands positioned for the new middle ground.

We see evidence of this trend in the auto industry, where every major player is actively pursuing what we call a soup-to-caviar strategy. Ford has broadened its coverage of market positions by an acquisitions and ventures strategy that has included capturing a stake in Volvo, Jaguar, Land Rover, and venerable Aston Martin. BMW is following an organic growth strategy, introducing its version of the Mini to capture the low end, and currently working on a 1 Series to fit between the Mini and the 3 Series, an X3 version of its X5 SUV offering, and a 6 Series coupe to fit, naturally, between its 5 and 7 Series.

Kraft built a brand pyramid on top of its famous Tombstone pizza by layering family-value brand Jack's on top of the pyramid in the early 1990s, then adding DiGiorno in 1995 on top of that, and placing California Pizza Kitchen (CPK) at the very top in 1998. The clear new-middle-ground winner for Kraft, however, in terms of both position and profitability, has been DiGiorno: a convenient meal solution aimed at adults accustomed to restaurant and takeout pizza. The brand has been a tremendous success for Kraft, growing the pizza division sales by 20 percent its first year and driving significant growth ever since.

DiGiorno, in fact, has followed the new-middle-ground strategy by extending the category's product positioning map to include not just frozen pizza, but delivered restaurant pizza. When DiGiorno was introduced in 1995, there was a clear gap between the best that frozen pizza could do in terms of quality, and the quality of delivered pizza. So besides expanding the company's thinking on quality, expanding the map allowed Kraft to consider challenging a then $19 billion market for delivered pizza, instead of just continuing to compete for frozen pizza's relatively tiny $2 billion market.[45]

While delivered pizza hardly seems a luxury today, it certainly was several years ago, at least when compared to the standard product served up by the frozen-pizza market, in terms of both cost and consumer attitude. People were just starting to get used to delivered pizza as an everyday occurrence and not something special, thanks to the advent of companies like Domino's. These low-cost, fast deliverers were also just beginning to pose a new and significant threat to frozen. Mary Kay Haben, in charge of launching DiGiorno for Kraft, told *Mediaweek* at the time, "When we first started there was that initial skepticism. Will anybody pay $5.59 for a frozen pizza given that they're used to getting two for $5? Even though people pay $10 for a delivery pizza, they did not want to believe that a frozen pizza would taste as good as restaurant pizza."[46]

One way in which DiGiorno worked to overcome the price issue was by intentionally targeting upscale families in 1998 with the DiGiorno/ PGA Tour Rolling Clubhouse. Since golf is a major sport of interest for the moneyed masses, the mobile clubhouse visited 124 cities that summer "to attract youths to the sport and families in general to DiGiorno."[47] The California Pizza Kitchen frozen line has been Kraft's next step in moving upscale, and though the line is fairly new to the market, results have been very promising. While Blair Boggs, senior marketing manager for the brand, rejects "gourmet" as a descriptor, he is comfortable with the appellation "upscale."[48] Though still early in its introduction, the line has been reporting strong returns.

Claiming the New Middle Ground

Commentators from Dorothy Parker to Frank Lloyd Wright have paraphrased Plutarch's aphorism "Give us the luxuries of life, and we will dispense with its necessities." In doing so, these commentators provide continuing insight into a timeless perception. Luxuries have always been rare, exquisite things that exist outside the routine of one's daily life. Necessities have always been mundane and uninspiring. And for most of history, consumers have had to choose between them; there was no middle-ground solution. Today, this is still true in too many categories of offerings in too many industries.

Yet, the rise of the moneyed masses is forcing marketers to stake out a new middle ground that bridges the gulf between luxury and mass-market positions. This middle ground, however, is not likely to remain a distinct third way for marketers for the long term. As is already becoming evident from developments in the restaurant, auto, and consumer packaged-goods industries, companies should look ahead with a view toward offering a seamless continuum of products and services optimized for very different customer needs, lifestyles, and, most especially, incomes.

Such a continuum can, and undoubtedly will, create some confusion. The distinctions between offerings will become increasingly subtle, requiring clearer messaging and positioning than ever before. Clarity is essential, because buying decisions will become more complex, as brands stretch to their limits and consumers are driven to evaluate a richer set of criteria when choosing from this profusion of options.

The downside of blurry messages to consumers is coming to the fore in the increasing competition between the Volkswagen and Audi brands. Since the late 1990s, many consumers have struggled to tell the difference between the Audi A4 and Volkswagen Passat, both of which include similar design, components, and price points.

But how will consumers receive the $100,000 Phaeton from "people's car" provider Volkswagen, when the Phaeton trumps Audi's previously exclusive luxury position? CEO Bernt Pischetsrieder explains it this way: "There was never a hierarchy between the two brands."[49] But it remains to be seen whether consumers will agree.

As the dust settles, we think that trends initiated by the conquering of the new middle ground will only bode well for consumers and marketers alike. Consumers will be rewarded with a general increase in the quality of their offerings, which will make their lives more convenient, efficient, and enjoyable. For companies, the new positions will provide a refuge from the price wars and commoditization that have soured the mass market. The hard-won production efficiencies of recent decades will now be applied toward the creation of higher-margin products and services that generate not just spending, but profitable spending, among many more customers for years to come.

3

Treat Some Customers
More Equal Than Others

Old Rule
Offer identical things, at a price affordable to all.

New Rule
Offer nearly identical things to all, at the price they can afford.

For many seasoned skiers, fresh powder is a kind of promised land. It's pure and thrilling, yet a skier often must have a degree of fanaticism to find it. Some skiers experience it by renting helicopters that will drop them on otherwise inaccessible peaks, whereas others trek for hours to reach remote bowls. The next-best option is to be among the first in the lift line—no small feat at most resorts. A skier has to rise before 4:00 A.M. to stand under the cold cover of darkness until the first rangers arrive.

Today, however, some ski resorts are offering a new path to this promised land. From Utah to Vermont, ski operators have recognized how highly prized this fresh powder is to some of their customers and have created a new revenue stream by offering this once priceless experience to these customers, at a price. Deer Valley ski resort in Utah, for example, offers the first hour of slope time to any individual or group of up to eight willing to pay a $1,000 fee. Called First Tracks, the program is ostensibly a lesson and includes a personal ski guide in the price.

Deer Valley is not alone. For $124, just about twice the regular lift ticket price of $61, Copper Mountain in Colorado gives skiers the right to enter the slopes fifteen minutes before the resort opens. Even better, this Beeline Advantage ticket allows holders to cut to the front of lift lines for the remainder of the day. For many skiers, this benefit is even more attractive than early entry, but it is also one of the most controversial perks that slope managers are peddling. Skiing, though pricey, was once considered a highly egalitarian sport, at least among those who could afford the initial cost. This attitude of egalitarianism held, despite the existence of tiered prices on lift tickets (e.g., multiday and "locals" discounts) for decades.

But the ability of operators to grow profits solely on differentiated prices (and not on differentiated offerings) has been diminishing rapidly as the number of skiers has remained flat. Struggling to increase revenues, many ski resorts now offer every amenity imaginable, for a fee. Valet parking, showers and club rooms, spas, line-cutting privileges, and private instruction are just some of the benefits skiers can reach into their wallets for—to the tune of $7,000 a year and more for the whole gamut of extras at some resorts.

A growing number of skiers are opening their wallets. But such programs are not sitting well across the board. Some skiers are even arguing in court that because many resorts reside on U.S. Forest Service land, such differentiated access is illegal. Even if the operators can win these suits, some correlative lessons remain: First, that profitable operation of a large-scale business can demand that customers be effectively segmented and charged to the limit of their willingness to pay. Second, that this type of segmentation is not an easy business challenge, largely because of the social implications of segmenting customers along those lines.

Dancing with the Ones Who Brought You

In chapter 2, we explored the benefits of taking a new middle position between the luxury and mass markets. But this approach is not always easy, or even possible, for many companies that are already deeply committed to serving mass-market needs with mass-produced, one-size-fits-all offerings. For these companies, doing so would require an impossible scaling back of existing infrastructure commitments. For many others—like the aforementioned ski resorts—the barrier is also social convention.

To see significant gains in profitability, these companies must find ways to either raise the profitability of all customers a little or achieve significant profit improvement from some of their customers. With one-fifth of all households now holding nearly three-fifths of all income, it behooves marketers at these companies to attempt the latter and to find ways to provide a differentiated version of their core offerings to those who can and will pay a premium.

Embracing this approach can border on heresy in some industries that pride themselves on even-handed treatment of their customers, but take note: The number of industries that assiduously maintain a single level of customer treatment is shrinking rapidly. In select hospitals, consumers can now find maternity rooms that resemble suites in the Four Seasons. Even governments are showing subtle favoritism by moving services like vehicle registration online.

In some cases, customers have organized boycotts to protest such segmentation efforts. Fortunately, there is ample evidence that differentiated offerings can ultimately result in legitimate, compelling benefits *across* the customer spectrum. For example, the higher prices charged to certain buyers have a dramatic impact on the bottom line of many companies. Whether they know it or not, most customers regularly enjoy the benefit of having their purchases and retail experiences subsidized by bigger-spending customers, in everything from high-end department stores to opera performances.

And these innovations rarely remain exclusive for long, tending to trickle down to mass-market offerings in a timeworn and predictable manner, as companies strive to increase their competitiveness. This pattern was reinforced in the summer of 2000 when American Airlines introduced expanded leg room for *all* its coach-class customers, not just its frequent flyers, as was the case on a major competitor. In September 2003, Dunkin' Donuts began competing more directly with Starbucks by offering a more affordable latte, advertising it as, "Latte for Every Tom, Dick and Lucciano."[1] We can even imagine competitive ski resort operators responding to the new premium lift tickets mentioned above by using man-made snow to produce slopes of fresh powder multiple times a day. The operators would then sell this newly abundant premium skiing experience to many more skiers, at price that would still garner a premium, but would be more affordable due to the growth in supply.

Serving Customers with Distinction

To differentiate existing offerings—some of which have decades of history with customers—companies need insights and strategies that emerge from real-life experiences. Our research led us to explore the paths companies have taken to differentiate their traditional mass-market offerings and their approaches to overcoming push-back from disaffected customers. We found a number of companies making dramatic inroads into new market segmentations, in some cases effecting sweeping changes in how entire populations viewed particular industries and offerings. But we also found companies that successfully handled initial adverse reactions in their customer base, only to fail in the long run because they couldn't make their new differentiated offerings more attractive than the old.

Our research reveals three strategies traditional mass marketers can employ to better capture the spending of the moneyed masses without sacrificing the former core mass market

Give customers the chance to spend more. Offer new premium versions, adding on product upgrades and differentiated service levels to existing offerings.

Honor customers with the recognition they desire. Create status levels that richly reward willing-to-spend customers in all of the ways they wish to be recognized.

Offer the right price to each customer. Use effective pricing tactics to achieve differential margins based on qualities that aren't intrinsic to the offering.

Each of these strategies affords consumers a different reason to spend more, and each varies in its complexity and appropriate usage.

Let Me Pay for This

How many times have you stood in line at a grocery store, wishing you could pay a bit more to be served immediately? Or ordered something that was out of stock and dreamed of paying a little extra to take the place of somebody willing to wait but whose order was being fulfilled immediately? Every day, millions of consumers are paying less than they might otherwise, simply because they have not been given the chance to pay more.

Despite this pent-up demand, most furniture companies still do not offer the chance to pay extra for a more certain delivery time. Telecommunications companies, for example, still keep their best customers on hold for twenty minutes or more, rather than devising a way to let them pay to be moved to the head of the queue. This is particularly surprising, considering how phone companies have turned customer-time-saving directory assistance into a nearly $6 billion market, with some firms' gross margins as high as 50 percent.[2] In fact, directory assistance is the second largest source of revenue for carriers, after subscriptions.

Reliable, timely service is critical to the moneyed masses, given their hectic lifestyles, which create a low tolerance for wasted hours. Companies have hardly exhausted the opportunities here, and capturing the opportunity need not cost more. In fact, being more responsive to customers can actually lower a company's cost to serve when done correctly.

Consider what Dell did when it came under fire from some members of the press for lapses in its call center for technical support. Overwhelmed by call volume, Dell began to package services to offer significantly better responsiveness—for those customers willing to pay more. In 2003, Dell executives began testing a priority-call-routing program that would provide customers with three years of preferred call-answering for technical support for $89. For an affordable price, customers short of time now have the chance to move to the front of the line.

Dell has also begun offering an option that decreases average call time by eliminating the need for representatives to stay on the phone with customers and guide them through a painstakingly long setup. For $119 to $139, Dell will send a technician to a customer's house to complete the setup in person.[3] The program probably won't earn millions, but it just might save millions. A typical company that spends $500 million annually on customer service can save $1 million each year by shaving a single second off the average length of a service call.[4]

Do companies that already hold a strong mass-market position face risks in moving upward into premium service levels in the manner we've just described? Yes, they face challenges similar to those facing companies that move up into the new middle ground with entirely new offerings. But we believe that premium service offerings also help such firms gently develop a value proposition suitable for the moneyed masses, without forsaking their existing operations and delivery mechanisms and without angering their core market.

Some managers may feel their offerings are too commonplace or too mature to be meaningfully differentiated any further for a well-heeled customer ready to spend. But Sam Hill, Jack McGrath, and Sandeep Dayal abruptly dispel this notion in their article "How to Brand Sand," describing how even commodities can be effectively differentiated through three simple changes in how they are sold.[5] The authors recommend focusing on adding *convenience for the user, greater consistency in delivery or performance,* and *customization* (which often requires no more than sorting existing products to ensure that customers get their preference).

Those authors' strategies are targeted largely at business-to-business commodities, but are equally appropriate for mass-market consumer goods in an increasingly affluent market. The relatively high number of earners in more affluent households creates consistent demand for convenience, which is compounded by the relative (perceived) value of their time. Two economists have made an interesting observation about time: It becomes more valuable as you become wealthier, no matter what, just because of the change in its relative worth.[6] The reasoning is simple but powerful. Time is fixed; we have no way of getting more. But material goods and income can essentially grow forever. As our ability to acquire goods increases, our inability to increase time becomes more pronounced, making time both perceptually and economically more valuable. The moneyed masses are increasingly recognizing the relative value of their time, and effective marketers must do so, too.

Perks!

The popularity and effectiveness of the rewards used in loyalty programs in the grocery, airlines, and entertainment industries are well documented. Membership is known to have its privileges. But leading companies are also making two important improvements to that formula to better serve the moneyed masses. First, where perks have become a critical component of an overall offering, some companies are *selling* access to their programs' status levels instead of making customers earn them. This creates a win-win for companies: more satisfied customers, plus a new segment of customers who are not heavy users, but who become every bit as profitable as a result of the additional fee for status. An added bonus is that companies are able to collect this profit contribution up front, like a wholesale club, at the time of membership and renewal, not in increments as the customer purchases.

Second, some companies are welcoming the high-status, heavy users of competitors' programs, offering them easy, costless access to the same benefits they enjoy elsewhere, plus the unique benefits of the companies' own programs. Marketers are coming to recognize that loyal customers of their competitors are not likely to be lured away by their standard offerings.

Selling Status

It can at times appear crass to desire loyalty status with a company just for the free benefits. The implication is that one is too cheap or impoverished to simply pay for these perks.

But many times, customers cannot gain access to these status benefits any other way (unless they're willing to pay a king's ransom). Consider the value of having an open seat next to you in coach on a moderately full flight, or the thrill of spending a night in the Lincoln bedroom at the White House. Until recently, neither was awarded without a great deal of proven customer loyalty. But both came to be more available in recent years, thanks to those astute enough to sell status.

In other words, the most entrepreneurial of managers have come to realize that there is a growing number of people willing to pay a fee to gain loyalty status. These consumers want to have access to the benefits of status without having to buy more of an organization's offerings than they really want to consume.

Recognizing this phenomenon, many airline companies have begun allowing their best customers to retain their cherished elite status by allowing these flyers to buy it. (Airline status has become so valuable to many frequent flyers that they often take what are known as mileage runs— unnecessary flights to distant places—just to acquire the mileage credit needed to retain their standing.) While these programs are meant to be a temporary fix to help loyal customers through a downturn in the economy and have been aimed at a small section of each airline's overall customer base, the programs also open the door wider to the edgy, but potentially highly profitable practice of selling status.

Of course, status levels need to maintain some degree of exclusivity. American Airlines, for example, has kept its payment program highly targeted, offering it only to existing status members and not allowing the purchase of an upgrade of status (e.g., gold members cannot buy platinum status). Certainly, status given too liberally is no longer status. But if an industry finds itself in a position where it refuses to sell for a substantial fee the right to better service, because it thinks *too many* customers will pay, it needs to rethink its service levels and segmentation strategies, for it is almost certainly leaving money on the table.

Conferring status, however, can mean more than just proffering tangible benefits. Sometimes it is about delivering intangible or at least indirect benefits, such as influence and control. Anybody who has ever tried to book a table at a top New York restaurant for any specific day knows this is nearly impossible except for people with instantly recognizable names or those who can afford to stay in a top hotel with a highly influential concierge. The relatively obscure and unconnected today have a third option. They can hold an American Express Platinum Card.

Beyond the pride one feels in being able to present such a card when the bill comes at an impossible-to-get-into restaurant, the card's value is in its ability to actually get these cardholders into the restaurant. The Platinum Card's fine-dining program holds a table reservation for its members at over 850 of the best restaurants around the world. Tables are available to members even on short notice, when these restaurants would otherwise claim to be booked solid. For the $300 membership fee and a yearly spending requirement, holders gain instant recognition and credibility, even in cities they have never visited.

Platinum Card holders also have access to a wealth of concierge services, including hard-to-get theater and event tickets and invitations to special, member-only events. Movie stars have never had it so good— which is probably what prompted Prince Charles to present one of the coveted cards to the object of his affections, Camilla Parker-Bowles.[7] While membership is still "by invitation only" (and thus still prestigious), most newly affluent have been, or can easily manage to be, solicited.

It's worth noting, too, that American Express has not limited its strategic use of selling preferential treatment to its top-tier cardholders. Even Gold Card members have special ticket-purchasing privileges. At Ticketmaster, for example, these cardholders can request tickets through a separate members section on the seller's online order form. Recently, holders of Gold Cards were still able to purchase choice seats to a James Taylor concert at the Boston Tweeter Center two hours after it sold out.

Hertz is another company that has found increased success by selling status as a core part of its business. Take the Hertz #1 Club Gold program. For a $50 annual membership fee, customers can avoid checking in at a counter and instead can go straight to their waiting car. This program differs from a premium offering in that the status is tied to the customer and not the purchase, so its benefits apply across all rental sales, whether a midsize for business or a weekend convertible for personal pleasure at a promotional rate.

In general, the hospitality and financial service industries have a head start in treating certain customers like stars. But companies in every industry can find ways to confer elite status on their customers who seek to pay more to be treated like ones.

Recognized Everywhere

One of the unique challenges of impressing high-spending customers is addressing the likelihood that these customers are part of the most attractive and best customer segment of many competing companies. They are therefore probably accustomed to the benefits that companies provide for their high-spending customers, whether they spend to that level with all companies or not. Because a saturation point exists when it comes to special treatment, the question for marketers must shift from "How do we give our most profitable customers status?" to "How do we counter the status conferred on this group by our competitors, or by other companies in general?"

Recognizing the status of customers in competing loyalty programs within your own company's offering is one way to meet this challenge. This approach has an added benefit: The moneyed masses will gladly help you learn about their status in other companies, giving your firm the opportunity to either meet or beat your competitors' offerings.

Such *courtesy status* is now routinely being given by airlines; many automatically grant similar status in their frequent-flyer programs to those who demonstrate elite status in a competitor's plan. United Airlines calls its courtesy program Go for the Gold. And though the practice is not well publicized, the airline has a well-developed process for reviewing customers' existing industry recognition and for conferring equivalent status. Outside the airline industry, similar reciprocal agreements have the potential to challenge established loyalty programs in businesses ranging from groceries to casinos.

The ultimate in pan-program recognition, however, may be American Express's recently introduced black card, called Centurion. Though it is again offered by invitation only, its target income of above $150,000 puts it within the reach of millions of households. One of the card's most attractive features, beyond all the dedicated concierge services and special events, is the broad recognition it delivers its holder in other companies' loyalty programs, for most or all of their shopping haunts. For one annual fee, members are automatically entitled to elite status on four airlines and in numerous rental car and hotel companies' programs—including those of the Ritz-Carlton and Four Seasons chains.

This status remains as long as members keep their card, regardless of their spending levels at those businesses.

The Price Is Right (Here and Now)

While differentiation is a prerequisite for premium pricing, it is just a first step. Getting paid for differentiation that is based on customer-valued benefits requires differential pricing schemes. Price discrimination is by no means a new concept. Nobel laureate George Stigler wrote about it back in 1966 in his *Theory of Price.* He argued that companies must differentiate on time, place, or appearance to achieve and sustain higher prices, or else all buyers will eventually migrate to the lowest prices available in the market. This downward migration is already happening for certain products: People who can afford to pay higher prices for these products are nevertheless flocking to lower-priced stores like Wal-Mart and Costco.

Optimal pricing has been a terrifically complex problem since the dawn of commerce. And pricing has only become more complicated with the advent of technologies that have enabled pricing innovations such as instant menu price changes (e.g., electronic menu boards), dynamic just-in-time couponing (such as what customers receive at most grocery store checkouts today), and real-time, inventory-driven rolling markdowns.

To help decision makers manage the complexity, most pricing texts recommend a linear approach to pricing strategy: Start with the company's strategic objective, such as optimizing market share, sales volume, or profit, and then work your way through a series of decisions about initial price and subsequent tactics that are based on such factors as competition and demand volatility.[8]

But even the savviest of existing pricing strategies needs to be revisited in light of the increasing significance of the moneyed masses. With incomes and wealth increasing, marketers must search for strategies that can cajole consumers into paying the higher prices they can now afford. Companies more than ever need to be sure their pricing strategies are driven by value-based thinking, not cost-plus thinking.

The affluent are likelier than most other customers to pay a higher price for at least two reasons. One is that they have higher search costs for price information. Because their time is more monetarily valuable (as shown earlier), any amount of time involved in finding a lower price is more costly to the affluent than to others. Search costs therefore increase with income, a relationship that is increasingly pressuring today's consumers to be less price-sensitive. Though technology has made searching for low prices easy, convenience and habit can still win out. One study of online shopping showed many consumers do not even click to check for a lower price at another online store, once they have become familiar with an easy-to-use online retailer. Price dispersion across the Internet for items like books, presumed to have become commoditized, remains high.[9]

Increasing affluence also leads to higher reservation prices. At least in theory, growth in income and wealth raises the absolute top price a consumer is willing to pay for something he or she wants, because consumer decision making is often driven by fluctuating budgetary considerations rather than actual prices. Consumers are known to regularly evaluate the real cost of an offering not on its price alone, but based on how much of their income they must give up to own it. While the moneyed masses are value-conscious in general, marketers should note that this is restricted to the customer's frame of reference. All else being equal, the higher the income, the higher the top price a consumer is likely willing to pay. This relationship holds especially when marketers factor in the customer's desire for convenience or need for immediacy. Such factors can drive consumers to pay substantially more than they otherwise might for a purchase, for example, for an all-inclusive vacation or simply for sunscreen at the beach, so long as the price doesn't exceed the upper limit they have set in their mind.

Pricing Down to Sell Up

On the flip side, there are also particular opportunities for marketers to *lower* high prices to increase spending and to grow sales. Many top luxury companies and high-end providers, challenged by an economic downturn, have searched for ways to fill unused capacity with more regular patronage from occasional patrons who cannot afford more frequent consumption at list prices.

Two tried-and-true strategies for discreet discounting should be considered. The first is couponing, which has recently even moved into the sphere of high-end restaurants. Sites like Restaurant.com sell coupons offering as much as 50 percent off at upscale eateries. And if that's not enough, customers can use an on-site link to eBay to bid for a coupon at an even lower price.

Similarly, Dinnerbroker.com is providing 10 to 30 percent discounts at select restaurants for off-peak dining reserved through its site (not surprisingly, the company also offers the reverse—last-minute reservations can be had for an additional fee of $2 to $10). The resulting chart on the site, listing the rates for each restaurant for each day and time, looks remarkably like a yield management system, so familiar in the entertainment and vacation industries. And indeed, yield management is the key benefit of these programs for participating restaurants. The system keeps the establishment full during slow times, which not only means higher revenues and better asset utilization, but also ensures that the restaurant will be sufficiently crowded for the complete enjoyment of full-paying customers. Bustle is, after all, a critical element in certain entertainment service industries such as cruise ships, theaters, and resorts. (Who wants to cruise on a ghost ship?)

Most of these programs are being kept relatively quiet for now, a practice that customers appreciate. (Many customers don't want to look cheap by brandishing a saver card or coupon). Online dining clubs like iDine, for example, are so subtle they require only that members register their credit cards and then dine when a discount is offered; the savings is automatically applied as a refund, which appears on the credit card statement.

The second flip-side strategy is to cultivate a secondary market. Not a new approach, this tactic is nonetheless invading new segments of some industries and causing great turmoil. Consider luxury hotels. The Internet is now host to dozens of hotel room wholesalers, including Hotels.com and Expedia.com. And, although only 9 percent of hotel rooms are booked through third-party Web sites, according to the *Wall*

Street Journal, the move has so worried the leading chains, that five—including Marriott, Hilton, and Hyatt—have gotten together to start TravelWeb.com to compete.[10] Luxury hotels have been reluctant to join the fray, appropriately fearing brand devaluation, but many are having a hard time avoiding the temptation, and those that have made the leap are unlikely to return to single-tier selling in an improved economy. A quick look at Hotels.com shows broad and active participation from even the most upscale hotels.

Companies must be careful with tiered pricing and online wholesaling, however, to ensure that the right set of consumers ends up patronizing the right tier. Leakage across tiers can result in a situation where the affluent wind up with the best deals and sidestep the marketer's higher-priced alternatives. This worst-case scenario will come to pass for hotel rooms if the more affluent and Internet-enabled crowd becomes the wholesaler sites' predominant patrons, rather than the truly price sensitive who would not be willing to pay the standard rack rate under any circumstance. This perverse effect is already a problem for medical care, where the uninsured poor tend to pay the ultrahigh published prices because they cannot avail themselves of the volume price discounts that insurers (and their generally more affluent customers) receive.[11]

Nonetheless, businesses should think expansively when planning a tiered marketing strategy because it is possible, on occasion, to enforce solid boundaries between tiers even across very large populations of customers. For example, the tradition of kamaina, or Hawaii resident, discount makes an entire state's population the second tier for participating businesses, as compared with tourists, who are obliged to pay more for these products and services.

At the same time, implementing tiered pricing requires careful, detailed analysis. The truth is, price discrimination may not always be the best strategy for optimal profits. Two U.K.-based economists have found that the benefit of capturing the extra amount some customers would be willing to pay but aren't, can be often outweighed by the additional costs involved in having to compete at a customer-by-customer level on price. "Only when . . . the increased profit extracted from the most loyal customers exceeds the loss in profits from the least loyal customers [who have abandoned the company because of the price changes can such an approach be profitable]."[12]

A River of Tiers

Any creative or aggressive pricing strategy carries risk. Companies must recognize important legal limits that guarantee the rights of all to fair— if not always equal—price treatment, even if consumer protection in this area is foggy, especially in the area of online price discrimination. They should not only stick to the letter of the law when determining what constitutes fairness, but also incorporate the consumers' perspective as well.[13]

A guiding principle, one that will help executives achieve this end, is to keep offerings reasonably available to all consumers. This avoids the illegal practice, once common in the lending and insurance industries, of basing decisions on geography and, consequently, the people living within those boundaries. That practice, known as redlining, has received renewed scrutiny as a result of the nature of selling on and through the Internet. Coined "Weblining" by an April 2000 *Business-Week* article, this practice has gotten companies in trouble when they limit their services based not on geography, but on the results of customer sorting *and grading* that today's data mining technologies provide. Banks such as Sanwa can now routinely evaluate customer requests, for example, to waive a check-bouncing fee, based on a letter grade its system pops up when a customer calls—A, B, or C.[14] First Union Bank's Einstein system, and a host of others, behaves similarly. Likewise, Fleet Boston Financial has developed a system that incorporates data purchased from external sources, such as credit bureaus, to calculate its customers' total wallet size, and then the company's share of it, using this information to guide its customer offerings and treatment.[15] All of these are now fairly standard practices, but they receive attention for their potential for abuse and negative unintended consequences.

To understand how troublesome differential pricing can be, consider Amazon.com, which was caught selling DVDs at different prices to different customers. Loyal customers, that is, those with purchase histories, were being charged higher prices than those Amazon considered first-time shoppers. This practice is not unusual by itself (new customers are conventionally offered low, introductory-rate specials), but today's conventional practices of rewarding loyalty had conditioned repeat customers to expect the lowest prices. Faced with substantial customer backlash at a time the company could ill afford it, Amazon.com had no choice but to call an immediate end to what it said was a simple test for price elasticity and to forswear doing it again, telling the *Washington Post*, "Dynamic pricing is stupid, because people will find out."[16] This was probably not a statement of immutable truth per se, but rather an indication of how far a company must distance itself from certain pricing practices when those practices, and the companies that apply them, fall out of favor with customers.

Another early Internet leader that managed to get in trouble with actual geographic redlining was Kozmo.com, the now defunct Web-based home delivery service. In a lawsuit, the company was accused of refusing to serve residents of certain predominantly African American neighborhoods, such as New York City's Harlem, while serving others in predominantly white, and mostly wealthier, neighborhoods.[17] In Washington, D.C., for example, a city two-thirds African American, two-thirds of the white population was eligible for service, but only one-eighth of the black population.[18] The irony is that the company had distribution centers in the neighborhoods it was accused of refusing to serve. Though its executives argued they were simply using Internet usage demographics as a basis for choosing service areas, the pattern of service that resulted appeared very nearly equal to redlining, with predictable results.

What's Fair Got to Do with It?

Even assuming that a company is implementing its marketing strategies entirely aboveboard, as it should, customers may perceive an unfair advantage for some segments and revolt accordingly. Consumers of all levels are often uncomfortable with distinctions in levels of product quality and service. Yet these attitudes are so emotionally charged, they cannot be easily typified. Why is it that so many of the same consumers who have no problem with first-class cabins on airplanes or box seats at ball games or the opera find themselves unable to tolerate grocery aisles dedicated to frequent shoppers and the prospect of movie theaters charging more for the best seats?

Marketing scholars have sought for years to understand consumers' attitudes toward differentiated offerings and the concept of fairness in selling prices, and insights are continuing to emerge. In their 1986 article, "Fairness as a Constraint on Profit Seeking," Daniel Kahneman, Jack Knetsch, and Richard Thaler ask the critical question for marketers seeking to serve the moneyed masses: "Why is it fair to sell a painting or a house at the market clearing price, but not an apple, dinner reservation, job or football game ticket?"[19]

The answers they have uncovered span an array of circumstances and causes. Sometimes the answer turns on the unavailability of a liquid resale market for the goods, as in the case of sporting event tickets. Other times it turns on whether the good is considered a life necessity or a basic right, such as electricity. But the authors' overall conclusion is powerful: Customer beliefs about the seller's rights affect business and can prevent companies from achieving maximum profit, regardless of the expected "rational" economic outcome.

To avoid making the kind of moves that result in customer backlash, companies need to anticipate and continually monitor customer response to differentiation. Our research included an exploration of consumer attitudes toward the appropriateness of differentiated offerings across a large number of product and service industries. We found overwhelming negative reaction to such offerings in certain significant categories. In particular, consumers apparently believe that some services are indeed basic rights. More than 70 percent of respondents reject differentiation in electricity, medical care, hospital care, and education.

Their discomfort with differentiation in these categories presents a strong marketing challenge. Unless companies in these industries target differentiation opportunities selectively and proceed with caution, they risk offending large numbers in their customer base. Not surprisingly, the more affluent households were far more willing to judge differentiated offerings as acceptable, with as many as 20 percent more respondents viewing them as acceptable in certain categories.

The wealthier among us do believe certain categories are fair game, and they are likely to look forward to more differentiated offerings in those categories in the future—an opportunity for fast moving companies. Notable were personal computers, home electronics, restaurants, automobiles, theme parks, and movie theaters. Firms with relevant offerings in these categories can move forward more decisively with tiers of new and better services aimed at a more affluent customer base, if they keep a watchful eye out for potential customer backlash.[20]

Choosing a Good Time, Really Good Time, or Great Time

Take theme parks, for example. Going on a theme-park-based vacation requires most visitors to accept the unpleasant fact that between rides, restaurants, and rest rooms, they are likely to spend the majority of their park time standing in line. In many popular establishments, from Walt Disney World to Knott's Berry Farm, the wait for the latest attractions can stretch to more than two hours. Delays are so long, park marketers now design elaborate preshows to entertain guests as they slowly wind their way toward the entrance. Theme parks have traditionally made one exception to waiting: for celebrities. As Eliot Sekuler, a spokesman for Universal Studios, explained to the *Orange County Register*, someone like Tom Cruise "obviously wasn't going to stand in line."[21]

But Universal realized that some customers were willing to pay more for better, faster access to its rides and attractions. In the same interview, Sekuler told the *Register*, "There are people whose money is less important than saving time and hassle."[22] In response, the parks developed new customer tiers that provide a taste of the celebrity experience. At Universal Studios Orlando, for example, individuals willing to spend $100 or more per person above the cost of park admission can buy a VIP program ticket. These pricier passes entitle visitors to a guided, semiprivate tour of a selection of park attractions, with priority entry and preferred seating privileges on each ride. For $1,700, an entire group can buy a private tour led by a resort VIP guide, who shows them the attractions of their choice.[23]

Launching the VIP packages has been important for Universal, though numbers are not easily available. With park attendance generally down since the late 1990s because of reduced family leisure travel, Universal, like most other theme-park operators, has had to find new ways of increasing park revenues. Although upscaling its in-park restaurants and shops led to a 72 percent increase in average per-capita in-park spending between 1987 and 1997 (up to $33.82), this growth has largely peaked.[24] Theme parks will be increasingly stretched to find new ways not just to grow attendance, which these programs do by creating a differentiated experience that a new segment of impatient or time-starved customers can enjoy, but also to dramatically increase per-capita spending.

A few leaders are taking the concept of differentiated theme-park services to the next level. They are creating environments in which the service tiers make every customer feel like a celebrity. Busch Entertainment adopted this approach when it launched Discovery Cove, an entire destination where services center on the needs of a prosperous customer base. Hate to stand in long lines, but feel uncomfortable standing in a priority entry line? Discovery Cove was designed to never have lines. It admits no more than a thousand visitors per day.[25] Dislike the constraints of a guided tour? At Discovery Cove, a five-to-one ratio of staff members to visitors ensures that help is never far away. In addition, the park provides unique attractions such as swimming with bottlenose dolphins in a tropical lagoon or snorkeling in a reef full of tropical fish.

None of this comes cheap. A basic pass for full-day admission costs $119, compared with just $49.95 for adults and $40.95 for children at Universal Studios Orlando. Customers who want to swim with the dolphins and tropical fish must be willing to shell out $219. But for a time-pressured, newly affluent family taking one of its rare vacations, the price tag could be a bargain.

A Prescription for Differentiation

What about the industries our research pegged as the least likely to receive customer support for differentiation strategies? Introducing tiered marketing in these arenas can be hard, but not impossible. These industries may in fact present the greatest opportunities, having avoided differentiation for so long that they have acquired significant pent-up demand for better offerings.

Few services, for example, are as politically, socially, or economically charged as health care. Yet in this stormy environment, one company, MDVIP, is flourishing. How? It has created a higher standard of medical service for those in the moneyed masses who appreciate and are willing to pay for this service. Along the way, MDVIP has overcome serious concerns on the part of consumers, industry participants, and civic leaders about the fairness of its offering. The company's experiences, recounted to us by cofounder Edward Goldman, provide lessons for other firms looking to create meaningful differentiation in categories for which doing so could be contentious.

MDVIP distinguished its services by developing what is now often referred to as *concierge* or *boutique* health care. MDVIP physicians restrict themselves to just six hundred patients, not thousands as is all too typical. The result is a higher level of service. The cost is a flat annual fee of $1,500. As Goldman explained when we interviewed him in March 2003, "Patients enjoy a more personal relationship with their doctor, greater convenience in managing their health, and a heightened focus on preventive care."[26] For example, patients often receive same-day appointments, are not rushed through one-on-one consultations, and even receive their doctor's beeper numbers and e-mail addresses for follow-up.

Goldman stresses that MDVIP's services, while certainly available to anyone, have proven most compelling for the more affluent. "A demographic of $100,000 to $300,000 is the market segment we are looking for. This is a large enough segment of consumers who both understand the value of increased service and are willing to pay more for it."

To support this targeted value proposition, Goldman deliberately priced MDVIP's services below the highest tier of the market: "My partner was recently at an event where he explained the MDVIP concept to another gentleman. The fellow replied, 'When I feel ill, I just jump on a plane and fly to a hospital in Manhattan. It has a wing named after me.' . . . Clearly, such individuals are above our target. There are other concierge health-care services for those people priced at $20,000 per year. We wanted to make our price point attractive to a broader audience. Fifteen hundred dollars is, after all, about what one could spend in a year on premium cable channels, or a nice dinner out each month."

Even when a company such as MDVIP has defined its offering and price point, it still must take additional steps to defuse objections from those who consider any segmentation inappropriate. Indeed, MDVIP's model initially provoked controversy from certain groups, particularly older consumers and some state and national lawmakers. MDVIP responded by crafting two clear messages. First, it asserted that by differentiating services, it was simply addressing an unmet need in the health-care market for preventive care. Goldman recalls, "We really stressed the preventive aspect of our health-care services—the VIP in our company's name stands for 'value in prevention'—and pointed out that federal programs did not offer it. There is no Medicare funding for preventive care, so if a patient needs it, they already must pay for it from their own pockets." With this reasoning, MDVIP asserted that it was not tampering with the basic rights that consumers wanted to see protected.

MDVIP's second message was one that holds true in many other industries—that, in fact, segmentation already exists in health care. Goldman asserts, "We pointed out that the health-care system already had several segments, including the uninsured and HMO [health maintenance organizations] and PPO [preferred provider organizations] customers. And there were also already great variations in the education and capability of doctors. In other words, we were not really introducing new distinctions to the market. We were simply getting a lot of flak for openly segmenting what was already a segmented market."

To ensure that such messages are effectively disseminated, marketers should emulate MDVIP's proactive communications approach. The company directly approached third parties, from congressional representatives to the media, to tell its story and explain its service offerings firsthand. "We wanted people to learn who we are and what we are doing from the source," says Goldman. "That way, if they received negative feedback from other people, they would already have a factual context." Today, he sees the fruits of MDVIP's efforts. "We don't hear the fairness arguments much anymore. Even many of those who once criticized us now understand the need for our services and acknowledge their right to exist in the market."

Patients have done more than accept MDVIP's services; they have embraced them enthusiastically. Since MDVIP's founding in 2000, the company has grown to include twenty-five practices in seven states, with forty more practices in the pipeline in 2004. "We have a lot of hay to make in these new markets," explains Goldman. With the business infrastructure in place, MDVIP is now able to focus on enriching its service offerings by partnering with complementary businesses in other industries, such as wealth managers and even luxury automakers, to jointly go to market.

Despite the challenges MDVIP has had to overcome, Goldman remains convinced of the market opportunity for those who create differentiated offerings for the growing number of affluent consumers: "It's an underserved market, but it can be tapped. If you develop an offering with the right points of differentiation, there is no question that these consumers will respond. In fact, they are a market that can make business easy."

Peace in Our Time

No matter the industry, effectively managing the social politics that often surround introducing differentiated offerings is critical to any entrant's success. Our research reveals three effective tactics used by successful companies for managing consumer backlash:

> *Discriminate on value proposition and behaviors, but not people.* Everyone we interviewed emphasized the importance of having distinct value propositions for each offering and presenting choices and trade-offs to consumers of all incomes. While the wealthy may be more inclined to be the typical consumer (they are the biggest consumers of almost everything more expensive), the offering should in no way discourage any buyer who finds the value-for-money proposition worthwhile. Similarly, rewards should be targeted always at those who behave in desirable ways for the business, not particular customers.

Communicate messages of business rationale clearly. It is rarely enough to know that offerings do not discriminate; consumers and related parties must understand the how and why of such propriety. Marketers must clearly articulate their rational of how the tiers and offerings are targeted fairly and must convey this message regularly, particularly to those inclined to be highly concerned about the issue.

Be discreet, be discreet, and be discreet. As is so often the case, being right is not enough when appearances imply wrong-doing. This is also true for the best differentiated offerings. While some amount of affluent consumption is for social effect, most of that effect is intended for income peers. The wealthy of every generation and society have always come to understand that bold displays of differential consumption are not only distasteful, but they can also be bad for future consumption. Ask Marie Antoinette.

Each company we have observed moving delicately—and successfully—into a tiered approach to marketing did so through a complex mix of these three tactics, balancing them as necessary over a period as they first tested the waters, then gradually accelerated the roll-out until the change had finally been achieved. We saw this pattern repeated across several industries, including several in which consumers told us it would be highly unacceptable to differentiate offerings.

When the Powder Settles

In time, many industries may make the transition successfully. Despite high levels of consumer sensitivity to differentiated offerings, financial service companies, for example, report few public relations snags relating to differentiated offerings. Alexander Labak, the chief marketing officer of Deutsche Bank, which launched new services in an effort to differentiate offerings, told us, "It has not been hard for people to accept that customers with more money probably have more complicated needs related to managing their finances. Discretion in marketing the program means avoiding any elitist note and instead promoting the wisdom of 'different strokes for different folks.'"[27]

Dan Egan, general manager of Tenney Mountain Ski Resort in New Hampshire, sees skiing going the same way. He told London's *Independent* in 2003 that line jumping is "just a minor irritation: it's about as upsetting as the early call first-class passengers get for a flight."[28]

But his assessment must be tempered with a recognition of his deeper, business-driven assumption—one that many companies will likely share—which may motivate him and others to be less cautious than they should. "Ski areas have no choice but to maximize revenue, and VIP programs enable them to keep the basic lift-pass cheap for normal customers."[29] This may be understandable enough to any businessperson—but try telling that to the customers.

PART TWO

The New Rules of Designing Offerings

4

Find an Occasional Use

Old Rule

Make the "special" in a version suitable for everyday use by the masses.

New Rule

Make versions of the "everyday" that are suitable
only for special-use occasions.

Most of us have experienced confusion at a formal dinner, wondering which fork or spoon to use for which course. But today's flatware choices are a far cry from what one would have experienced at a traditional Victorian dinner party. These banquets frequently entailed more than twelve courses, and up to twenty-four pieces of silverware might adorn each place setting. Each piece had a unique purpose and would have been chosen from the well over one hundred types of individual silverware in use at the time to accompany particular dishes and ingredients.

Take the soupspoon, for example. There wasn't just one style; there were spoons designed for clear soups and spoons designed for cream soups. There was also a spoon just for ice cream (there was an ice cream fork, too, in case the treat was on the more frozen side). For the more exotic dishes, rarely seen today, the host could also be expected to supply guests a custom-purposed utensil; witness the marrow spoon, sardine fork, and terrapin (turtle) fork.

Such specialization continued with the knives, which could easily number as many as eight at the table, each with a different design, for cheese, fish, game, roast, and fruit. Each knife would have its own knife rest, and each place setting would be rounded out with individual butter picks, salt dishes, and—when the season called for it—game shears.

Stemware was equally varied, having as many as eight pieces arrayed in two rows of four, or diagonally when fewer. Specially designed glasses were used for water, Chambertin, Latour, and champagne. There was also a green glass for sauterne, a sherry glass, and a red glass for Rhine wine.[1]

All this variety served to highlight the wide assortment of exotic, expensive dinner ingredients being presented. Guests were subtly made aware that while these ingredients were costly, they were commonplace enough in the host's home to justify their own tools and vessels.

Yet, this remarkable variety was not limited strictly to the highest levels of society. According to the Rogers Historical Museum, even average families could afford significant variety in their tableware: "A peek at the 1897 Sears, Roebuck & Co. Catalog (the 'Cheapest Supply House on Earth') shows an attractive dinner service for twelve, one hundred pieces total, which cost all of $11.50. With an average income of $75 to $100 a month this one-time purchase was an affordable luxury for a family."[2]

The extravagance of the Victorian table—in flatware, stemware, and other tableware—illustrates how affluence has historically spawned enjoyment in profuse specialization of everyday products and how others of more modest but growing means have emulated the wealthier contemporaries. Though we rarely use marrow spoons today (if ever), we continue to spend our wealth on a profusion of products that are highly specialized but seldom used. We do this both out of appreciation for what this specialization can bring—the ease of eating crab with an appropriately designed pick, for example—and for the prestige of ownership, which is as enjoyable and important for us today as it was in Victorian times.

To the Victorians, having many versions of an item, each designed for a particular purpose or occasion, was an understated and consequently acceptable way of displaying and enjoying the benefits of wealth. It was an almost sensible form of flagrant overconsumption. It was inconspicuous in that no item was particularly ostentatious; an item was simply designed for an intended purpose. Each precisely met a gustatory need. Yet the practice was conspicuous, mostly by what was implied by omission. Observers were left to imagine what else the possessor must own if he had a coat just for fishing, and another just for hunting. Though few of us own terrapin forks today, the desire to show sophistication while enjoying the benefits of specialized products continues, particularly among the new affluent.

New Skins for Old Wine

Consider the simple wine glass. The Austrian firm Riedel (rhymes with "needle"), which has been creating glass and crystal for nearly three hundred years, made a significant contribution to glassware consumption in 1973, when Claus Riedel introduced a series of ten glasses, each painstakingly designed in its size and shape to enhance the flavor and bouquet of a certain type of wine. After selling as few as 2,000 glasses in the United States in 1989, Riedel today sells over 1.5 million glasses annually in the United States and 5 million worldwide and offers more than eighty different glasses in its collections. These glasses range in price from roughly $8 a stem for the Overture series up to $85 a stem for the Sommelier series. And like those of the Victorians, each glass is dedicated to one of an array of wines: Bordeaux, Burgundy (including one for grand cru), Syrah, and chardonnay wines, to name just a few.

Another area in which the affluent are driving tremendous market growth through specialized product usage is cookware. Hugh J. Rushing, the executive vice president of the Cookware Manufacturer Association, told the *New York Times*, "Growing male interest in cooking is one of the bright spots in the kitchen retail market. . . . Men tend to have no problem buying a special pan for paella, if the recipe calls for it, whereas women will make do with a regular skillet or pan."[3] He also noted that specialty cookware sales are up 17 percent since 2000.

The affluent are not the only ones to take advantage of specialization in offerings, of course—everyone enjoys using the right tool for the right task. But the moneyed masses do enjoy these specialized gadgets more often, and with less concern about paying a premium for the privilege. This assertion was borne out in our research, which uncovered data supporting the logical belief that high-income earners own more of everything—and more nearly identical versions of things—across a large number of categories, from cars to shoes. This distinction is important in understanding that product innovation through specialization, while likely to be attractive to a broad range of consumers, will have its largest impact first on those who consume the most, and at the highest prices.

Our research shows the moneyed masses are especially likely to purchase goods for occasional use, because of their indeterminate social status. Their needs can range from a bowling shirt to a tuxedo. And owing to their purchasing power, they are quite likely to have both in their closets. In our predominantly anonymous society, consumers use possessions to communicate information about themselves and to achieve a sense of belonging in any given locale.[4] We dress to fit in; different products or product types fit our different roles. The trend creates what one scholar has termed "a cohesive society of perfect strangers."[5]

And the number of scenarios one can choose to be a part of proliferates. So the need for ever more *information-bearing goods* (goods that communicate outwardly the owner's appropriate knowledge about the occasion) also increases. In generations past, the merely affluent were spared the expense of consuming simply to communicate status and gain acceptance. Not only did earlier generations have more class information available (because of smaller social circles and the use of heraldic titles, for example), but sumptuary laws made pretending to be in another class—through clothing and other outward symbols—a crime. Today, ever increasing populations and broad physical and social mobility have made "fitting in" in many venues a large and acceptable part of everyday life. Even the notable exceptions, such as the move to casual dress in offices—thought to allow people to wear what they wanted and, presumably, already owned—have quickly transformed into occasions to reaffirm one's status. *Business casual* is code for a new standard that pressures employees to acquire entirely new wardrobes of information-bearing clothes.

Well Heeled

Shoes are a classic example of products that have increasingly conveyed important, if implicit, information about their owners. Consider for a moment: Men may own two or three pairs for work, a pair for casual wear, and a dress pair. They may also have a pair for black tie, if they own a tuxedo. Then there are the sports shoes—tennis, running, cross training, golf, and perhaps even skateboarding. Add in ski boots, hiking boots, and winter boots, and the average man can easily own twelve to fifteen pairs of shoes, for one pair of feet.

And that's a very conservative estimate. Though few can match the 1,060 pairs of shoes belonging to the former Philippine president's wife, Imelda Marcos, the average American woman in fact owns 30 pairs of shoes.[6] Consumption researchers Elizabeth Shove and Alan Warde compare the choices of footwear for today's and yesterday's athlete: "We can now buy running shoes, training shoes, squash shoes and tennis shoes, whereas the previous generation just bought plimsolls [sneakers]."[7] More exactly, the National Sporting Goods Association lists no fewer than twenty-four athletic shoe categories alone.

What's more, the number of pairs owned continues to grow. The number of shoes sold in the United States now equals five pairs per person, *per year*, up from an average of 2.5 in 1920.[8] Much of this shoe fetish can be attributed to the disproportionate buying of the moneyed masses, whose share of total shoe purchases is disproportionately higher than their share of feet. Lou Ripple, director of sales and marketing for high-end shoemaker Allen-Edmonds, shared his view of the trend with us:

> Years ago, somebody would buy a pair of black shoes and they would buy a pair of brown shoes and that's pretty much what they had, and most of the shoes were dress shoes. When their dress shoes got to be kind of beat up, then they'd become their casual shoes or they'd wear them to cut the grass.
>
> What has happened over the years is that there have been many different kinds of shoes developed. So, customers really have a wardrobe of shoes. What we saw was twenty years ago, you'd have people who said, "All I have is Allen-Edmonds shoes. That's all I wear. That's all I have in my closet," and you could have people who had anywhere from six or seven pairs to twenty-five or thirty pairs.
>
> As different companies came out with different types of shoes, we found our customers saying, "Well, I have Allen-Edmonds for

my dress shoes but then I have some Timberlands, I have some Rockports." You know, they have different shoes that they wear for different occasions, and over the years, we've introduced more different styles for more different occasions. So we now capture that customer who used to wear Allen-Edmonds just for dress or just bought the dress shoes and now has dress casual and casual shoes. And they're returning to where they may have all their wardrobe back to Allen-Edmonds shoes now because we have shoes that address all those occasions.[9]

Two Feet Under

How can a company create advantage in an arena full of products designed for every occasion? In the crowded, competitive market of shoes, one would expect to find it difficult, if not impossible, to create much new opportunity or innovation. But recently and in the past, both incumbent and new companies have managed to grow their businesses dramatically by exploiting new footwear usage occasions. The key in all these cases has been attentiveness to subtle trends and a quick response.

In 1987, incumbent Nike introduced a shoe that would spur the development of an entirely new category of footwear, the "water sport" shoe. Being attuned to the market, Nike noticed that one of its failed lightweight running shoe lines had become a favorite of people who windsurfed. These customers were searching for—and couldn't buy off the shelf—a shoe that would be comfortable and provide traction while in water, but would also be durable and provide cushioning when the wearer was walking over rocks and gravel on land. Nike promptly modified the shape of the failed running shoe and added neon colors, and voilà: The Aqua Sock was born. The first 50,000 pairs sold out in less than a month, and production quickly jumped to 3,000 pairs a day.

Competitors quickly followed. Omega, known for foul-weather gear and flotation devices, introduced the Reef Runner, and Reebok the Kahuna. It is not entirely surprising that water sport shoes took off. Water-focused activities, though always popular, were in a period of rapid growth. In the late 1980s, the National Sporting Goods Association noted that swimming ranked first among participant sports and passed other activities like aerobics, walking, and bowling. Windsurfing, boogie boarding, and volleyball had all also picked up noticeably in retail sales.

A spokesperson for Nike explained at the time: "The unexpected success of our Aqua Sock convinced us that there was a big market for product in and around water. Windsurfers and small-boat sailors are on the leading edge, setting trends in sports." Completing the bigger picture, she added, "We see [Nike] not as a shoe or apparel company, but as a sports company. We want to be in touch with leading-edge consumers and give them the product they need."[10]

But not everyone was highly impressed by Aqua Sock's sudden success, or by the opportunity it demonstrated to serve the unmet need for shoes worn only occasionally, for that matter. In 1989, two years after Aqua Sock's introduction, Stephan Encarnacao, head of marketing and research for Converse at the time, opined, "It's good for people to take their sport seriously and to immerse themselves in it. But you can take this thing too far. I wouldn't want us to take ourselves so seriously that we really believe you need a croquet shoe."[11]

Maybe we should not take *ourselves* that seriously, but taking *occasional use* seriously is another matter—one that might have saved Converse from the ultimate fate of bankruptcy. In 2002, after ninety-three years as a grand "Made in America" shoemaker, Converse was forced to shut its factories, having lost all but 2 percent of the market. According to Rick Burton, director of Warsaw Sports Marketing Center at the University of Oregon, Converse, "rode the basketball horse too long," by choosing to stay mired in its Chuck Taylor All-Star high-top.[12] Designed in 1923 by a former high-school all-state player, the All-Star had led Converse to command 90 percent of the basketball shoe market by the late 1960s. Though it was once the shoe of choice for professional players like Wilt Chamberlain, it quickly fell into decline with the introduction of leather into sport shoes. And by the mid-1980s, even endorsements from famous players like Julius "Dr. J" Irving and Larry Bird could not stop the decline of the brand or the company.

By contrast, since Nike's introduction of the Aqua Sock in 1987 (two short years before the Converse comment was made), the company has grown from a $1 billion company to a $10 billion company. Along the way, Nike has introduced shoes and apparel targeted at women, hockey, and golf. With the acquisition of Hurley International LLC, Nike has ventured into two of the potentially hottest arenas for occasional-use sporting goods: skateboarding and surfing. And in September 2003, the company acquired none other than Converse.

New occasions for athletic-shoe use, based on emerging unmet needs, appear remarkably far from being exhausted. The fragmentation of participants in traditional sports like baseball and football into dozens of "X sports" like mountain climbing, snowboarding, motor-cross, and skateboarding continues to generate tremendous opportunity and margins, particularly for fast-moving new entrants. As Galbraith points out in *The Affluent Society*: "So long as the consumer adds new products—seeking variety rather than quantity—he may, like a museum, accumulate without diminishing the urgency of his wants. Since the average consumer owns only a fraction of the different kinds of goods he might conceivably possess, there is all but unlimited opportunity for adding such products."[13]

Bringing Occasional Use Home

Even some of the most expensive items in the typical household budget are becoming occasional-use necessities. The automobile, a rare and coveted luxury possession less than a lifetime ago, has changed its consumer significance today. Not only do we seek to own an automobile, but we also seek to own many of them. Although the superrich have always had their collections of Rolls Royces or Bugattis, this trend has moved considerably further down the line. It was cemented a few years back, when the number of licensed automobiles outgrew the number of licensed drivers in the United States. By 1998, the ratio had climbed to 1.14 cars per driver.[14] In just three years, from April 1999 to April 2002, the number of three- and four-car households jumped 31 percent, from 10.9 million to 14.3 million.[15] Not surprisingly, the affluent are fueling this market. Research by J. D. Power and Associates shows that of the 13 percent of new-vehicle shoppers who are considering luxury makes, 40 percent already have three or more vehicles.[16] The increase has come from consumers buying all sorts of vehicles that are not intended as their primary mode of transportation—convertible sports cars, pickup trucks, muscle cars, and antiques. From 1998 to 2003, the number of car models offered increased by more than 50 percent, giving consumers unprecedented selection and specialization. Alaska has even created a special occasional-use license plate for these cars, allowing reduced taxes to be paid on these cars because of their reduced-use status.

To accommodate such a shift, the affluent home has had to change as well. In 2001, 18 percent of new housing units had space for three or more cars, up from 11 percent in 1992, the first year the U.S. Census tracked this figure.[17] Not that this space is entirely dedicated to cars. The garage is increasingly being used as household self-storage (a trend accelerated by the growing preference for finished basements we mentioned earlier). At least one company, appliance maker Whirlpool, has jumped on this opportunity, shifting focus from washers and dryers to its new Gladiator GarageWorks line. This line's offerings include everything from workbenches to cabinets to tool walls and even a garage refrigerator. Not just a smaller version of the in-home kind, this appliance has been specifically engineered for use in a garage, having a built-in heater to keep its contents cold but not frozen, even when it is surrounded by a temperatures well below freezing.

This discussion brings us to another, still more expensive occasional-use necessity: the residence. Even the home itself, usually the largest single purchase a consumer makes in his or her lifetime, is increasingly being purchased in multiples, for part-time rather than full-time use . . . and by more than just the superrich. An estimated 6.4 million American households (roughly 5 percent of households) own second homes today, but perhaps more importantly, nearly 10 million households are expected to have them by 2010.[18]

This trend is being driven in part by the baby-boomer generation's purchasing vacation homes in preparation for retirement. But the purchase of these homes, and everything that goes with them, will remain a significant sales opportunity for some time to come, boomers or no, for those companies that see the opportunity and design their products to this particular market.

Rising to the Occasion

How can companies infiltrate and conquer the occasional-use market? A number of companies have capitalized on it by concentrating on two distinct strategies. In doing so, they have managed to achieve great business results relative to their competitors.

Create new usage segments. Successful companies excel in uncovering new uses within established, traditional usage behavior segments and categories.

Improve the fit. Companies can concentrate on honing their offerings to better fit a specific occasion. This creates additional distinction for their brand and offerings, based on their ability to overcome specific underlying component challenges of use.

Finding the Use Within the Use

An important strategy for defining and capturing new occasions is to split an existing category of use by some aspect of its use—or some attribute of its users. At each step, much like how a Russian nesting doll is taken apart, a deeper level of unmet need is revealed and then a product developed to satisfy it.

The history of shampoo is instructive. The origin of soap is dated as far back as 2,800 B.C.: An early form of it was found in clay cylinders in an excavation of ancient Babylon. While the recipe for the contents is clearly inscribed on the containers, its intended use was not recorded. It seems to have been used in its earliest days as a hair treatment and styling aid. According to the Soap and Detergent Association, "Biblical accounts suggest that the Israelites knew that mixing ashes and oil produced a kind of hair gel."[19]

Modern shampoo, in contrast, was invented (or reinvented) only quite recently. Back in 1930, John H. Breck Sr. introduced his eponymous shampoo after decades of research at his clinic in Springfield, Massachusetts.[20] His product was an unexpected departure from the then-current practice of using on one's hair the same bar soap that one used on one's body. By calling on users to differentiate their use occasion, and by outlining the benefits of doing so (Breck suggested that using bar soap on hair caused hair loss), he was able to create a significant new business, one based on customizing a product for a particular segment of its existing use.

Except Breck took it even further. He continued to segment shampoos by devising different formulations for dry and oily hair. His son Edward also led the targeting of shampoo at women with his world-famous "Breck girls," who appeared in Breck shampoo advertising starting in 1936. The brand has proven so strong and closely associated with shampoo in consumers' minds that it is being resurrected today after more than a decade of decline and ultimate removal from the market in 2000.

Although Breck eventually became associated with a low-cost, bottom-shelf product, for thirty years it was, remarkably, *the* premium brand and a salon favorite, commanding a premium price. And though more than nine out of ten Americans currently claim to shampoo daily, Breck's success is even more notable when considered in the context in which it was introduced.[21] A separate soap for hair care was considered quite a luxury in the midst of the Great Depression.

Additional subsegmentation of shampoo continued by other companies in the years that followed Breck's introduction, so that the first movers gained significant advantage. For example, in 1953 Johnson & Johnson introduced its No More Tears baby shampoo. Targeting this particular use involved a real soap breakthrough, however, with the company introducing amphoteric cleansing agents to consumer use. Though these agents are not as effective as traditional soaps, they are extremely mild, which makes them quite literally *easy on the eyes* and perfect for a baby's sensitive but presumably not-too-dirty skin. Designing this new category of cleaners for this user segment enabled Johnson & Johnson to capture a category it still dominates today, more than fifty years later. Within six months of its introduction, Johnson & Johnson had captured 75 percent of the baby shampoo market, a share it held as recently as 1995, when a rise in both birth rate and affluence in the United States permitted competitors to successfully sell marginally improved products at a price two to five times that of Johnson's Baby Shampoo.

Johnson & Johnson continued to see the opportunity in different-use shampoos, eventually establishing a leading position in the area of dandruff control.[22] But in one case, the continuing opportunity to create baby versions of other products curiously escaped the company, at least for a time. According to Euromonitor, "Johnson & Johnson is the baby care company in the U.S. with a dominant and leading position in all sectors *bar sun care products* [emphasis added]."[23] Instead, Schering Plough dominates sun block formulated for babies, with its Coppertone Water Babies and Coppertone Kids brands capturing over 50 percent of the total market in 2001. This market grew 50 percent in just four years—from $60 million to $95 million from 1997 to 2001—yet the appreciable differences between adult and child sun-care products are hard to define.

The next logical step in creating more shampoos for occasional use is slowly occurring. Companies are beginning to target shampoos for different occasions experienced *by the same user*. For example, there are now shampoos one should use after going to the beach, after using a pool, and even before going out clubbing (for extra body). And other opportunities for proliferation abound. Today, shampoo makes up only 33 percent of the industry known as hair care, which encompasses styling products (including hair sprays, mousses, and gels), hair color, and home-permanent and hair-growth products.[24]

In an "Aha!" moment much like the shampoo discoveries, toothpaste manufacturers just recently made the disconcerting (to the manufacturers) discovery that many families share a single tube of toothpaste. In an effort to correct this problem, the companies have started introducing toothpastes targeted not at problem areas, such as breath freshness, whiteness, or plaque, but at users. Procter & Gamble recently introduced a for-women-only toothpaste under the name Crest Rejuvenating Effects. The product is targeted at 30- to 44-year-olds—a more mature and higher-earning segment—and backed by a $50 million promotion campaign.

Procter & Gamble acknowledges that the new product offers essentially the same benefits as its other offerings. But the vanilla and cinnamon notes in the taste, the increased tingle while brushing, and the teal hues of the new packaging are expected to make women appreciate a product designed just for them. Procter & Gamble is also hoping for a rejuvenating effect in Crest sales, which slipped in the late 1990s to competitors like Colgate-Palmolive, which focused on cosmetic attributes such as whitening, while Crest targeted more functional attributes like tartar control and gum care.

Interestingly, P&G has acknowledged that men are unlikely to "get" the idea behind for-women-only toothpaste. But the company draws comparisons to the Gillette Venus razor, another product that does essentially the same thing for both sexes, but which has been successfully differentiated in the market and has created tremendous value for its creator in the process.

Still, it is important that the differentiation sought be grounded in real, consumer-valuable differences—to fulfill unmet marketplace needs—as in the case of a nonirritating baby shampoo. Failure to adequately provide new value to consumers can lead to backsliding into shared usage. While shampoo is not likely to go away anytime soon, the convenience of having only one washing agent versus the benefits of segmented products is helping "all-over" body shampoos make headway in Western Europe. These products accounted for almost 7 percent of total use in 2002.[25] Yet, this shift has not been a total wash for the soap industry; the direction of the shift has been to the higher-priced and more quickly used shampoo-style product, not back down to bar soap.

Making the Offering Fit the Occasion

Making a product suitable to a particular use occasion requires that it be made distinctly different in ways linked to specific customer needs. Whether or not every buyer values or uses the unique features of skateboarding shoes, there can be no denying that they are not simply a tennis shoe made up to look good for skaters. For example, the unique needs of skateboarders, particularly for wear resistance to combat the constant friction with the board, and padding in unusual places like the tongue to soften board flips, has kept designers scrambling to use the latest materials in their construction. A list of these requirements reads like a chemistry textbook—polyurethane (PU), ethyl vinyl acetate

(EVA), thermoplastic rubber (TPR), and polyethylene, for starters. The designers have also sought out new technologies that can be applied to shoes to create the right shoe for real skateboarders. Airwalk's Verus technology uses plastic beads developed by The Dow Chemical Company, for example. The beads are formed into geometric cones and molded in opposing formation, giving the shoes tremendous durability. This technology beats out the air-and-gel technologies of other leading manufacturers, because the air-and-gel structures tend to break down under constant stress. Skateboarding shoes may look to some like rebadged canvas loafers, but technically speaking, they are anything but.

This same interest in creating real attenuation to usage can be seen in any number of specialized products. One need only visit a Williams-Sonoma store to understand the possibilities. An industry executive we spoke to about this topic was passionate about her Williams-Sonoma-supplied asparagus steamer, using it solely for that purpose and swearing that it preserves the tips better than any of the countless other methods she had tried. As the item description at the Web site explains, the key to cooking asparagus perfectly is to use a tall pot that holds the asparagus upright, "allowing the bottoms to boil while the tips steam."[26]

Sur La Table, a store for professional chefs and other cooks, has dozens of items specifically designed for use with fish, including bone tweezers and bone pliers (remarkably similar to a pair of needle-nose pliers, but that is to our point). It also has fifty-seven different types of spoons, including measuring, soda fountain, and grapefruit (gold plated for a putative festive touch). Perhaps its designers were inspired by the Victorian table?

In a move that may help boost the fortunes of the long-suffering apparel industry, clothing makers are finally coming around to exploring the real ways in which clothes are used, which today often means in conjunction with a slew of electronics. Pagers, cell phones, personal digital assistants (PDAs), and the like are currently all crammed into pockets that have not changed appreciably in design since the late 1700s—that's more than two hundred years!

This is starting to change. Seventy-five per cent of American men own a pair of Dockers khakis, for example, but only recently have these consumers had the chance to own Dockers Mobile Pant, with side and back pockets ideal for storing a cell phone and PDA. And Levi Strauss, which makes Dockers, is not a particular newcomer to the concept of creating technology-relevant clothing. Back in 1995, it partnered with electronics maker Philips to begin exploring wearable electronics. The result of this partnership was ICD+, its Industrial Clothing Division, whose first products are available at selected European retail outlets.

And pants are just one example of efforts under way to create clothing better suited to today's electronics and use occasions. Apple and Burton Snowboards have partnered to create a parka with an embedded iPod MP3 player. "It's a handsome, perfectly normal-looking winter jacket, with one difference—a fabric panel on the left sleeve with a set of raised audio control buttons."[27] Such news comes none too soon to menswear, a $51-billion-a-year industry that has seen sales of its traditional fair—suits, blazers, and trousers—fall by 10 percent between 1998 and 2001, from $5.3 billion to $4.7 billion.[28]

Understanding Occasions

How can companies gain the insights they need to improve the fit of their existing offerings to specific occasions, and to create new offerings for new occasions? They must first come to better understand customers, their occasions, and the unmet needs inherent in those occasions. Leading companies have actively pursued and invested in the capabilities that allow them to have better knowledge and deeper understanding of occasions and use environments than their competitors.

A number of techniques have proven useful to these companies, including:

Immersing themselves in the actual use of products—including intense observational research; and

Hiring "heavy user" employees—people who are enthusiastic users of all products in the category being marketed to, who bring deep insight and knowledge into the core of the organization.

These techniques may seem obvious. (What responsible company doesn't study how its customers use its products?) But there's more "there" there than meets the eye.

Occasions in the Mist

Capturing the opportunity in a product's usage occasion requires the ethnographic approach of a cultural anthropologist—seeing products and services in the context of their consumption, from the consumer's perspective. Many marketers and executives may dismiss this recommendation, knowing that their companies' have already made tremendous investment in developing customer knowledge and believing that existing capabilities must therefore be adequate. But consider the soft-drink market. Could there be a product category more researched, with its usage more considered? Yet, it was not until 2002 that Coke introduced its Fridge Pack, soda cans sold in packaging that improves the drink's consumption from a refrigerator.

With the change in the traditional four-by-three-can packaging design into a six-by-two formation, more soda can be stored in the often empty back of the fridge space. Easier access to this space comes from a unique, forward-facing dispenser design. This change is not selling soda per se, but rather selling an information-bearing product: soda to be consumed specifically out of a refrigerator. But soda has been consumed at home out of refrigerators for decades. Why did it take manufacturers so long to fit the product to the occasion? In fact, they didn't.

Alcoa, the aluminum company, originally came up with the idea as a way to increase sales of its cans. By going into people's homes and watching how they used canned soda, researchers learned that most people were only loading three or four cans at a time into their refrigerators. Though in the aluminum can business, Alcoa's engineers then set out to design a better, more refrigerator-friendly package for soda, settling on the fridge pack. They believed that if they could increase the number of cans in the refrigerator, the result would be increased availability and therefore consumption, as well as increased user satisfaction from fewer restocking episodes.

Alcoa was right. Coke Consolidated, Coke's second-largest U.S. bottler, saw sales of twelve-packs grow by 25 percent after introducing the new packaging in August 2001. The change contributed one point to the bottler's 2.8 percent volume growth the following year. Two other Coke bottlers, including the largest, have also started using the Fridge Pack. A spokesperson for Coke Consolidated observed, "When we saw it, we wondered why nobody had thought of it before."[29]

The Fridge Pack also shows two ways that companies can innovate for occasions: through packaging and through product. In some instances, like the Fridge Pack, greater value results when companies exploit occasions through packaging. And as the New Coke experience shows, innovating to occasions in packaging may also be a lot less risky. At the very least, companies should consider both approaches.

Applying a similar technique, Starbucks was able to take another simple, everyday product—chewing gum—and bestow on it a special-use status that enabled the company to charge an unheard-of premium for the product. In the process, the company created the new category of after-coffee specialty gum.

How did Starbucks do it? First, it recognized the explosive market growth in specialty mints—technically, *breath fresheners*, in candy industry parlance—being driven by the increased consumption of strong coffee such as its own product. Erin Brennan, an Altoids spokeswoman, explains the mint-coffee connection: "When Altoids arrived in America, they were most successful in the Northwest. It must be the coffee." Altoids made $118 million in 2000, eclipsing the $66 million figure for LifeSavers.[30]

This success drove Starbucks to introduce its own mints, which it has now followed up with gum. Although the company will not release exact sales figures, a spokesperson did say the original mints did well enough to justify introducing new flavors and styles, and that Starbucks has been very happy with the success. The real number has been over 1.7 billion (!) mints sold to date.[31] The result of the after-coffee mints' leading to after-coffee chewing gum is that a once-ubiquitous product—with an average selling price of maybe fifty cents for a five-pack of Wrigley's—has become more strongly flavored and sells for $1.95 a package, a new-middle-ground price improvement any maker could love.

Everyday items modified even slightly for an occasion regularly command such tremendous premiums. Golf shirts, though in most cases only slightly modified from traditional polo-style shirts, can command two, three, and even four times their price. What better way to find an inroad into a polo-shirt-stuffed closet than to create a requirement for a different kind of shirt for an increasingly popular sport?

Nurturing Employee Users (and Vice Versa)

Most employees in most companies have experience with everyday products, like dish soap. But if you're designing, manufacturing, or even selling high-performance mountain-climbing parkas, you'd better have people in-house who have experienced the product and who understand its use. Serving more specialized occasions requires a more specialized employee. Rare is the company that manages to define and dominate an industry without passionate employees immersed in the product.

Employees of Patagonia travel the world both to test its products and to cultivate new ideas. And the story of Nike's beginnings, with founder Phil Knight teaming with his celebrated coach Bill Bowerman to create a better shoe just for runners, is legendary. The next trend in shoes may also come from personal passion. Kevin Beard, a leading shoe designer for K-Swiss, Reebok, and adidas, has taken his experience and started a new company around his passion for amateur auto racing. Named Piloti, after the Italian word for racing driver, Beard's company makes highly authentic race car driving shoes (most styles come with fire-resistant Nomex linings) worn by a number of Formula 1 and NASCAR champions. Now available at mainstream retailers like Nordstrom, the shoes are seeing a growing number of competitors, including major brands adidas and Fila, which have introduced lines of their own.

Wet suits originated with another equally enthusiastic founder, or in this case, equally enthusiastic founders. As the company Web site explains, Bob and Bill Meistell of Body Glove were two avid surfers and divers in the earliest days of the sports: "Bob and Bill needed to find a way to combat California's cold water. They tried a variety of ideas, including electrically heated flyers' suits from war surplus, but those would burn up and wool sweaters lasted only as long as they remained dry, which wasn't too long. Finally in 1953, they found some insulation material, which was used in the back of refrigerators. This material was called neoprene and was used to make the first practical suits."[32]

For companies that make top-quality, highly targeted products, it is critical that as many employees as possible—from salespeople to product developers to scientists in R&D—are immersed in the usage of the company's products and other products of the category—in a way that goes far beyond mere observation. The benefits of employee immersion hold true, for example, in the bicycle industry. After two hundred years of use and development, cycling is an industry one could reasonably believe to be "occasioned out." But as recently as the mid-1970s, with the introduction of mountain biking, the industry was reinvigorated. Today, the mountain bike segment represents nearly half—42 percent— of the $5.6 billion U.S. market for bikes and parts. This new use for bicycles also led to the decline and eventual bankruptcy of the venerable hundred-year-old brand Schwinn, replaced in the market by early enthusiast-led innovators like Trek and Cannondale.[33]

Michael Larson, retired vice president of design and engineering at Sram, a Chicago-based maker of high-quality, high-end bicycle parts, explains the value of employee enthusiasts:

> We were looking for people who were enthusiasts as a bare minimum. These were not occasional users but people deeply committed to some type of cycling. The advantage is their incredible insight and their ability to think up a better mousetrap. They have personal end-user experience with the product.
>
> When one looks at very robust product development methodologies, it all starts with understanding the voice of the customer. If you are the customer yourself, you have incredible internal insight into your organization, about how the product is used, what the current limitations to the current product lines are, et cetera. I have found most creative engineers and technical people, whenever they use a product . . . are doing a pretty technical product review. They'll tweak them, they'll fix them.[34]

As an added benefit, Larson says, these employees tend to be more resilient. Enthusiasts use their own enthusiasm as a motivating factor to deal with the normal ups and downs of a business. You tend to overlook the negative stuff if you dig the product you are cranking out, especially if you are the user.

One example of how usage experience paid off was when Sram created a twist shifter for mountain bike use. It was recognized early on that the device would need to be smaller, require less rotation in use, and have a better transition into the handlebar grip than the shifters used on other bicycle types. These three needs were captured in the acronym SRT, which eventually became the product name.

Larson explains that the development of Sram's innovations happen quickly, because the developers are also people who love the category: "We are the people who went out there, rode, and came back with the design parameters for different conditions (the need to design a way to avoid accidental shifts, for example, when a shorter shift rotation is used). Enough of them to get a good handle on what it took. When the product is something you interact with, you iterate at supersonic speeds, the feedback comes incredibly fast."[35]

A risk, however, particularly in a smaller company, is insufficient external market testing, created by an overreliance on internal expertise. Enthusiasts can become overprotective of their own product baby. One product that should have been a terrific success at Sram suffered from being overengineered and was never introduced because it was judged too expensive to produce, given its likely sale price. Says Larson: "Internal expertise can clog the system. People hang on too long, because they are emotionally attached, making doing something less than perfectly more troubling than if they are designing a flange, let's say, that nobody they know will ever see; they stop worrying about how real customers will use the product."[36] Even much larger companies can suffer from similar employee myopia. We have heard this complaint echoed to us by marketing executives from leading computer and chip manufacturers, where product developers and scientists have been known to fall in love with a technology while losing sight of the market.

And though our discussion so far has focused primarily on designers and entrepreneurs, the best, and even the largest, companies strive to have an understanding of customer occasions at all levels of the business. The Home Depot and Nordstrom, for example, dominate their industries in part because they hire salespeople who can empathize with customers and who have a similar base of needs and experiences in their own lives. One Talbots executive told us how much the company values the positive customer experiences that result when a store hires a good customer who is well connected in the neighborhood. She said that this hiring practice happens frequently, because of the culture the stores bring to their locations.

The failure to have employee users can also have the reverse effect. Executives of a number of mature global companies have bemoaned to us how nobody in their company seems to be passionate about the company's core product anymore, and how this is keeping them from innovating and serving the market in the way they would like. And though many companies now require their executives to interact regularly with customers, some companies inadvertently shelter their employees from being true users of their products. For example, many automakers offer their employees special acquisition and service plans that keep them out of local dealerships and away from the typical buying and ownership experience of their product—potentially denying them the experiences that lead to insights for continuous improvement and business growth.

The Not-So-Real Deal

A deep understanding of real use, which is so important in product design, does not always equate with a deep understanding of customers. Inevitably, the market of those who truly have an occasion gives way to a greater market of those who wish to use a product's distinctive characteristics merely for fashion purposes. For example, the lowly bowling shoe enjoyed a recent fashion craze, with versions by design houses Prada and Hermes. The fashion versions have outsold the authentic versions in revenues, but also (surprisingly) in unit volume. Skateboarding shoes, too, have successfully made the move from being a valued piece of sporting equipment to fashionable street shoes.

But don't misconstrue. These second and third levels of potential buyers—the aspirants and fashion leaders—in fact underscore the power of designing for occasional use, even if the actual user base appears at first to be small.

Many high-end products sold to the mass market are rarely used for their intended purpose and are instead supported by an evergreen desire for authenticity in product by those who can afford the best. How many of the 150,000 Land Rovers sold each year ever sees a forty-five-degree rock incline outside the dealer lot? That dealers need to create these test environments—rather than pointing customers to a suitable testing spot nearby—serves only to highlight the improbability that any of these vehicles will see the conditions for which they were made. Nevertheless, authenticity is a must, as it serves the unmet needs of both the core and secondary markets—the first demanding real capability, the second seeking fashionable affinity with those who use the product to its fullest potential.

Many companies are already benefiting by providing the moneyed masses offerings designed for occasions that these consumers will probably never see, but that are considered worth preparing for—like coats for summiting Everest (getting more common every day, right?!) and stoves for preparing the kind of gourmet meals that demand six burners (some high power, others with perfect simmer capabilities). Categories and companies that have successfully leveraged this desire to, "Be Prepared," as the Boy Scouts say, include cookware (All Clad), waterproof clothing and gear (Helly Hanson), dive watches (Ulysses Nardin), and tools (Snap-on), to name just a few.

And a few companies are in fact built around the idea of products for occasions that buyers know they will never see, but don't really mind missing. Purveyor J. Peterman has had tremendous success with an entire catalog devoted to authenticity without actual occasion, selling things like real rancher's jackets, Canadian hockey shirts, and World War II parachute jumpers' coats. As the company states in its published philosophy, "People want things that . . . have romance, but a factual romance, about them . . . things that make their lives the way they wish they were."[37]

More Occasions to Come

There is no shortage of occasions to target, and there is the distinct promise of more to come. In fact, five clear trends among the moneyed masses conjure up markets that are ripe for this type of innovation.

Going Back for Seconds

This opportunity comes from the affluent trend to owning seconds—as well as thirds, fourths, and fifths—of everything, from clothes
to cars to homes. The trend to a single bathroom per bedroom as a minimum in today's home designs (not to mention multiple half baths)
should serve as a sign. Homes with 2½ baths or more have grown steadily
from just 16 percent in 1970 to 55 percent in 1999.[38] Atherton, an affluent
town in California, has an average of eight rooms per household while
averaging just 2.8 occupants (this is nearly three rooms *per person!*).[39]

Recognizing the new attributes affluent consumers will look for, or
will need, in a product when purchasing a second (or third, or fourth . . .)
one is a key to future occasional-use success. Companies have already
begun changing the design of refrigerators to increase the number people own. They are making these secondary and tertiary appliances
smaller, and designing them with special features to provide cold drinks
everywhere, from inside a media room to the basement to inside a car.
These uses, along with specially designed wine refrigerators, are supplementing sales of the traditional, one-only kitchen refrigerator. Televisions have been designed for every room in the house as well, even for
under a kitchen cabinet. Intended use, different for each product
owned   whether it is the first or second or third—is again critical to
absolute saturation of the market.

The Care and Feeding of Oneself

The new focus on the care and feeding of oneself will be another significant opportunity. Characterized by Robert Putnam in the best-seller
Bowling Alone, Americans have moved away from traditional social and
civic interactions to more individual pursuits and activities. The moneyed masses have taken cocooning to heart and are actively grabbing
onto once-shared facilities and making them their own. Evidence of this
trend can be seen in the creation of sumptuous spa baths and media
rooms in homes with relatively few occupants to enjoy them. Usage is
being reshaped around individuals, as seen in the continued trend

toward single-serve packaging of everything. This already includes myriad offerings, from one-cup coffeemakers to single-serving microwavable hot fudge to individually packaged jelly for the home (advertised as being "just like in a restaurant").

Consider the sale of children's playground equipment, in which a few swings and a clubhouse from companies like ChildLife and Rainbow Play Systems can start at $3,000 and quickly move up into five figures. Structures such as these, once reserved for public playgrounds, now appear regularly in the backyards of the well-off—so regularly that one can find entire neighborhoods with a similar structure in every yard, often separated by less than a hundred feet (and, unfortunately, a five-foot fence).

Where can this trend lead? Companies must search the ranks of shared enjoyments and consider what can and will be moved figuratively and literally in-house. Equipment once reserved for health clubs, including saunas, steam baths, and multihead showers, are now regular fixtures in new home construction. And near the home, the possibilities are growing as well. Home putting greens, of both the synthetic and real grass variety, are exploding in number, as are personal backyard skating rinks (including poured concrete bases, halogen lighting and ice resurfacing attachments for the riding mower). In the winter of 2004, Snow-Station, LLC couldn't keep up with demand for its $2,000 Backyard Blizzard home snowmaker, a product that makes even skiing and sledding an at-home sport for a growing number of consumers.

Signs of Aging

Demographic trends can be mined for telling signs of occasions to come. The aging population portends everything from changes in meal times and foods to be consumed (important for the restaurant industry to note) to increased leisure travel.

Apparel maker and lifestyle purveyor Tommy Bahama appreciates the increase in leisure travel of older, more affluent adult Americans and has moved brilliantly to exploit it. Founded in 1992, the company has a target audience that is clear from a glance at its fashion models. No bikinied teens or surfer dudes here. The recurring visual is of an older couple of indeterminate age—him significantly gray, yet distinguished and vibrant, her attractive, but clearly mature. Recognizing that many can afford, and are taking, tropical vacations to exotic island resorts, but only a few can afford to turn the trips into a lifestyle, this company has focused on simulating these occasions by bringing the resorts closer to home.

Tommy Bahama may at first appear to be a simple lifestyle purveyor, but it is in fact much more. Unlike true aspiration marketing, Tommy's hook is not to provide a taste of an unattainable or distant good life, but rather to serve as a complement for a lifestyle many already share in, if even in differing amounts. Unlike Ralph Lauren, whose lifestyle images are attractive but largely unattainable, Tommy's clothing serves aspirants and actuals alike. It outfits those taking tropical vacations and who are uncertain how to dress, as well as those who have returned and seek to recreate the mood and experience through their attire.

This focus on participants is core to the company's origins: Two of its founding executives met when they purchased neighboring vacation homes in Naples, Florida, and the brand's first real success came in the opening of a combined restaurant/retail space in that city, one known for its large population of retirees and senior vacationers. As we've said, there is a strong attraction to dressing the part for an occasion, especially once you are in it.

Tapping this emerging market has resulted in over $300 million in sales, with a target of $1 billion by 2008, a number many analysts find extremely reasonable. And graying need not be the end of the occasional-use road, so to speak. In 2003, the *Wall Street Journal* documented the opportunity for postmortem consumption, a "tomb boom" that includes high-end mausoleums with everything from digital photos and voice recordings, to cafés and exhibition space for local artists.[40]

Embedded Occasions

Golf courses and health clubs—in a move to become even more posh—are serving up everything from massages to gourmet restaurants. This arrangement allows consumers to combine and embed experiences, layering them into a more complex experience tailored to their immediate desires. This trend is a shift in when and where the experiences and their related goods and services are consumed. Companies that can define the important differences that result from this shifting of time and place and can redesign the offerings for better fit will find new ways to capture new value in what others will see as essentially old offerings.

The Desire for Occasions of a Lifetime

As consumers grow older and more affluent, the occasions they seek become more uncommon and personally significant, and therefore more expensive and less frequently enjoyed. The result is one of the largest opportunities in new occasions: selling once-in-a-lifetime experiences. What companies in this market are losing in repeat business, they are making up in the growing numbers of moneyed customers who are aspiring to, and finally living out, their fantasy activities. Want to travel in space? Dennis Tito did. He accompanied a Russian expedition. The cost: $20 million.

Twenty million is an intimidating sum, yet other experiences possessing relatively equal marvel are far more attainable, especially as a once-in-a-lifetime splurge. Flying a MiG-25 will get you to the very edge of space, but is far more affordable at $27,000 (including accommodations at the five-star Metropol Hotel in Moscow, training flights, visa, and tourism from Incredible Adventures). Prefer going the other direction? Diving two miles below the surface of the ocean to see the *Titanic* runs $36,000 (without heart-of-the-ocean necklace). Deep Ocean Expeditions has five other choices, including submersible trips under the Arctic for $10,000. Prefer the South Pole? Adventure Quest will fly you there on a sixteen-day escapade for $25,000.

The point is, there is no point on the planet really off limits. Scaling Everest is still pricey at roughly $65,000, but jungles, plains, deserts, and ocean floors have all given way to tourism. And it is not just the places, but the activities that matter. Flying at Mach 2, driving over 150 miles per hour, dog sledding, and even simulated Army Ranger missions can now be experienced for a fee. All of these adventures drive not just increased tourism dollars, but demand for the products that go with them, from specialized apparel to climbing gear to newly designed submersibles.

Adventure travel is not just for men having midlife crises, either. Lower on the testosterone scale, but equally attractive and expensive, are high-end nature, eco-, and cultural travel, like bird-watching in the Galapagos and historian-led trips to places like Syria. With a market estimated to be at least $50 billion (with some saying upward of $125 billion), opportunity abounds. Although the average male spent 3 percent of his life in retirement at the turn of the last century, today he is likely to spend upward of 30 percent as a retiree, with time on his hands for just such adventures. What's more, women account for an estimated 65 percent of adventure travelers and tend to be older and married. Some of the biggest growth is coming from cross-generational trips, including grandparents and grandkids.

The opportunity for creating once-in-a-lifetime experiences reaches down to restaurant meals, cars, and even furniture, where high-end providers can expect—and seek opportunity in—a growing number of onetime splurge buyers for what become true wide-scale, or plenary, indulgences. The challenge for marketers is to create offerings so desirable, consumers cannot imagine going through life without having experienced them at least once. How will your offering be remembered, when all is said and done?

A Time to Close

Though some have characterized it as social satire, Thorstein Veblen noted in his 1899 book *The Theory of the Leisure Class* the important relationship between the use of a good and the status conveyed to its owner: "Even in articles which appear at first glance to serve for pure ostentation only, it is always possible to detect the presence of some, at least ostensible, useful purpose; and on the other hand, even in special machinery and tools contrived for some particular industrial process, as well as in the rudest appliances of human industry, the traces of conspicuous waste, or at least of the habit of ostentation, usually become evident on a close scrutiny."[41]

And while his wording is ponderous (literary critic H. L. Mencken described his work, saying, "It was, and is, impossible to imagine worse

English, within the limits of intelligible grammar"), Veblen's subsequent caution to his readers is, in a business context, instructive.[42] "It would be hazardous to assert that a useful purpose is ever absent from the utility of any article or of any service, however obviously its prime purpose and chief element is conspicuous waste; and it would be only less hazardous to assert of any primarily useful product that the element of waste is in no way concerned in its value, immediately or remotely."[43] The lesson then for business is to not shy away from needless adornments in offering design, but to look first for the use that grounds the vanity.

5

Introduce a New Math of Ownership

Old Rule
Produce less-expensive versions of luxuries to sell to the masses.

New Rule
Introduce new models of ownership that make a wealthy lifestyle,
and even real luxuries, affordable to the masses.

In an imposing Georgian mansion, just steps from the Colorado State Capitol Building, resides an elite but little-known school whose graduates can expect to earn as much as $150,000 per year.[1] The curriculum reveals some similarities to a business program, with lessons in administration, finance, human resource management, and team building. But these graduates are not M.B.A.s bound for investment banks or consulting firms. They are estate managers and are destined for the homes of some of the nation's wealthiest individuals. The school is the Starkey Institute for Household Management, and its students are trained (among other things) to supervise the activities and possessions of very wealthy households.

No longer the tuxedoed valet personified in Sir Pelham Grenville (P. G.) Wodehouse's stoic Jeeves, today's estate managers, as they're called, behave more like the chief operating officers of small companies.[2] Their primary responsibility is to supervise the procurement, use, and disposition of the goods and services that flow throughout a household. So on any given day, they may be found taking inventory, coordinating maintenance and storage, hiring and firing staff, meeting payroll, and overseeing construction projects. And although some estate managers still see to traditional tasks such as ironing the morning newspaper (it keeps the print from rubbing off on an employer's fingers), they are much more apt to be found coordinating the scrupulous care of art and antiques.

Graduates of programs like Starkey's are in great demand because of what some might say is an enviable predicament of the megarich: Owning everything one has ever wanted is not just a blessing; it is often a heavy burden. Each oceanfront home, vintage car, or precious piece of artwork requires someone to care for it. As many wealthy individuals tell us, you don't own your possessions . . . they quite often own you. The best estate managers enable their employers to enjoy the benefits of ownership without its nagging obligations. Put another way, these people add tremendous value to their employer's possessions.

Marketers would do well to consider that value carefully, because the upkeep of one's possessions is no longer a problem for the megarich alone. Our affluent society, most of which cannot afford to employ a full-time household manager, has amassed an unprecedented quantity of material goods. And people today have much less time to care for everything they own than they did even twenty years ago. In 2000, the average American worked almost one hundred hours longer per year than in 1980.[3] After such hard work, few consumers relish the thought of returning home to spend precious leisure time cleaning, repairing, or organizing possessions. What's more, research conducted by Yankelovich Partners confirms a growing "claustrophobia of abundance" caused by the fact that "people just feel overwhelmed by [their] stuff."[4] The growing burden of ownership on the affluent, left unchecked, *will hinder their future spending.* The moneyed masses may elect *not* to purchase certain goods, recognizing they have insufficient time or energy to maintain them. Or they may make the purchase, but quickly become dissatisfied with the product, the brand, and the company because they are unable to properly manage ownership, an equally unappealing alternative.

Unless marketers find a way to lessen the burden.

The Burdens of Ownership (and the Opportunities Therein)

The first and most obvious challenge facing people who own a great deal of "stuff" is where to put it all. Based on moving industry statistics, the average U.S. household has over 5,000 cubic feet (nearly four tons) of stuff. But therein lies an opportunity for builders: Americans have been constructing more spacious homes than ever before. The median square footage grew from 1,605 in 1985 to over 2,100 in 2001.[5]

Storage areas within the home are also growing larger and better equipped. California Closets, which began selling custom home-storage solutions in 1978, grew sixfold between 1996 and 2002.[6] The company now sells over $155 million worth of storage solutions a year to its prosperous customer base.[7] Meanwhile, the National Association of Home Builders reports that traditional pantries—not just oversized closets, but full, walk-in rooms for stockpiling kitchen goods—have become the most sought-after amenity in upscale homes.[8]

Of course, storage is only one of the challenges the moneyed masses face with increased ownership. Here's another: More expensive things are usually harder and more complicated to own. For example, a Swatch watch can have its battery changed in seconds by its owner, whereas an Omega diver watch must be sent insured to Switzerland so that the manufacturer can repressurize and seal it. Cashmere must be dry-cleaned. And while the care and maintenance of a snow shovel is straightforward, servicing a thirteen-horsepower self-propelled snow blower is not. Tossing it in the trunk of a car and hauling it to the dealer is not an option. Just lifting a blower can sometimes take three or four people. Savvy marketers will find opportunities for new revenue streams in all these problems consumers face.

To help marketers assess these new opportunities, some researchers are taking a more comprehensive view of household management. Most notable among them are Thomas Boyd and Diane McConocha at Miami University's Richard T. Farmer School of Business. Boyd and McConocha believe consumer marketing should take a page from industrial marketing, viewing *the household* as the buyer, just as organizations—and not just their individual members—are considered buyers. The researchers have created an ownership model they call the

Inventory Ownership Cycle, which compares household operations to materials management.[9]

All marketers are familiar with the first three of the model's seven steps—preacquisition (i.e., evaluation), acquisition, and use—but the subsequent four are seldom examined in sufficient detail:

- Storage

- Maintenance

- Restoration (taking an item out of storage, preparing it for use, readying it for storage, and then returning it to its place)

- Disposition (disposal)

Although these four steps are often invisible to consumer marketers, they are important to consumers and particularly critical to the time-starved moneyed masses. Each of these ownership components can require the investment of considerable time and effort, thereby determining whether an item is considered easy or burdensome to own. These, then, are important areas of differentiation that companies can focus on to better serve the ownership needs of today's consumers.

Reinventing Ownership

Goods and services that solve the burdens of the final four ownership steps have a powerful consumer appeal. Boyd and McConocha offer the example of the automatic dishwasher, now a fixture in 54 percent of American homes.[10] The maintenance benefit that all dishwashers provide—keeping dishes clean with less effort than hand washing—is obvious to both owners and manufacturers. Yet, some manufacturers have found that busy consumers also rely on their dishwashers to *store* dishes—both dirty and clean. Some people even prefer to reuse dishes directly from the dishwasher, rather than take the time to return them to kitchen shelves.

This extra storage benefit within the product's cycle of ownership has become one of the top valued features of a dishwasher from New

Zealand–based manufacturer Fisher and Paykel. The company earns a significant price premium in the market for having designed a dishwasher that is known for its ability not just to clean dishes, but to store them for easy use. The model, called the Dishdrawer, features separate pullout drawers so that consumers can wash and store two loads of dishes separately: one dirty and one clean. Even at a price of $2,000— ten times the cost of some entry-level dishwashers—many affluent households have been willing to pay extra to never have to return dishes to cabinets again.[11] Fisher and Paykel does not disclose Dishdrawer unit revenues, but North American sales grew by 16 percent in 2002 alone, while overall profits have tripled.[12]

But changing the product itself is just one way to seize the opportunity to provide more customer value throughout the ownership cycle. Another is by enhancing ease of use. Many marketers do this by altering the packaging as well the product—creating no-drip pouring spouts, for example. A third way is by improving post-sale support. Marketers have captured value here by streamlining their return processes, and by bundling in free routine maintenance, as many premium automakers now do.

There is a fourth option, as well, which builds on improving the ownership experience, but which is much more radical. It entails challenging the preconceived notions, both of buyers and of marketers, about what truly constitutes ownership, and asking what the value proposition of owning something should be. A few leading companies are doing this. And based on their experiences, we have identified three strategies companies can exploit to combat the customer's perceived downside of purchasing a given offering.

> *Distribute the rights (and responsibilities) of ownership among several consumers.* No longer just the domain of telemarketers pushing cookie-cutter Florida condos, fractional ownership now succeeds in making expensive, maintenance-intensive purchases more affordable and manageable for myriad products, such as luxury boats and exotic automobiles, by enlisting fewer, more affluent owners, distributing larger shares, and enhancing the flexibility of ownership.

Offer innovative payment options. The moneyed masses are
often asset rich but liquid-cash poor, eager not to tie up large
amounts of cash for a purchase (money that might yield
better returns elsewhere), and preferring to enjoy the
benefits of a product without ever actually paying in full for
ownership. As a result, marketers should look to introduce
new payment options that increase flexibility in the timing
of payments, such as leasing, pay-as-you-go, and all-inclusive
flat fees, into their repertoire.

Dramatically shorten the duration of ownership. Many
consumers, including the affluent, insist on keeping many
possessions long beyond the time the items are most useful
(or fashionable), though the owners can easily afford
replacements. Effective marketers in the furniture, consumer electronics, and apparel industries are driving out this
commercial inefficiency by constructing incentives for
consumers to replace goods much sooner. (We explore
the value of the alternative, the lengthening of the duration,
in chapter 6).

Each strategy must be assessed with the unmet needs of the moneyed masses in mind. The goal is to solve the problem of expanding the
customer's ability to consume, while also allowing the customer to
retain the valued sense of ownership so coveted to begin with (and
avoiding any negative associations the moneyed masses may have with
arrangements like rental centers, for example). We'll go into each of
these strategies in detail.

Sharing the Rights (and Responsibilities) of Ownership

In India, elephants were once the preferred form of transportation for
royalty, and few people would ever dare to dream of owning such an
animal. The hurdle was not simply the price of the elephant; it was the
enormous cost of its care and feeding.[13] The ruinous effects of elephant
ownership were so well known to Thai kings that they would use the gift

of a white elephant (sacred and therefore unable to work for its keep) as a punishment to those out of favor, an experience so financially painful we retain the expression for many such goods today.

Fortunately, marketers are realizing that by selling *portions of the rights* to such an item, while retaining responsibility for its general upkeep, they can lighten the burden of ownership and significantly broaden demand. Such *fractional ownership programs* are finding increasing success among the moneyed masses. While any significantly expensive item can be sold fractionally, from jet airplanes to jewelry (not a bad idea), four particular product categories—cars, boats, entertainment offerings, and vacation homes—demonstrate how this approach is managing to bring even the most extravagant of possessions into the hands of those who are merely well off.

Planes, Yachts, and (Exotic) Automobiles

Fractional jet ownership, begun in the early 1960s, had become so popular by the mid-1990s that Warren Buffet's Berkshire Hathaway bought NetJets (now Executive Jet) in 1998 for nearly a billion dollars.[14] Chicago-based Exotic Car Share has recently begun applying the same concept to the most elite models of rare, antique, and luxury automobiles. Through a new equity ownership program, individuals can buy a one-fifth share in cars such as a Ferrari 360 Modena Spider, a Lamborghini Murcielago, or a Bentley Arnage T.

As founder and CEO George Kiebala told us, the extension of fractional ownership to cars was a logical step: "Until recently, you could fly on a fractionally owned jet to your fractionally owned beachfront timeshare, where you sailed on a fractionally owned yacht. What was the missing piece in this picture? The car."[15]

Indeed, elite cars fall squarely into the category of desirable possessions that are highly burdensome to own. For every day spent cruising down sun-splashed roads, the typical Ferrari (particularly one owned by a Chicagoan) spends many more days sitting in a garage, where it racks up insurance, storage, and maintenance costs. Yet, although the car remains out of sight, it cannot remain out of mind. Like a fine thoroughbred, the garaged Ferrari needs constant exercise and care to stay in top condition. And to retain a sleek, shiny exterior (who daydreams about driving a dirty Ferrari?), the vehicle requires constant cleaning and buffing—more meticulous care than can be trusted to the local car wash. It is easy to see that few among the not-filthy-rich could have the time, money, or patience to devote to such a possession.

That's where Exotic Car Share comes in. Each share owner receives seven weeks of drive time per year by making an up-front investment of $7,500 to $60,000, depending on the car model, and paying an annual maintenance fee of between $7,500 and $15,000.[16] While this figure is certainly expensive, the fee is not much more than many affluent enthusiasts spend annually on their hobbies. Kiebala notes, in fact, that his customers come from every walk of life, occupation, and income range. What they all share, however, is a passion for cars.

What can make participation even more affordable in the long run is the residual value of the car. After three years, the owners can choose to keep the same car, upgrade it to a new model, or cash out and be reimbursed for the resale value. The ability to sell the vehicle means customers can recoup much, all, or even more than their initial investments. Kiebala notes that a Lamborghini purchased for $300,000 might be sold for $250,000 three years later—representing a drastically reduced depreciation cost of just $10,000 per owner, or roughly $3,300 per year—no worse than the family sedan. And should the car appreciate in value, as exotic ones often do, the owners stand to make money for the privilege of driving one.

Kiebala's experiences as a marketer offering fractional ownership deals have not always been easy. For example, Kiebala recounts that although the company was able to take advantage of the precedents set in other categories with regard to setting up enforceable terms and conditions of shared-ownership contracts, Exotic Car Share had a difficult time finding insurers that were comfortable with the concept: "We negotiated with insurance companies for a year and a half before finalizing their participation. It took a while because they had no precedent for insuring what we wanted to do."[17]

He also noted that it was difficult initially to demonstrate to manufacturers and dealers that the benefits of broadening the customer base through his program would outweigh the potential downside of brand dilution caused by the increase in accessibility. (Dilution will be a concern for any marketers attempting this approach with a product or an offering that is not their own.) Dealers, for example, are often the initial suppliers to such programs and must be convinced that the immediate sales opportunity (coupled with having a far greater pool of consumers who appreciate the benefits of their products from real firsthand experience) outweighs the risk of cannibalizing sales from customers who would have bought a whole one outright.

Exotic Car Share's program is far too new for us to declare a certain success. But Kiebala is optimistic: "Fifteen years ago, if someone were flying in a corporate jet, you thought that they must own it. Today, you assume instead that it is fractionally owned. There is an opportunity to achieve the same paradigm shift at the highest end of the automobile industry. I think that ten years from now, when people see a Lamborghini on the road, they will also assume that the driver has an equity share."[18]

Despite the obvious challenges of the approach, fractional ownership programs in general continue to catch on. Today they exist in a variety of arenas, including even one of the most time-honored bastions of elite luxury: yachting. Yachts are so notoriously expensive that even avid owners refer to them as "a hole in the water I pour money into." But companies like World Yacht Federation in San Diego are making it possible for aspiring boaters to purchase a portion of a million-dollar yacht. For between $70,000 and $85,000 (plus $6,000 for maintenance and insurance annually), fifteen buyers get the use of the boat for three weeks each year—or twenty-one days of unencumbered smooth sailing.[19]

More Like a Mutual Fund

There are any number of ways to offer fractional ownership deals. Rethinking the rights implied in ownership, for example, has led some professional sports organizations to tweak their season-ticket value proposition, which was once the province only of die-hard sports fans and the very wealthy. Consider the San Diego Padres, which have begun offering new, partial-season options (including 40-, 20-, and even 4-game versions, versus the full 81-game season) that help buyers avoid the hassle of reselling tickets they are unable to use. The Padres have also created a new tier, the Founders Club, which delivers a key new perk of owner-ship. For a onetime fee, Founders Club members may pass on their sea-son tickets to whomever they choose. Other season packages revert to the club if they're not renewed. By allowing this transferability, the team wisely and intentionally fosters the perception that its fans actually hold equity in their team's stadium.[20]

Another approach is to sell a share not just in one piece of property, but in a group of many properties. In the real estate arena, for example, rather than selling a fraction of a single residence, luxury hotel compa-nies like Ritz-Carlton and Four Seasons have created residence clubs that offer shares in a closed system of vacation resorts. For $28,000 and a $1,000 annual maintenance fee, a family can vacation at a Four Sea-sons residence in Scottsdale, Arizona, one year and in Mexico the next.[21]

One high-end provider, Private Retreats, offers its 190 members access to twenty-six resort homes from Hawaii to Hilton Head. As one customer happily explains on the company's Web site, participation "really is like having 20 second homes."[22] Another provider, Exclusive Resorts, contends, "For what you'd pay in property taxes on a single vacation home…you can have an 8th, 9th, 10th. . . ." The company car-ries the provocative tagline, "A Lifestyle Investment," and describes itself as, "the intelligent way to balance lifestyles and investment agendas."[23]

These plans tend to be more successful than traditional time-shares because they involve high-quality properties in well-known destina-tions; they offer larger shares to a smaller, more exclusive base of own-ers; and they have the support of large, trusted brand names. Additionally, customers are being offered much greater flexibility in converting their ownership stake into a variety of paybacks. This is especially valuable for those in the moneyed masses for whom partici-pation is a fairly significant investment. Marriott and Disney have cre-ated new points-based systems that let consumers "cash in" their fractionally owned properties in exchange for other products and serv-ices. Families may choose to give up the use of a time-share in exchange for points that they can spend on affiliated hotels, cruises, and airfare packages offered within the program. Peter Giamalva of Resort Condo-miniums International, a major time-share-trading organization, explains: "It's more like buying currency than buying a timeshare interval."[24] And this approach need not be limited to identical properties, either. Creative marketers could easily bundle shared ownership of cars with condos, let's say, or any number of possessions.

Such flexibility reduces the stress of the commitment to buy (when purchase means a financial reach) and allows ownership to evolve as customer needs and desires (and ability to pay) evolve. Yet the average income of time-share owners reflects the success of this approach in appealing to an upscale customer base. In 2002, 46 percent of time-share owners had a household income over $75,000 (versus 25 percent of all Americans) and 23.5 percent had incomes over $100,000 (versus 14 percent of all Americans).[25] Consistent with this general owner affluence, the number of high-end residences sold through fractional ownership programs has grown sharply. Market researcher Ragatz Associates finds that sales at private residence clubs increased 115 percent in 2000 and even 24 percent in 2001, a turbulent year for the travel industry.[26] Clearly, the once-modest time-share has been successfully elevated for a more discriminating, affluent consumer.

Offer Innovative Payment Options

In colonial times, buying something on credit was considered shameful evidence of class pretension.[27] But in the early part of the twentieth century, credit became an important way of enabling more consumers to pay for the expensive items that were suddenly being made available to them by the industrial revolution. In the process, the use of credit propelled the business concepts of liquidity and leverage into mass-market consumption. By 1925, just a few years after auto manufacturers introduced installment plans, three-fourths of all cars were being purchased with loans.[28] And in 1950, the launch of the first credit card from Diner's Club helped seal credit as a fixture in the consumer landscape, attracting 1.25 million customers in its first decade.[29]

Our research has found that developing new payment plans, and extending existing ones into new product and service categories, enables the affluent to partake of an offering's benefits like owners, without the responsibilities and financial consequences of real ownership. Companies should therefore evaluate the potential for new payment arrangements—pay-per-use, leasing, and flat all-inclusive fees are a few examples—to drive revenues in conjunction with developing their existing or planned offerings. While these approaches are not new in many industries, they remain surprisingly absent or nascent in others.

Pay as You Go, Go, Go

Consider the love-hate relationship between affluent urbanites and their automobiles. Cars can provide a connection to the world beyond a city's limits, yet they are expensive and inconvenient to own in an urban environment. Transportation researcher Runzheimer International estimates that the average New Yorker spends nearly $700 per month on the ancillary expenses related to car ownership, including some of the highest insurance and parking rates in the world.[30] Yet how much use do these consumers get for their money? Industry watchers point out that the average American family uses its car no more than one hour a day.[31] And the average moneyed New Yorker is likely to use it only a few hours each weekend, on a jaunt to IKEA or East Hampton.

To address this imbalance, a start-up called Zipcar has launched a pay-per-use service that provides urbanites of all income levels in Boston, New York City, and Washington, D.C., easy access to cars for short-term round-trips. For a $75 annual membership fee and usage charges, Zipcar's customers can reserve cars online, pick them up from locations in nearly any neighborhood, and use them in increments as small as a single hour. The company's unique payment model differentiates Zipcar from traditional rentals. Its customers are charged only for the exact hours they reserve the car. The flat fee includes all gas, maintenance, and insurance, while ensuring parking at reserved company spaces throughout its cities of operation.[32]

Nancy Rosenzweig, Zipcar's vice president of marketing, explained to us how the service eliminates the burden of car ownership: "Once you become a member, it takes fifteen seconds online to reserve a car. Then you use the car as needed and pay for it as needed. Once a month, you'll see the charges on your credit card bill."[33]

This ease-of-use value proposition has resonated with affluent city dwellers. While Zipcar's customer base is economically diverse, encompassing everybody from students to retirees, Rosenzweig discloses that households earning over $100,000 "are among the earliest adopters of our service, as well as the most loyal and frequent users." They account for anywhere from 19 percent of Zipcar users in Washington to about 40 percent in New York City (versus roughly 14 percent of the urban population). Those figures are noteworthy because, while these customers could certainly afford cars of their own, as Rosenzweig explains, "They only need a car once in a while and don't want the hassle of owning one. They see Zipcar as much a part of the urban infrastructure, and as simple to use when needed as an ATM machine." The pay-per-use model has proven so compelling, in fact, that many Zipcar users forgo automobile ownership altogether once they start using the service. About 15 percent of Zipcar members have given up their cars since joining the service, while another 25 percent have deferred an automobile purchase.

The pay-per-use concept is particularly attractive to customers who are inclined to look beyond standard ownership behaviors. Rosenzweig advises that the young and educated tend to be this type of consumer. "These consumers are very independent-minded and willing to try new things—they appreciate new services that can enhance their lifestyles." A full 98 percent of its customers are college graduates, while 40 percent hold graduate degrees. Evidently, for educated consumers (who tend to affluent or on the way to becoming affluent), pay-for-use is a smart choice.

A New Lease on Life

Another attractive proposition for many moneyed consumers is leasing, because it allows them to pay for the ongoing use of an item in installments. Offering a kind of ownership via this approach is especially effective for marketers selling very expensive items or goods that have a fashion component to them that might make long-term ownership less desirable. The approach is also particularly effective for companies whose products have complicated service and resale processes or highly uncertain residual values.

One arena in which all of these factors combine to make leasing a cinch is the high-end automobile sector. Recognizing that some people have a strong desire to always drive a new car without having to deal with the hassle of selling or trading in old ones, luxury automobile companies have created a wide variety of leasing schemes. These not only make sliding behind the wheel of a new BMW, Jaguar, or Mercedes more immediately affordable, with a short commitment, but also remove the hassle and expense of maintaining the car and selling it for a fair price.

Such schemes have hit their mark: About 56 percent of luxury cars (those costing more than $30,000) are leased, compared with 26 percent of all cars.[34] Meanwhile, some luxury brands have begun presenting entirely new leasing offers that would have been unthinkable a few years ago. For example, one can now drive a Maserati Coupe GT for an attainable $999 per month (with about $10,000 cash due at signing).[35] Such initiatives are not inexpensive, but empower the moneyed masses to aspire, and to enjoy.

Another category that we believe has the potential for explosive growth via leasing arrangements is art (which, not surprisingly when you think about it, has many properties similar to luxury cars). Consider the Virginia Center for the Creative Arts, which is one of many galleries now offering leasing options to individuals as well as business customers. The center offers *Night Shopper,* an oil-on-linen painting by Marlene Baron Summers, at $3,500 to buy or $35 a month to lease. And according to the center's Web site, "Purchasing a work of art can be an intimidating process; it is a major aesthetic and financial decision. Leasing art eliminates the burden of purchasing while allowing you the flexibility to change your mind. At the end of the lease period, you have the option to return, renew, or purchase."[36] And that's just the beginning. Other marketers of high-priced goods with illiquid resale markets are also beginning to test the leasing waters, sensing that such programs will increase sales to the moneyed masses. For example, Saul Hymans, an economics professor at the University of Michigan, recently proposed at a furniture industry conference that manufacturers begin offering three-, five-, and ten-year lease terms for high-end consumers.[37] While some analysts questioned the appeal of preowned furnishings (and indeed, images of some current furniture rental businesses don't conjure up thoughts of affluent customers), one Merrill Lynch vice president pointed out a successful precedent: the antiques market.

Although these early industry discussions have not yet resulted in new programs, we will likely see the day when, for example, an executive household that relocates frequently may never actually buy a set of furniture. Instead, it might lease a number of traditional Thomasville Hemingway collection pieces for a multiyear assignment in Washington, D.C., and a roomful of contemporary Roche-Bobois furniture for its next tour of duty in Los Angeles.

Price Fixe-ing Things

In some categories, companies can eliminate the need for affluent households to buy and use entire ranges of products altogether by replacing them with a single, all-inclusive *service,* priced at a flat fee. Some economists are beginning to argue that such arrangements (which are actually a combination of a new take on payment and a new value-charged sales proposition) are not only more convenient, but more efficient. Here's the logic: According to analyses of so-called household production, the value of an affluent person's time is often too great to be spent on buying individual component products and services and on performing routine tasks such as lawn care and laundry.[38] These economists argue that many household activities should be outsourced, even for those who are not particularly rich.

To understand how this all-inclusive model is already working, look to the growing number of personal chefs. The ranks of this group have grown from a few hundred in 1997 to more than 7,000 in 2002, serving in excess of 100,000 households.[39] The American Personal Chef Association estimates those numbers will grow to 25,000 chefs serving 300,000 clients by 2006.[40]

Unlike private cooks, who work for one wealthy client, personal chefs often cater to several households at once. For a few hundred dollars a week, they shop for household groceries and prepare an agreed-upon number of meals, such as weekday dinners. Meals are prepared in-home or for drop-off (less mess), and the chefs are now being hired for special meals like an anniversary or for weeks at a time (e.g., during a vacation) or as an ongoing service like a nanny. The chef service allows the family to transfer responsibility for buying and processing the majority of its food purchases. Instead, it simply receives healthy, tasty meals that are ready to eat.

Upscale food retailers should take note of this trend, as more buying decisions are being made by personal chefs preparing food on behalf of affluent families. One could imagine Whole Foods supermarkets, for example, establishing and marketing its own network of affiliated personal chefs who use the chain to identify moneyed customers and, in exchange, agree to buy all their ingredients at the stores.

Kitchen accessory manufacturers might also see opportunity in selling to a new class of buyer, the home professional. This takes the same idea that manufacturers had for small office/home office versions of business machines and moves it into the world of cooking and beyond.

And food is just one category. Marketers in other fields should also anticipate service categories that could take shape around their product lines, deciding now, ahead of the curve, whether to cast their lot with emerging players or to offer the new capabilities themselves. At best, companies exploring this approach may create a lucrative new business opportunity. At a minimum, they should be able to prevent new service intermediaries from developing unchecked influence over customer buying decisions.

Here's another arena in which the appeal of flat-fee services has fueled an ever growing market: the hotel apartment, a living concept that was originally popularized in New York City in the 1920s. Today, new condominium buildings operated by high-end hotel chains are winning residents by promising direct access to the all-inclusive service levels that made the parent companies famous, from housekeeping to dog walking to valet parking. According to Delta Associates, nearly 2,000 such units exist in eight cities, with another 1,400 units currently under construction.[41] Prices range well into the millions, but start at several hundred thousand dollars, about the price of a home in the surrounding suburbs. Having such amenities allows these residences to command a sizable premium. A 2002 study found that hotel condos appreciated an average of 22 percent faster than similar units without the service affiliation, while The Residences at the Ritz-Carlton in Georgetown cost 64 percent more than equivalent units elsewhere in Washington.[42]

L'Addition, S'il Vous Plait

John Gourville, a professor at Harvard Business School, and Dilip Soman, of Hong Kong's University of Science and Technology, have carefully studied how the timing of payment methods can encourage consumers to renew offerings. The key, they say, is to time payment requests appropriately to ensure the regular consumption of goods and services being paid for. Companies that do this successfully, Gourville and Soman find, grow sales, establish switching costs, and increase customer satisfaction.

While some have argued that consumers dislike being reminded of their payment obligations, Gourville and Soman maintain that spreading payment over the life cycle of a contract or lease is, in fact, a powerful tool for companies: "Payments that occur at or near the time of consumption increase attention to a product's cost, boosting the likelihood of its consumption. By contrast, payments made either long before or after the actual purchase reduce attention to a product's cost and decrease the likelihood that it will be used."[43] The authors found that consumers who pay for their health club memberships on a monthly, not annual basis, for example, are by far the most likely to consistently make use of the service—and therefore renew when the term is up.

Firms offering flat-fee services can also take this approach one step further. When a payment includes a series of product and service charges—as is the case in an automobile lease—marketers should consider itemizing each cost. Gourville and Soman have found that this practice increases the offering's perceived value. For example, a personal chef who bills an affluent customer at a flat fee, yet itemizes individual food and preparation costs, reminds the customer of all the things he or she *doesn't* have to do, buy, or own. The customer will be more likely to appreciate the value of his or her expenditure this way, and rehire that chef when the contract comes up for renewal.

Shortening the Duration of Ownership

When asked to name the most enduring commitment we are likely to make in our lifetime, our thoughts turn naturally to marriage and spouses. Although this belief is romantic, some furniture industry executives say it is often very wrong. The longest attachment most of us are likely to have is to that dining room table—the one that we bought for our first home and that we still gather around on special occasions today. This artifact precedes and outlasts many marriages. Christian Mathieu, external marketing manager for international furniture retailer IKEA, told us, "We have found that people have the same number of spouses as dining room tables—literally. They average about 1.5 of each in their lifetimes."[44]

Statistics further support Mathieu's contention by illustrating the tendency of consumers to cling to household items, regardless of the ownership burden. One study estimates that consumers keep sofas for an average of eight years, bedroom furniture for up to twenty years, and dining room furniture for more than twenty years.[45] The International Housewares Association finds that this curatorial tendency applies to many smaller household goods as well. Consumers buy a teakettle once every ten years, and a bread box once every thirty years. By contrast, the average marriage lasts a paltry seven years.[46]

Hanging on to a possession for years—or even decades—may at first seem like a practical and efficient decision. But often, neither companies nor consumers benefit. The disadvantages for companies are obvious. Low purchase frequencies limit revenue potential and diminish the potential average lifetime value of customers. Yet, consumers are not well served by lengthy ownership, either, IKEA's Mathieu contends: "We've found through in-home interviews that most people hold on to furniture that they dislike. Not only do these items fail to express the owners' personal style, but in many cases, they no longer serve a useful function."[47]

Such behavior reflects a breakdown in the ownership cycle. Even the affluent continue to maintain and reuse a product when the effort far exceeds the return, despite being well able to afford a replacement.

Mathieu explains some of this consumer behavior: "It's an irrational behavior. Sometimes it is motivated by the sense that just because items are old, they are classic and have some heirloom or sentimental value. But, there is also a fear of change involved. A consumer may wonder, 'If I change my sofa, then what else will I need to change in my home?'"[48]

Redefining the offering in ways that provide consumers with incentives for making more frequent purchases can create new revenue opportunities. These new offerings must, however, first break down the obligation consumers feel for retaining their current possessions. A shift away from long-term ownership in a number of categories has already begun. Witness the trend in remodeling to "serial renovators," estimated by some to be 40 percent of buyers, who constantly replace their purchases with the latest must-have items.[49] Even homes are becoming increasingly disposable, with consumers regularly making teardowns, once typically reserved for houses older than thirty years and under 2,000 square feet, out of million-dollar homes.[50] Many of these teardowns are admittedly hastily built McMansions sitting on prime real estate, but that only serves to reinforce the changing belief in a home's being consumable rather than durable. And there are likely even more such transitions on the way.

We see five effective approaches for shortening the duration of ownership, all of which work even better when combined. Marketers can

- teach consumers to demand continued value from their purchases,
- speed the pace of innovation in a category,
- offer versions tailored to less frequent use,
- shorten time-to-market of offerings and inventory, and
- facilitate and accelerate product disposal.

Changing Hearts and Minds

The first step in changing purchasing behavior is to directly challenge the consumer mind-set surrounding long-term ownership. Marketers must teach consumers to demand more from their possessions, insisting these items continually earn a place in their home. International furniture retailer IKEA has made an ambitious effort to convey just that message by spending nearly $50 million on a television advertising campaign that satirizes the sentimental attachments consumers develop to old, and often ugly, home goods.[51] When the ad's protagonists replace their furniture, a narrator chastises viewers for feeling badly for the old items. "You are crazy," he tells the audience.

Mathieu, responsible for the campaign, explains: "The campaign was a way to encourage consumers to leave behind their durable-goods mind-set and think of furniture as soft goods. We challenged them to expect items that are attractive, functional, and reflective of their own taste and style."[52] While IKEA shared this message with all of its customers, it also directly targeted the affluent—who can afford to replace their furniture more often. The company supplemented its television ads with twenty-four-page booklets in upscale magazines such as *Dwell, Vogue,* and *Wallpaper.*[53]

When does it become an imperative for a company to shake up its entire category, rather than making a nice-to-have investment in changing consumer behaviors? For IKEA, one important business driver was the need to support its aggressive expansion in North America. Mathieu explains the logic: "Soon, we will have even more stores concentrated around cities such as Toronto and New York. To support that density, we cannot simply skim from our existing customer base. We have to challenge the category as a whole and try to change its behaviors, while at the same time educating consumers about IKEA."[54]

Companies should not undertake such an effort, however, without a clear understanding of its risks. Perhaps the greatest danger is investing in a behavior change that will not produce any visible results for years to come. IKEA knew that it could not accept such a delay. "Retailers can't wait years to move a category," Mathieu confirms. To ensure near-term results, IKEA started by developing a clear vision of what it hoped to achieve. The wristwatch industry provided one guide. According to Mathieu, "We considered how Swatch, for example, changed its category. The company transformed watches from rare purchases into more affordable items that consumers bought as fashion statements."

IKEA then constantly checked its progress against its goal through market research. Mathieu continues, "For example, we tracked changes in the way consumers responded to the question, 'Do you prefer furniture that is timeless and classic or furniture that expresses your personal sense of style?' For the first time, in December of 2002, more consumers said that they preferred the latter. While we can't attribute that change to marketing alone, it confirmed that we were moving in the right direction."

A second challenge facing companies is the perception that, by encouraging shorter ownership cycles, the company is promoting waste and damaging the environment. This issue was taken particularly seriously at eco-friendly IKEA, says Mathieu: "First, we had to clarify that we are not advocating disposability. We are against waste. Our idea comes from a different place. It is that, if you have an old desk that is no longer functional or attractive, you should buy a new one in order to create the home you want and need." IKEA stands behind its assertion through a commitment to eco-friendly disposal, for example, by eliminating brominated flame retardants in its furniture to make the pieces more easily recyclable. The company also has many high-profile sustainable forestry partnerships and initiatives with organizations such as the World Wildlife Foundation and Global Forest Watch.

In spite of the challenges, companies that commit to changing the customer mind-set toward ownership can enjoy substantial rewards. Mathieu told us, "We saw increases in many of our major business metrics both during and after the campaign. Brand awareness, perception, and consideration all rose. So did store traffic and sales. Overall, this has been a very successful strategy and we feel that taking on such a large challenge has paid off."

Innovate a Reason for Discontent

While efforts such as IKEA's are producing results by encouraging consumers to swap out products they no longer value, other companies will not succeed with even the most articulate marketing campaigns unless they also offer consumers regular, compelling product innovations. After all, consumers cannot be expected to discard possessions more frequently without new desirable alternatives. The consumer electronics industry is one segment that has evolved to this strategy successfully. It is hard to imagine now, but consumers were once reluctant to replace their electronics. Radios and televisions were once considered lifetime purchases, and in the 1960s and 1970s, consumers were still reluctant to buy new ones unless theirs broke. As recently as the 1980s, stereos were expected to have a useful life span of fifteen years or longer. These items even *looked* permanent, with many being built into wooden frames and cabinets. Home electronics didn't just resemble furniture; they were furniture.

Buying behaviors have changed dramatically since then, with consumers now buying and replacing electronics frequently, to take advantage of new innovations. The digital video disk (DVD) player has had the fastest penetration of any such item: 25 percent of U.S. homes in just four years, by 2001. Our research finds that today, consumers consider home electronics the most innovative product segment of all.

What did the electronics industry do to increase the pace of purchases that others in more staid industries can follow? Generally speaking, we attribute the change to several broad manufacturer initiatives.

First, the industry has accelerated the development and marketing of new offerings. Electronics have come a long way from the days when breakthrough products entered the market once per decade—such as the television in the 1950s (although it was first publicly introduced in 1939), the audiocassette in the late 1960s, and the videocassette recorder (VCR) in the 1970s.[55] Now, new products are developed and marketed frequently and aggressively, with Intel regularly crediting its success to a willingness to cannibalize its own product lines, often with no more than incremental improvement. While there is no single tally of annual product launches, the growth of the Consumer Electronics Show, now about ten times the size of the first conference held in 1967, reflects the increased activity.[56]

Second, the consumer electronics industry has been expert in seeding demand with announcements of forthcoming offerings, but doing so in a way that does not destroy demand for products already in the market. Although consumers are accustomed to learning about what they will be buying in a few years from consumer electronics and auto shows, other industries have yet to create such a consistent way of communicating to their customers their commitment to a pattern of continuous innovation. Are consumers well aware of the innovation *to be expected* in the sporting goods industry, for example, and are they convinced that sporting goods will continue to be improved through innovation for years to come?

Finally, manufacturers have worked to lower price points more aggressively to spur market growth and broaden demand for new offerings. For example, lower prices are accelerating sales of high-definition televisions. Brad Jones, a spokesman at the Consumer Electronics Association, points out, "Sales [of high-definition televisions] have exceeded forecasts by 70 percent, partly because prices have plummeted, so that a $4,000 set is now available for under $2,000."[57] Contrast this with the difficulties experienced in the 1970s with the launch of the VCR, which debuted on the market with a $1,000 price tag that remained high, delaying widespread consumer adoption until the early 1980s.[58] Today, manufacturers are doing a better job of finding price points that sustain margins while expanding accessibility to the merely affluent consumers who want them.

Throwaway Ideas

Shorter ownership cycles can also be created by a focus on single-use and limited-use versions of products, which often better serve customer needs. For example, millions of us have purchased disposable cameras to bring on a vacation or to a family gathering. But few of us are likely to realize that these items now represent an annual business worth nearly a billion dollars.[59]

How did camera manufacturers create a successful single-use version of a product that consumers had only known as a long-term, highly considered purchase? First, they uncovered unmet needs: several instances when consumers wanted to take pictures but, for various reasons, could not or did not do so with their traditional cameras. They identified two types of consumers in particular—tourists who had mistakenly left their cameras at home, but did not want to invest in buying new ones, and individuals pursuing outdoor activities and who were afraid to damage their expensive Minoltas or Nikons.[60] With these pro-files in mind, manufacturers created a single-use version of a camera that would serve customers in these specific situations.

Most marketers probably think the next step was a huge investment in new technology and product design. Yet, surprisingly, accommodating single-use products was not a significant challenge for camera makers. The earliest disposable cameras were little more than pieces of cardboard and plastic casing wrapped around a roll of film.[61] So while finding the best product packaging undoubtedly required work, the core technologies at use were readily available.

The trend to creating fulfilling single-use products is pushing into some surprising categories. A handful of Walgreens locations in Southern California recently began offering the first disposable cell phones. Created by a start-up firm named Hop-On, the phones cost $40 apiece and are sold with an hour of prepaid calling time.[62] The ideal result for manufacturers is that the spread of disposable cell phones will change the way consumers view the entire product category. The proliferation of single-use models could encourage consumers to view their primary cell phones as more expendable, too—increasing the likelihood that they will be frequently upgraded or replaced.

The evolution of goods from durable to disposable items may, at first, seem like a drastic shift. But the ownership benefits are clear. This is a dramatically different mandate, however, from the concept of planned obsolescence—the practice of making products more disposable by increasing the likelihood that they will break and need replacement—something Vance Packard rightfully decried in his 1959 book, *The Waste Makers*. What we are proposing is that companies create a breadth of products optimized for different frequencies of use (likely driven by usage occasions), capturing the revenue and margin benefits of offerings that are purchased more frequently.

Shortening Time to Market

Product development should not be the only focus of innovation. Some companies, particularly those whose offerings are not technology driven, need to place equal or greater emphasis on increasing the innovation's speed to market. Products that are subject to fashion, for example, can increase purchase frequencies by bringing new styles to consumers at unprecedented speed. The apparel business has already used this approach to change buying behaviors. Once, new trends originated from a handful of influential designers. Most consumers had to wait years before mainstream manufacturers identified the most popular styles, designed their own versions, produced them, and shipped them to store shelves. By then, the style makers had often moved on. Only the wealthiest individuals could afford to buy the latest fashions of the season and to do so every season.

No longer. A handful of leading clothing chains are now able to offer the latest styles, colors, and cuts at moderate prices within weeks of their appearance on runways. Madrid-based clothier Zara claims that it can bring a product from design stage to store shelves in as little as two weeks, compared to six for most competitors.[63] As a result, Zara is able to release a massive amount of products—11,000 different models of clothing for men, women, and children in just one year—and quickly refresh its selection.[64] Tracy Mullin, CEO of the National Retail Federation, explains the advantage of a shortened time to market: "It's like you walk into a new store every two weeks."[65] The company confirms that no single item is available for more than one month.[66]

The rapid appearance—and disappearance—of cutting-edge items has drawn consumers to stores deliberately located in affluent areas such as New York's SoHo and Miami's Aventura Mall. Although Zara spends little money on advertising, sales have boomed.[67] In the third quarter of 2002, parent company Inditex—whose financial performance is dominated by Zara—experienced growth of over 30 percent in net income, while sales rose 25 percent.[68] Zara opened almost fifty new stores worldwide throughout the year.[69]

How can companies emulate Zara's success in achieving speed to market? By optimizing their supply chains for agility, not just low cost. According to chief financial officer, Borja de la Cierva, "The most important factor for us is time to produce and distribute our products."[70] To that end, Zara has developed technologies and processes that enable it to replenish directly from point-of-sale data. The company then relies on a number of local suppliers operating near its European stores to manufacture and distribute product.

While using European suppliers is more expensive, Zara claims that it enables increased responsiveness, which has nearly eliminated excess inventory and warehousing costs. Its overall profit margin, 10 percent, matches those of the highest performers in the apparel industry.[71] Such success illustrates that rapid product releases, based on timely and fact-based assessments of what the customer wants at a given moment, can convince consumers to buy more goods, more often.

The Power of Resale

Sometimes the barrier to overcoming buyer reluctance isn't just mental; it's also physical. While consumers may have no problem donating last season's Zara sweater to the charity bin, it is considerably harder to get rid of other goods, particularly big-ticket items like furniture and home appliances. Consider a perfectly good working stove that has gone out of style or become obsolete. Allowing an appliance store to keep it for free is not appealing, and curbside trash collection is problematic. What's more, even if curbside pickup is easy, the sending of a functioning stove, no matter how worn, to a landfill feels horribly wasteful and damaging to the planet.

In these categories, the missing ingredient to increasing purchase frequency is a liquid resale market. Resale networks provide consumers with simple, established ways to identify interested buyers and recoup a portion of their investment. For proof of the impact of effective resale markets on buying behavior, we need look no further than the Internet. eBay has attracted over 55 million registered users by offering a market-place for goods that were once difficult to sell at a fair price through traditional means. These items include, according to one snapshot count, listings for 927 boats and about 1,300 pianos.[72] But eBay is hardly a repository of leftovers for bottom feeders. The presence of the affluent is very evident from recent listings that showcase upscale items, including everything from a $500 Burberry trench coat to a $329 tee time at the Tiburon golf course in Naples, Florida.

Amazon.com provides an equally interesting study of how a high-profile resale market can help to grow transactions in a *single* product category. The company's decision to broker the sale of used books and CDs has made it easier for consumers to buy and sell tomes that were once abandoned on bookshelves, consigned to trash heaps, or relegated to the dusty bins of secondhand bookshops. Though Amazon.com introduced its resale site features only in November 2000, astonishingly, used books now account for more than 15 percent of the company's overall book sales.[73]

While not every product category can count on an Amazon.com or eBay to step into the secondhand business, there are measures that companies can take to foster their own resale markets. Supporting resale markets that already exist is a valuable first step. New York's Strand, the world's biggest bookstore and a famous refuge for well-heeled Manhattanites, launched an online presence that made its collections available to visitors of Amazon.com, Abebooks, and other leading Web book outlets. After just one year, the Strand's Web site contributed 15 percent of the company's total sales and a whopping 34 percent in its rare-books trade.[74]

In some cases, companies can take a more active role in donation and disposal services, like those currently run by both for-profit and nonprofit companies. For example, organizations—from the National Kidney Foundation to local animal shelters—regularly solicit tax-deductible donations of used cars, which they either keep or sell off for cash. The problem for marketers, however, is that such efforts facilitate only the disposal of goods, not the early replacement. Consumers tend to wait until late in their ownership cycle to donate items. These "gifts" are often barely functional and are, according to the chief operating officer of the Better Business Bureau, simply "donations of convenience."[75]

By stepping in more aggressively, marketers can transform disposal services into resale opportunities that better serve both consumers and charitable organizations alike. Dell has begun to exploit this opportunity by launching on its Web site a series of offers that discourage consumers from simply throwing away unwanted hardware.[76] Instead, Dell provides consumers with compelling incentives to trade in or donate their old PCs, such as coupons that can be redeemed for future purchases and product exchanges. The old models, depending on their condition, are recycled or donated to a nonprofit. In addition, Dell has joined a small group of manufacturers that encourages the dropoff of used electronics at select Best Buy locations, in partnership with the U.S. Environmental Protection Agency.

Through such efforts, manufacturers can increase the efficiency of product disposal while benefiting customers, their bottom line, and the environment. For example, thanks to Dell, customers can now get rid of their old PCs sooner and replace them with new models at more attractive prices, a process we call *accelerating markets.*[77] Dell gains an opportunity to market directly to consumers on the verge of product replacement. And, best of all for the environment, far less used hardware ends up as trash in landfills.

Adding It All Up

Winning the loyalty of affluent consumers means more than developing products and services they will want to buy; it means developing offerings (in whatever form of product or product/service package necessary) they will want *to own.* This requires devising offerings that easily integrate into households already burdened with prosperity—those with an increasing number of goods, yet limited resources to manage them. When the founder of the Starkey Institute, Mary Louise Starkey, describes the value that her estate management graduates provide to wealthy clients, she speaks in glowing terms. Estate managers do not just care for homes or ensure that a family entertains properly, but also manage their quality of life.[78] Companies seeking to cater to the moneyed masses must do the same.

6

Grow the Return on Consumption

Old Rule
Offer the masses new consumables and new investment opportunities.

New Rule
Offer new consumables that perform like investment opportunities.

Hollywood has produced no fewer than six screen adaptations of the novel *Brewster's Millions.*[1] In the most recent version, the star is challenged to spend (not just give away) $30 million in thirty days, in order to gain a far larger inheritance. What's the catch? He cannot buy a single tangible asset as part of his spree.[2] He has to consume the money by purchasing only nondurable goods, like restaurant meals, entertainment, the services of a personal trainer, or airfare.

Though the movie is only a fantasy, its underlying assumption—that it is difficult to consume one's way out of significant wealth—contains a kernel of truth. One economist has observed that Bill Gates could absolutely "consume" $10 million a day, and still not erode his net worth.[3] But here's the point that marketers need to absorb and act on: Monsieur Gates is not likely even to try to spend significant amounts of money (in relative terms, of course) on ephemeral pleasures. When the wealthy spend prodigiously, it is often on durable items with intrinsic value, such as art, real estate, and collector's items. These purchases have a propensity to maintain their value over time and to even go up in price.

Show a Little Appreciation

Most of us are not in Bill Gates's income bracket, or even close. But the behavior holds for even the less-than-ultrarich—on several fronts. A study by the National Bureau of Economic Research, for example, confirms that consumers save more money, both in real dollar terms and as a percentage of their income, as they move up the income scale. Estimated savings rates range from less than 5 percent among consumers in the lowest income quartile, to over 40 percent among the top 5 percent of earners.[4]

What's more, as households accumulate wealth, the appeal of spending on additional raw, nondurable consumption fades. Research conducted by Christopher D. Carroll, a Johns Hopkins professor of economics, finds that as consumers become more affluent, they increasingly enjoy wealth accumulation purely for its own sake (not because of a desire to save for a rainy day or to build a dynasty by giving it away to their children, for example). As a result, these consumers are likely to consider carefully the impact their purchases have on their net worth. Paraphrasing Carroll's words, the desire for purchases with even a modest intrinsic appeal will eventually exceed the waning lure of an extra dollar of non-durable consumption.[5]

Yet even seemingly lavish nondurable consumption can offer intrinsic appeal when it serves as a signal of the owner's ability and may therefore be viewed by the consumer as an investment: Robert Frank, author of the book *Luxury Fever,* explains how this can happen. "To the extent that wearing the right watch, driving the right car, wearing the right suit, or living in the right neighborhood may help someone land the right job or a big contract, these expenditures are more like investments than true consumption."[6]

Today's increasingly affluent consumers, in other words, are looking to purchase goods (and services) that exhibit an investment-like structure capable of enhancing wealth over time. We surmise that this eye toward investment is at least partly what drives more than 70 percent of the respondents in our consumer research surveys to report that they do a lot of research before making a significant purchase.

Profitable Consumption

The broad-based desire to make consuming more like investing exhorts marketers to demonstrate the enduring value of their offerings. They must articulate an offering's return on consumption—the benefits that extend beyond its predictable use. Our research reveals three specific strategies, based on the innate properties that characterize investments, that leading companies are using to profit from this growing consumer preference:

Pay dividends to your customers. Promise, for years into the future, dividend payments to those who buy and continue to own your offerings. These dividends can take the form of periodic cash payments, but are also known to include promises of recurring, and at times seemingly random, dispersals of free valuable goods and services.

Improve your customers' productivity. Every businessperson understands the benefits of making a capital investment in tools and machines, the idea being to increase the productivity of other inputs such as labor. Now is the time to include capital-investment-like offerings in your product and service lines—offerings that promise to improve the earnings potential and overall productivity of affluent consumers and their children.

Create value by extending a product's real and perceived useful life. This approach is particularly relevant for categories of goods where fashion and innovation are not easily accelerated, limiting the opportunity to shorten the duration of ownership (one of the strategies presented in chapter 5). In such cases, companies can lengthen the delivery of value by endowing goods with an heirloom quality, making them collectibles that span generations or increase in resale value. Another way is by launching warranty and refurbishment programs that ensure long-term, undiminished delivery of the value promise embedded in the original purchase.

Paying Dividends on Consumption

It took the wild stock market ride of the late 1990s to remind American consumers what financial planners have known for generations: that dividends are a highly effective vehicle for delivering consistent investment returns. A recent survey by Kiplinger's Personal Finance, in fact, found that 48 percent of consumers now consider dividends an important factor when they choose equities.[7]

An increasing number of public companies are coming on board; in 2003 Microsoft announced its first dividend payment since going public in 1985, a period of almost twenty years. Now it's time for marketers to follow suit. While executive boards determine whether a stock pays a dividend, marketers can allocate dividends linked to the companies' offerings. To ground these efforts, they should focus on the dictionary definition of the word *dividend,* which has two distinct shades of meaning—the offering of anticipated benefits ("a share of a surplus; a bonus") and the offering of surprise benefits ("an unexpected gain, benefit or advantage").[8] Leading providers of *consumption dividends* are paying both.

Share the Wealth

Thanking customers for their patronage at the end of transactions, from retail checkout lines to call-center conversations, has always been a standard business practice. Yet some companies are expressing their gratitude far more eloquently and effectively: with a check. Their strategy is to pay an appreciable "dividend" to their most profitable customers, returning to them some portion of the customers' total spending. This approach is helping companies convert their customer relationships from a series of one-off purchases and promotions into a financial bond that rewards customers for their purchasing and continued product ownership. Although cash-back initiatives have been around in the credit card industry since the 1985 launch of the Discover Card, manufacturers and retailers are now adapting this approach to engender the loyalty of top-spending consumers in their categories. Some of these programs intentionally use the term *dividend,* hoping to benefit from the cognitive connection consumers will draw to investment returns.

Clothing retailer Talbots, for example, has had great success using dividends to increase spending and loyalty among its customer base. In 1997, the company began a pilot program called "Classic Awards" for Talbots charge card holders in six Northeastern states. The pilot enjoyed great success, so Talbots launched the program nationally in 2001. For every $500 a customer spends during the year, Talbots refunds $25 in the form of an Appreciation Dividend. Other benefits of the Classic Awards program include a 10 percent discount on any single purchase during the month of the customer's birthday.

Of the many ways that a company can reward customers, why choose financial dividends? In Talbots' case, executives believed that dividends would be particularly compelling for its target customers. Many of Talbots' most loyal devotees are well-educated professional women who understand the value of investment firsthand. Margery Myers, Talbots' vice president of corporate communications, told us, "Talbots has always considered 'investment' to be a central theme of the company. This is evident both in the steadily increasing dividends we have paid shareholders and in the way we position our clothing—which returns value to its owners in the form of enduring quality and style. So, when we were looking for a way to demonstrate customer appreciation, it made sense to call our rewards Appreciation Dividends rather than simply points."[9]

While dividends enable consumers to enjoy a bankable return on their consumption, they also deliver two important benefits to retailers. First, they provide a powerful incentive for customers to focus their spending on retailers that offer such programs. At Talbots, Myers says, paying dividends has been credited with helping the company grow their share of customers' spending in the category. "The Classic Awards program has helped us to move many of our less frequent customers into our core customer base. These are the individuals who spend the most time shopping in our catalogs or stores, and buy most of their apparel from us."[10]

Second, dividends help drive transactions through what is typically the retailer's most profitable payment channel—its store charge card. At Talbots, the introduction of dividends has created a significant boost in purchases made on its store charge card, which is used to keep track of customer spending for dividend payouts. Myers told us, "Between 2001 and 2002 alone, the Classic Awards program helped us to increase the percentage of sales conducted on store charge cards from 36 to 41 percent. In addition, the expansion of our core customer base through the program has had the added benefit of generating incremental finance charge income as well as savings on third-party bank card fees."[11]

Make It Up in Volume

Marketers should note an added benefit of dividend programs: enhanced pricing control. Properly structured, dividends act like volume discounts, only the purchases are made over time and the reductions are granted only after the customer reaches the target volume sales level. By varying the requirements and dividend payout, a company can better control the average price paid by its top-consuming customers. In this way, companies can fashion a quasi-segmented pricing scheme for higher-spending customers, while offering all customers an incentive to spend up to their potential.

Marketers must not, however, confuse this opportunity with the more complex issue of dynamic pricing. As noted in chapter 3, that practice generally refers to offering different prices to customers for the same product, based on a real-time assessment of their needs and demands. Although that approach gained traction in the early days of the Internet, companies must tread carefully to ensure that they do not run afoul of customers' principles or legal mandates. The size of price cuts and the type of personal information used to determine dividends must never cross the line of unfair price discrimination.[12] Dividends do, however, offer a realistic chance to steer clear of such inequities because they do not affect individual product prices and they are not determined by the customer's personal profile.

Surprise Me

Dividend programs need not be monetary to be successful. Car dealers have recently proven the value of semiregular gifts as an effective payback for customers. Consider the rise of Jeep Owner Appreciation Days. Started in 1999, the program provides customers with free ski-lift tickets to select resorts in New England on designated days, roughly one each week throughout the winter. The tickets are given to the driver and one passenger of any Jeep, no matter what the vehicle's age or model. This magnanimity frequently results in the dividend's being paid on purchases that occurred ten or more years ago. Jeep launched this program, in partnership with the New England Ski Areas Council, to reward customer loyalty and to connect the product with a lifestyle. By tying the dividend to a winter sport, Jeep also cleverly reminds customers of a distinct value of owning a Jeep—easy travel in snow covered terrain.

Do Jeep owners really take advantage of this dividend? Yes, and in large numbers. Two participating resorts recently reported over six hundred Jeeps filling their parking lots on these days. A few of these customers had traveled five hours in the snow just to get there.[13] Jeep's success illustrates that dividends need not always be mailed to the consumer, or deposited in their accounts. Presented with the right enticement, consumers will drive hundreds of miles to pick them up.

Improving Consumer Productivity

Sometimes investments are made not for a direct financial return—as in the case of equity securities—but rather to improve the productivity or returns on other investor holdings. Textbook examples from the business world include tools, factories, and equipment. While these produce no new revenue on their own, they enable companies to achieve higher, more efficient levels of production.

In the consumer realm, offerings that emulate these types of capital investments promise more effective social and economic performance for individuals and their families. The return on purchasing these goods and services is often an enhanced quality of life, or a newfound ability to accumulate greater wealth. With this in mind, we see three consumer capital investment opportunities, centered on the sources of consumers' productivity and having proven appeal to the affluent: personal education, skill building for one's children, and health improvement and management.

The Wealth That Can't Be Stolen

Ben Franklin once said, "An investment in knowledge pays the best dividends." That appears to be as true today as ever. Few capital investments provide returns as attractive as education does. While the average high school graduate had a household income of $60,300 in the year 2000, that amount increased to $84,000 for those holding a bachelor's degree and to $104,200 for those with graduate degrees.[14] Education also offers other appealing, if less predictable, resources for getting ahead. Alumni networks, for example, help to generate job leads and accelerate career paths. An academic association can positively influence one's associates and colleagues. And the weight of degrees can also serve to motivate one's children to achieve equal or greater education and income levels.

But while most people can appreciate education's returns, marketers should be keenly aware that the more affluent the consumers, the more likely they are to invest in it. Education was the fastest-growing category of spending among top-quintile earners between 1984 and 2000.[15] This is not surprising, considering that affluent parents are far more likely to send their children to college than their middle- or lower-income peers. They are also increasingly likely to participate in the growing trend of donating a large amount to a college or university (or in some cases even the "right" preschool), in the hope of gaining admittance for a child. In this way, the child becomes what is known, euphemistically, as a "development applicant."[16]

But the affluent are also top buyers of all sorts of personal enrichment courses. They are more likely to participate in adult education programs than any other income group (a linear relationship exists between income and participation), including part-time degree work, career skill building, and personal development. In 1991, nearly 49 percent of adults with household incomes exceeding $75,000 had taken some kind of adult education course during the previous twelve months, versus 27 percent for those with household income in the $20,000 to $25,000 range. By 1999, that number had grown to almost 57 percent for the high income earners, while the lower income group grew to 36 percent participation.[17]

It follows, then, that marketers wanting to take advantage of the appeal that capital investments have for the affluent should incorporate an educational component within their offerings. The most compelling of these offerings offer a high level of skill development, provided by expert sources, in an "upscale" environment.

One good example is the Skip Barber Racing School, which was founded to train professionals for car racing careers. The institution offers a driving school in partnership with Dodge aimed at a broad range of consumers who it promises will "develop the skills to prepare for any obstacle or challenge encountered on today's roads."[18]

During a two-day course that costs $1,195, students can expect to learn road safety techniques few other drivers are likely to understand, from heel-and-toe downshifting to threshold braking, all the while at the wheel of a thrilling, high-powered Dodge Viper. The exclusive driving knowledge, wrapped in an upscale experience, fulfills the desire of affluent consumers for capital investment by providing them with tools to better protect their own safety and that of their families while driving.

The exploding popularity of elite cooking programs illustrates another approach for providing education that can improve specialized skills in everyday life. Some of the most successful of these courses offer budding chefs direct access to experts from whom most people can only dream of learning. Consider the internships provided to enthusiast amateurs by L'Ecole des Chefs Relais Gourmand. For between $1,100 and $2,600 (U.S. dollars) for two- and five-day programs, customers work on the job in some of the world's most prestigious kitchens— learning cooking techniques from Michelin-starred chefs in France and elsewhere around the world.[19] The success of this and other programs has fueled a sharp increase in demand for cooking vacations. According to the ShawGuides, an annual cooking vacation guide, the number of these vacations grew from 271 in 1992 to 632 in 2002.[20]

Marketers need not break ground on entirely new schools or programs to make the connection; creativity can suffice. One example: Popular cooking courses are now being set up as part of executive retreats. In Scottsdale, Arizona, the city's Culinary Institute allows senior executives in town on business to watch students prepare a gourmet meal and to ask questions every step of the way.[21] The fees remain a low $75 to $95—CEOs could certainly afford a far higher price tag—but the state tourism office points out that the program fosters an appreciation of Arizona that benefits the local economy.[22] While few of these CEOs are likely to use the experience to assume cooking duties in their own households, their schooling does put in their cultural cap a feather that they would not have time or initiative to earn from a more demanding culinary program.

Retailers have embraced "edu-commerce" too. Bookseller Barnes & Noble has established an online "university," offering over fifty free online courses on subjects from guitar playing to Shakespeare. Adventure supplier Eastern Mountain Sports has taken the lessons outdoors with its affiliated climbing and kayaking schools, and Williams-Sonoma has for years offered in-store cooking classes and demonstrations. The goal of these programs is not just to have students purchase the required materials from the sponsoring company's store (or Web site using provided links), though that is definitely a leading goal, but also to grow primary demand by training a new cadre of educated, enthusiastic consumers.

Finally, the trend has not been lost on traditional providers of education. The number of institutions granting two- and four-year degrees has already increased by about one-third in almost thirty years, growing from about 3,000 in 1971 to 4,182 in 2000.[23] Part of that growth has come from new entrants. Kaplan, Inc., once known as admissions advisers, has seen its revenues grow from under $100 million to over $600 million by becoming "one of the fastest growing players in the booming business of for-profit higher education."[24] The company now serves over 40,000 students in the mostly two-year trade schools it managed to open or acquired in just five years.

Do It for the Children

All parents want the best for their children. Many even live vicariously through them (proof can be found by spending even just a short time on the sidelines of any youth soccer game). But affluent consumers often tend to their children's needs in a way that separates them from their less affluent predecessors: Their consumption decisions on behalf of their progeny are often capital investments.

Affluent parents are increasingly seeking out market offerings that enhance their children's athletic and cognitive abilities, those that promise to improve their children's chances of success later in life. This new focus on children's productivity can be seen in the decline in children's free time. Between 1981 and 1997, the amount of time kids between the ages of three and twelve spent doing "nothing"—that is, playing, watching television, or engaging in other leisurely pursuits—fell sharply in favor of scheduled, structured pastimes. Research from the University of Michigan found that time spent watching television fell 23 percent, while time playing indoors declined by 16 percent.[25] By contrast, study time rose 20 percent, and time spent in organized sports grew 27 percent.[26] The shift in children's activities represents a loss of twelve hours of free time each week, a dramatic increase in commitment to productivity by the economic standard applied to all workers.[27]

In keeping with these goals, parents are signing their children up for private lessons to catch up with—and even pull ahead of—peers in critical areas in school development such as reading, writing, language, and mathematical skills. Nationwide, commercial tutoring has become a $3 billion industry.[28] One of the industry's leading players, Educate, Inc., operates more than nine hundred and fifty tutoring facilities throughout North America under the brand name Sylvan Learning Centers. With most locations in or near affluent towns, the lessons do not come cheap. Hourly rates for personalized teaching begin at $35 to $40 an hour—more than what 80 percent of U.S. households earn for themselves on an hourly basis.[29] Yet, the growth of Sylvan attests to the willingness of many parents to spend thousands of dollars each year on improving their children's academic performance.

Even offerings once solely dedicated to children's leisure are retooling their programs to capitalize on parents' desire for capital investments. The number of summer camps offering academic lessons, for example, grew by 15 percent between 2001 and 2003.[30] It is no longer unusual for kids to take College Board Scholastic Aptitude Test (SAT) preparation classes or language immersion courses alongside more traditional summer pursuits such as horseback riding. At one camp, Pine Forest in Greeley, Pennsylvania, parents spend $7,300 for a 7½-week program that includes SAT tutoring.[31] Parents can be sure they're getting their money's worth, since the camp provides them with a copy of their child's practice SAT results.

An equally explosive market is to be found in the moneyed masses' desire to give their children every imaginable athletic edge. Two-thirds of American children participate in organized sports, camps, and related activities. For greater spending, private sports camps have sprouted up to ensure talented children (or well-patronized ones) can hone their skills particularly well.[32] These programs include pricey lessons with former professional players and skilled amateurs. For example, quarterback guru Steve Clarkson's football school charges students $1,500 for a summer sports camp.[33] Another firm, Georgia-based Velocity Sports Performance, has begun to franchise its operations and expects to achieve $50 million in revenue in 2004, with outlets in at least seven states. A gold package at the outlet, which includes twenty-four training sessions over twelve weeks, will set a parent back $750.[34]

What do parents expect in return? Though it in no way diminishes demand, sometimes the willingness to spend on sports camps is driven by loftier ambitions than, say, improving a child's batting average. One father whose children attend baseball and basketball camps told the *Fort Lauderdale Sun-Sentinel*, "I'm not looking for a return on investment. . . . [T]he return is that it makes you a better citizen and provides all the good things you get from team sports."[35] For many, "all the good things" includes the social skills and discipline that can increase interpersonal effectiveness and, perhaps, help with college admissions down the line. Not a multimillion-dollar contract with a sports franchise, but a return on investment all the same.

Helping parents cope with the stress of child rearing in the midst of these educational investment trends presents a marketing opportunity of its own (and represents, in fact, another continuing education phenomenon). The market for parenting coaches, and for the schools that train parent coaches, was small but is growing rapidly. The exact number of these coaches is unknown, because no formal training is required, but one school, Parent Coaching Institute, L.L.C., now offers parent coaching certification through a 12 to 18 month distance-learning program. Graduates typically charge upwards of $75 an hour to discuss by phone how anxious parents can overcome issues ranging from defusing sibling rivalry to dealing with school officials.

All of these expenditures may ultimately prove worthwhile, however, because whether they recognize it or not, parents who go this route are preparing to enjoy a concrete return on consumption from the investments they make in their children. In his book *Accounting for Tastes*, Nobel Prize–winning economist Gary S. Becker argues that the most compelling benefit is, in fact, receiving care and assistance in old age: "[Parents] may try to protect themselves against ill health, unemployment and other hazards of old age by instilling in their children a willingness to help out if that becomes necessary. . . . [P]arental spending on children partly depends on the anticipated effects of childhood experiences on adult attitudes and behavior."[36]

Becker argues that parental expenditures on their children's education and skills could yield, in the long term, a higher return on investment than would savings. To that end, spending on sports camps, academic outlets, and other skill-building activities for children represents indirect saving for old age. A dollar spent on children today could enable parents to reduce bequests and increase their consumption when elderly.[37]

This type of analysis may strike some readers as insensitive, but at its root is a truth that most of us should be able to identify with—having successful children can ensure greater stability and comfort in our own future. This relationship does not necessarily create direct commercial opportunities (although Becker points out that it would be a boon to create an enforceable contract that guarantees children will care for elderly parents). But it does reinforce a point: To improve offerings that parents will view as investments in their children, marketers should emphasize the benefits that will accompany those children into adulthood. One can only suppose a better-adjusted, more successful adult will be better able to return the favor, delivering better care for his or her parents if and when needed.

Our First Wealth

Health is often described as a blessing, but as far as affluent consumers are concerned, the poet Emerson was not far off the mark in saying, "The first wealth is health."[38] Good health helps one to fully enjoy life, but it is often also necessary if one wants to sustain a successful career and provide for a family.

And, like other forms of wealth, health requires ongoing attention and investment. Affluent consumers recognize this, and those in the top quintile of household income have increased their spending in the health category in real dollars by 18 percent since 1984 (the only category of expenditure besides education to grow).[39] Much of this increased spending is likely due to Baumol's cost disease. (A New York University economist, Baumol recognized in the 1960s that low relative productivity growth in certain industries that rely on human capital tends to drive up relative wages, and thus prices and spending, in those industries, e.g., education, insurance, health care and entertainment.) But at least some of the increased spending in health care has gone to innovative new medical offerings that promise to detect, preempt, or resolve health problems outside the boundaries of the traditional medical establishment.

Body imaging, once prescribed only by doctors for immediate medical purposes, is just one of these new offerings now available at for-profit clinics, and it has gained traction among affluent consumers seeking early detection of illness. Ventures such as Full Body Scanning, Inc., offer a menu of imaging services that—for prices often approaching $1,000—alert consumers to the presence of dreaded abnormalities. Other companies have transformed the prenatal ultrasound into a product offering. These entrepreneurs recognize that while parents value the medical benefits of the scan, they also deeply cherish the opportunity to see their children for the first time. For-profit ultrasound centers such as Innovative Imaging in Yorba Linda, California, now charge about $200 to give parents a first look at their unborn baby, completed with take-home images on videocassette and CD-ROM.[40]

Even certain operating room procedures have now been driven into malls around the country. The promise of a life without glasses is driving high demand for corrective eye surgery. An estimated 2.6 million people have already had laser-assisted in situ keratomileusis (LASIK) eye surgery, a fifteen-minute procedure in which a laser is used to reshape the cornea to correct nearsightedness.[41] In recent years, it has become possible to correct one's vision in less time than it takes to change the oil in one's car. Although the surgeries can cost as much as $2,000 per eye, some of the mall centers will now discount as low as $500 each, a price point aimed squarely at mass-market consumption.[42]

The exercise and dietary industries provide additional fertile ground for targeting consumers with plausible investments in their future health. Back in the 1980s, the term *personal trainer*—meaning someone hired to establish, enforce, and accompany a workout regime—did not exist in everyday vocabulary. In 2000, it was estimated that more than 5 million Americans worked with a personal trainer on their exercise regimen.[43] Rates in some gyms can start at over $50 an hour and easily approach the $100 mark for highly skilled or specialized professionals. One of the latest trends is to hire former military drill sergeants to design and enforce these salubrious regimes, for those who need a little bit of extra coaxing.

The desire to stay in shape and be physically active is driving another tremendous growth business: elective surgeries for aging boomers who have blown out a body part from overexertion. Rates of replacement surgeries and arthroscopic reconstructions are soaring, as weekend warriors endeavor to return to the field. Rebuilding the Six Million Dollar Man of today is more affordable than ever and can be attractive to marketers because much of the work is covered by insurance companies, which see the surgeries as a small price to pay to keep their aging customers physically active, thereby reducing the risk these customers will have a more debilitating, and costly, illness later in life.[44]

All of these health improving businesses have experienced tremendous growth. The proliferation of eye centers has helped drive a doubling of the LASIK industry every year between 1995 and 1999, when nearly 1 million of these surgeries were performed. Likewise, at least one industry trade publication expects that by 2008, the number of body imaging shops will grow from fewer than 100 today to over 4,000— located everywhere from mini-malls to spa centers.[45] But while rapid growth can drive the creation of a new industry, marketers must be sure to carefully time their entry. In the imaging industry, for example, rapid expansion has already led to a supply that far outstrips demand (particularly in the down economy in the last few years) and a damaging price war that has caused a shakeout in the industry. While this situation has been good for growing demand among mass-market consumers, it has been horrible for investors.[46] Yet, others companies, confident of a recovery, are using the dustup as an opportunity to buy distressed assets cheap, positioning themselves as leaders for what they consider a promising future.

What does all of this mean to a marketer peddling cereal, cameras, clothing, or movie rentals? The potential to bake wellness into any arena of offerings is enormous. Packaged food has already embraced the trend, with calcium being added to orange juice, and oatmeal being created just "for women's health." But health and safety is a concern that can be addressed as part of any purchase, from cars that are more crash-test safe, to refrigerators that filter the water they dispense, to carpets that are toxin- and allergen-free. Better health is an unmet need we all have, and one the moneyed masses are highly disposed—both financially and intellectually—to act on.

Providing Long-Lasting Value

Anyone who has bought a new car knows that it is anything but an investment. Some cars lose as much as 10 percent or more of their value the moment they are driven off the dealer's lot—with their value generally continuing to decline from there. *BusinessWeek* reports that, three years after purchase, a Ford Thunderbird retains just 29 percent of its value.[47]

But some goods have properties that cause them to retain their value over time. Near-luxury cars such as the BMW 3 Series retain as much as 60 percent of their value three years out. Some even appreciate in value with time. The opportunity for marketers is to embed similar attributes in their own products. Consumers must be able to use and enjoy an offering without actually consuming it, like a diamond that never wears out or a bottomless cup of coffee that is forever being refilled.

We observed two specific strategies for reducing or eliminating depreciation in offerings:

Create heirlooms. Create treasured possessions or at least emulate the scarcity, customization, and materials that make items used every day retain their resale value.

Establish innovative service agreements or warranty programs. When individual products cannot be made to last for generations, because of unavoidable wear, assure consumers of consistent functionality for an attractively long period.

Create Heirlooms

The promise of heirloom quality has long motivated the affluent to open their wallets. Although the idea that every possession must be worth passing down to future generations has not predominated since Tudor England, the *beau idéal* of long life for timeless possessions continues to appeal to affluent consumers today. Asked in a survey to rate the motivations behind their most expensive purchases, consumers in households with incomes exceeding $100,000 cited, first and foremost, "I don't mind spending a lot of money on something I'll have for the rest of my life or can leave to my children."[48]

Perhaps no marketer has leveraged the heirloom principle as successfully as watchmaker Patek-Philippe. The company actively markets its timepieces as items to be passed on, as manifest in its tag line: "You never own a Patek-Philippe. You take care of it for the next generation." Companies that want to emulate this positioning must support their claim, as Patek-Philippe has done, by having in their portfolio some products of exceptional and lasting value. Patek-Philippe produces certain scarce, and many times unusual, highly specialized products. For example, in 1989 it created its Caliber 89 to celebrate the company's 150th anniversary and labeled the watch the world's most complicated portable timepiece. The watch offers thirty-three separate functions and has 1,728 distinct parts.[49]

Other companies are now starting to communicate to customers a sense of timelessness by creating a small number of superpremium, top-of-the-line versions of their products. Examples range from automakers like Cadillac with its new ultra-high-end Sixteen, to spirits makers like Chivas Brothers, which recently produced just 255 bottles of its Royal Salute 50 Year Old.

Another important criterion of an heirloom is something only time can bestow—a proven track record of appreciation. So there is no time to lose. Patek-Philippe owners have decades of evidence that their timepieces are also valuable assets. Auctions are filled with examples of these possessions' increasing in value. The rare Split Seconds Chronograph owned by Duke Ellington sold at auction in 2002 for $1.6 million— about a million dollars more than it had fetched at a sale just four years earlier—but various models sell constantly. While most consumers cannot afford the company's most elite offerings, the money they spend on a Patek-Philippe will likely be returned—with ample interest in many cases—if they ever want or need to sell it.

While the watch market may seem like a natural candidate for heirloom status, companies in other industries are also adopting tactics to imbue their offerings with investment appeal. Developments in the high-end pen market provide a road map for manufacturers who want to transform their own everyday, functional items into something of lasting value. The idea of the pen as a mass-market status symbol dates only from 1920, when a manager at Parker Pen Company reputedly brought founder George S. Parker to the roof of a high building and pointed out the luxury cars below. If consumers would purchase something as utilitarian as transportation for a status symbol, he argued, then the pen could also be reinvented as a status item.[50]

For pen marketers, the first step toward heirloom status was the significant upgrading of the materials used in manufacturing. Initially, this meant embracing the durable, high-tech material ebonite—so common today it is used to make bowling balls. Use of this material supported the successful introduction of the $7 Lucky Curve Duofold pen. At the time, the pen was more than twice as expensive as other models on the market (an early example of a company succeeding by moving to a new-middle-ground price position), and it helped Parker to increase sales from 1 million to 24 million in just three years.[51] The key was in making the product more durable, that is, more physically able to deliver undiminished use over time. By offering the prospect of undiminished value and use over a long time, quality pens from makers like Waterman, Montblanc, and Montegrappa were now seen by consumers as a durable rather than disposable purchase.

Keep It Ticking

Many companies' products simply aren't suitable for lifetime owner-ship. Changes in technology make it unlikely that a consumer would want to retain a television set for decades, which explains the shift in TV packaging from burled wood cabinets to pennies' worth of plastic. And changes in fashion mean that few consumers would want to commit to wearing the same clothes for the next ten or fifteen years, even if the clothing didn't wear out. (You can't bank on "retro" appeal.) Marketers of these and other like goods must take different approaches to provid-ing undiminished use if they are to benefit from the consumer desire for lasting value.

Long-term, comprehensive warranties and other innovative service packages are one alternative. In a classic article from the *Journal of Consumer Research,* Terence A. Shimp and William O. Bearden of the University of South Carolina conducted research that established a connection between warranties and consumers' fear of financial loss.[52] They found that exceptional warranties—those with very generous terms—were powerful tools for reducing consumers' perceptions of risk in purchasing an innovative new product.

In our analysis, this tendency means that warranties also promote a sense that a purchase can serve as an investment—that there is some guarantee of uninterrupted functionality, and therefore value, and that the consumers believe they can recoup their money (similar to a resale value) if the product somehow fails in their or the product's lifetime. Lands' End and L.L. Bean have built their reputations on the power of such warranties, using tag lines like, respectively, "GUARANTEED. PERIOD" and "We Guarantee Everything but the Weather." This type of policy does not come without a price, however. Because of his guarantee, founder L. L. Bean had ninety of his first hundred sales of waterproof boots returned to his store after they failed, which required him to take out a loan to make good on his promise. Yet, the resulting goodwill helped make the company the great success it is today.

Refurbishment programs are a particularly compelling—and potentially lucrative—twist on the concept of a warranty. And few companies have profited from this approach as handsomely as Allen-Edmonds, the upscale shoemaker. Allen-Edmonds has long held an attractive affluent customer base, selling $300 pairs of shoes to a highly focused demographic target: businessmen with an annual income exceeding $100,000. Though these customers can afford the best, and lots of it, one of the company's most successful business lines is a program that lets customers send in their worn shoes for what the company terms "recrafting." For as little as $95, the company will remove old soles, heels, welting, cork foot beds, and laces from a pair of shoes and replace them with entirely new materials direct from the factory.[53] Lou Ripple, director of sales and marketing for Allen-Edmonds, told us in a 2003 interview, "As a result, we don't just repair the shoes. We basically re-manufacture them. It is as close as you can get to receiving an entirely new shoe."[54]

Since Allen-Edmonds introduced the program in the early 1980s, its affluent customers have responded enthusiastically. According to Ripple, customers appreciate the company's ability to dramatically extend the useful life span of their shoes through recrafting: "It's not unheard of for us to have customers recraft the same pair of shoes five or six times." As a result, recrafting now accounts for a sizable portion of the company's volume. Allen-Edmonds now recrafts 1,200 pairs of shoes per week; by comparison, it produces about 7,000 new pairs during that same period. Ripple points out that the service is also highly profitable: "With margins around 50 percent, it has become an important profit center for the firm."

Recrafting's success has reached beyond its popularity as a discrete offering. Ripple feels that its existence has helped Allen-Edmonds to better position the quality and longevity of all of its products: "It has become a great selling tool. A lot of our customers tell us that part of the reason they buy the shoes is that they can be recrafted. It reinforces the perception that these products are going to provide value for a long time, which is important to our customers."

The experiences at Allen-Edmonds illuminate two challenges that other firms considering refurbishment programs must plan for. First, the companies must ensure that providing repair capabilities does not detract from the efficiency of manufacturing operations. At Allen-Edmonds, manufacturing executives were initially concerned that the different processes required for recrafting could harm productivity on the factory floor. Ripple told us, "Part of the solution was to choose a pricing level that would account for any potential disruptions and still ensure a profitable service. So we asked the manufacturing executives how much we would have to charge in order to make the service worthwhile for the company—and realized that the market would support an even higher price."

Ripple admits that the program's efficiency has also been helped by the fact that the Allen-Edmonds manufacturing facilities remain in the United States, with both talent and raw materials nearby. Firms with manufacturing operations distributed overseas will need to manage the added logistical challenge of routing products between the customer and the resources that repair them.

A second issue that firms selling through third parties must address is potential channel conflict with third parties, such as distributors or retailers. Companies will need to allay the fear that extending a product's life through refurbishment will hurt sales of new offerings. Ripple says that Allen-Edmonds, too, faced initial concern from its retailers: "Understandably, they told us that they were interested in selling customers new pairs of shoes, not helping them to fix old pairs of shoes."

To ensure that recrafting did not reduce customer foot traffic to retail partners, Allen-Edmonds involved the stores in its program. "We distributed what we call Recraftpaks to the stores," explains Ripple, "so that customers could fill out a card with their information, drop in the shoes, and have it all sent to us postage-paid." To the retailers' delight, "they found out that customers would come in and ask retailers to send out their old shoes, then buy a pair of new ones on the same visit." With this innovative approach, Allen-Edmonds helped retailer partners to share in the benefit of increased sales.

Allen-Edmonds's unique value proposition of durability, supported by the lucrative recrafting program, has helped the company to grow sales by 10 percent annually throughout the 1990s while increasing profitability.[55] It's proof that providing affluent consumers with access to undiminished use can create new and more profitable income sources. And, in Allen-Edmonds's case, the success occurred despite a highly challenged industry that saw the bankruptcy of some of its leading companies.

The Bottom Line

Through tangible assets such as real estate, securities, and modern art, and intangible assets such as knowledge, good health, and family, the moneyed masses are increasingly experiencing and enjoying the benefits of greater wealth accumulation. Goods and services that grow consumers' wealth will be particularly welcome in these households; offerings that do not will begin to face greater skepticism as their short-lived returns become more apparent.

To gain a return on consumption, many durable goods will need a step function improvement in their overall quality, with a concentration on innovations that increase their intrinsic value and longevity of ownership. The hope is that we may one day see an appliance, or even a pair of shoes, being bought by consumers with investment or arbitrage opportunities in mind. If this seems a stretch, consider Porsche automobiles. Though the cars are clearly a luxury when bought new, ownership at every level is so highly valued, an astounding (though some owners say unsurprising) 60 percent of all of the maker's vehicles remain on the road today.[56] This is an enviable record for a product prone to technological obsolescence and plain old rust.

At the same time, services and nondurable goods will need to provide greater evidence of their future returns to attract the moneyed masses. Universities, for example, might need to shift from reporting the starting salaries of their graduates to reporting on the attractiveness of their career paths and average salaries ten or twenty years down the line—better demonstrating the lifelong value of their course work. In short, marketers must become more than inventors and promoters; they must become their customers' investment managers as well.

PART THREE

The New Rules of Customer Reach

Think Global, Retail Local

Old Rule
Make retail stores a destination for the masses, by having
the biggest variety, assortment, and discount.

New Rule
Serve the masses locally in their usual destinations,
with the convenience, layout, and assortment you know
they want and the prices you know they will pay.

In 1852, French merchant Aristide Boucicaut opened a store in the heart of Paris, in the hopes of capturing some of the city's burgeoning affluence. The store started out in the customary way, dedicated to a single category of shopping, in this case, custom lengths of fabric. But Boucicaut then had the idea to include additional merchandise in his store, such as women's apparel and accessories, and to give each type of good its own dedicated area, until—voilà—the world's first department store was born.

To the horror of neighboring proprietorships, the new store, called The Bon Marché (roughly, "good value" or "bargain") took Paris by storm, prompting merchants around the world to launch their own adaptations. Tweaks of Boucicaut's version of the department store came to dominate urban shopping districts for most of the twentieth century and continue to anchor most suburban malls today. Boucicaut's department store reinvented merchandising and, in the process, ushered in the era of mass retailing.

It was not the size of Boucicaut's store and the breadth of product line that was scandalous at the time. The store's insistence on giving consumers of all backgrounds equal access to the same product selection was equally unprecedented. Unlike earlier merchants, The Bon Marché and other department stores opened their doors to all social classes and both genders (shocking at the time).[1] And sales personnel were expected to be polite to every customer, no matter his or her origin. Even a hint of discourtesy was considered grounds for dismissal at The Bon Marché.[2]

Displaying products with clearly marked, nonnegotiable prices was another first. This approach eliminated the need for customers to ask the socially embarrassing question "How much does this cost?" and opened the door for the previously unheard-of practice of comparison shopping (a behavior department stores encouraged because they could achieve lower prices through volume).[3] And browsers were no longer obligated to purchase, a situation that introduced the masses to the idea of shopping for enjoyment and fanned the burgeoning flames of aspiration-driven consumption.[4] As Robert Tamilia, a University of Quebec professor with a concentration on retail management, points out, "The department store, by its democratization, made people aware of the existence of a wide range of consumer goods known previously mostly by the noble and the rich. The department store put these goods on display for the world to see and to want."[5]

In recent decades, Boucicaut's palaces of consumption (so called for the enormous scale and lavish decoration of the edifices once built to house them) have given way to unadorned big boxes for selling to masses of consumers. Discounters such as Wal-Mart and Costco have replaced department stores as the dominant mode of retailing, taking retail democratization and price competition to an entirely new plane.[6] Now more than ever, consumers can see, want, and even afford most of the goods in mass-market stores.

Yet, this latest degree of accessibility has come with important business trade-offs. Profitably sustaining low price points requires massive economies of scale and the sale of high volumes of extremely standardized goods. As a result, many retailers are serving up relatively undifferentiated offerings to all their customers, regardless of who they are, what they need, or what they might be willing to pay.

Although this new level of standardization has hardly deterred certain price-sensitive and lower-income consumers, our research finds that retailers have lost the interest and confidence of many consumers along the way, especially among the more affluent.[7] Boucicaut was able to drive sales by removing the obligation to buy, thereby encouraging browsing and window shopping. But that lever is no longer a powerful driver of foot traffic. Approximately 70 percent of consumers in households earning more than $100,000 a year say that they do not enjoy shopping when they have no specific purchases in mind. And the number remains surprisingly high, 61 percent, for those with lower incomes.

This trend may be related to our finding that over half of all consumers wish their most frequented stores had more product offerings in general. And nearly 55 percent of all consumers view the retail experience as a highly transactional occasion, agreeing with the statement "Most retailers do not care about my satisfaction after I have left their store." The number increases to a disappointing 70 percent for those with the highest incomes—customers who, one would presume, are currently receiving the highest level of postpurchase support.

Tuning a Channel for the Moneyed Masses

There is good news, however. New mass-market consumers would spend more—and more frequently—if retailers presented them with higher-quality offerings that better fit their needs. A full 70 percent of all consumers assert this, with the numbers inching higher for those with higher incomes. Nearly a quarter of those earning more than $100,000 wish that there were more expensive (and correspondingly better) products in the stores they frequent, and almost no consumers at any income level have any interest in the addition of lower-quality, less expensive offerings to their preferred retailers' assortments.

So the imperative for retailers is clear. They must preserve the advantages that brought them mass-market success—customer-facing features like accessibility, selection, and service and operational features like supply-chain efficiency—while serving a far more diverse and upscale set of needs. That means making a direct appeal to more affluent consumers, with steps ranging from determining and delivering better in-store assortments, to the creation of more highly tailored retail outlets within their local environments.

To see how marketers can profitably update their approaches to retailing for the new mass market, we will first consider how new locations and formats are better serving more profitable segments of customers while continuing to serve the mass market. We will then explore how the less drastic approach of changing assortments within existing locations and formats can drive impressive improvements to the bottom line. Finally, we'll look at how new retailing technologies are becoming critical to retailer success in optimizing locations, formats, and assortments to make the most of the moneyed masses.

Though we'll discuss these approaches primarily in the context of the traditional retail store format, the thinking behind each technique can be readily applied to other channel formats, such as catalog, direct sales, and online retailing. Although the idea of multichannel selling (i.e., opportunities for integrating these channels) lies outside the scope of this book, we have discussed it in other publications.[8] Much of what follows, however, can be applied to a multichannel approach to marketing.

Embracing New Store Locations and Formats

In retailing, reaching the right customers still begins with the famous three rules of real estate success: location, location, location. But until recently, few stores have been located or formatted to have intrinsic appeal to the moneyed masses. Big-box stores and regional malls have traditionally located in affordable "edge" cities, like Framingham, Massachusetts, and Bridgewater, New Jersey, to ensure low-cost real estate and easy automotive access. Meanwhile, upscale specialty retailers have continued to opt for the rarefied—and not broadly accessible—environs of places like Manhattan's Fifth Avenue and Beverly Hills' Rodeo Drive.

Today, though, retailers and real estate developers are together pioneering innovative mall concepts and store formats designed with the everyday needs of the moneyed masses in mind. Using three lines of attack, their strategies are: to locate in "lifestyle centers"; to exploit small-box formats; and to launch separately branded, more upscale store chains.

Lifestyle Centers of the Just Rich Enough

While malls are nearly synonymous with egalitarian shopping, America's first planned shopping centers were in fact located in the wealthy planned communities being developed outside major cities, and were accessible only by the rare luxury, the automobile. The first shopping center, opened in 1931 in the tony development of Highland Park, outside Dallas, was a handful of stores built around an inner space intended to function as a town square. Ever since, however, developers have competed to make their malls bigger and more inclusive, to support the arrival of the mass exodus from the cities to the suburbs. (By the 1990s, Simon Properties had bested all competitors, with its 4.2-million-square-foot Mall of America. Located in Bloomington, Minnesota, the facility includes a seven-acre amusement park and draws over 40 million visitors a year.)[9]

But while the mall concept blossomed, two entrepreneurs came to realize that affluent consumers prefer an entirely different shopping experience, in both format and location. Specifically, in the mid-1980s, Memphis-based developer G. Dan Poag realized that neither he nor his peers found shopping enjoyable. The mega-malls that were proliferating at the time, recounts Poag's business partner Terry McEwen, a seasoned leasing executive, "were too big, featured only a few appealing stores, and sometimes felt unsafe. People disliked fighting the crowds and dodging groups of teenagers just to get their shopping done."[10] Exclusive retail strips, on the other hand, were useful for an occasional purchase, but lacked the breadth to satisfy everyday shopping needs.

And so Poag and McEwen teamed up to fashion the concept of the lifestyle center and in 1987 opened their first such endeavor, The Shops of Saddle Creek, in Germantown, Tennessee, an affluent suburb of Memphis. Germantown's demographics are typical for the communities that host the most successful lifestyle centers today. As McEwen explains, "Germantown features a large, rapidly growing number of households earning more than $100,000. These households are not just desirable from an income perspective; they fit a specific profile. They comprise busy professional families willing and able to spend more for quality goods."[11]

What is distinctive about the lifestyle center's approach to retailing? McEwen explains that while lifestyle centers can vary a bit, they share some common characteristics, including "open-air shopping, a mix of upscale national chains and specialty stores, and features designed for the needs of a busy lifestyle, such as convenient access to each store directly from the parking lot."[12] Aesthetically, lifestyle centers are a far cry from the walled retail fortresses often found in suburban hubs. They feature a Main Street–style look with distinctive architecture and extensive landscaping. To provide a more manageable scale, lifestyle centers are also less than half the size of regional malls—often between two hundred thousand and five hundred thousand square feet.[13] This judicious choice of size helps them to fit right in to the same affluent communities that often reject larger-scale developments.

McEwen points out that the format, from its very inception, was intended to reinvent the mall experience for the needs of "merely affluent" consumers. But as lifestyle centers have taken hold in Germantown and elsewhere, Poag and McEwen have gained additional insight into affluent shopping behaviors, which has translated into further tweaks on the location and design of the centers. McEwen explains, "We found from research that our customers value two aspects of the shopping experience above all: The first is convenience, and the second is safety."[14]

The desire for convenience was only to be expected, but safety? It is hardly a top-of-mind issue among marketers. Yet, according to McEwen, "safety is a critical success factor for affluent retail locations. Focus groups and customer intercept studies reveal that a full 71 percent of lifestyle center shoppers are women, and that they are more comfortable when they have a short, direct line of sight between their car and the store they are visiting. At malls, they perceive that there is a lot of crime, a fear which is not helped by the groups of people hanging around and a general discomfort with parking garages."[15] Newer lifestyle centers reflect those insights.

The number of lifestyle centers is currently small, but growing rapidly. In fact, the International Council of Shopping Centers (ICSC) expects the number of lifestyle centers to double to about sixty developments by 2005.[16]

And while some marketers may worry that opening smaller locations in lifestyle centers could hurt revenues or margins, many retailers already operating in such malls report impressive financial returns. McEwen notes that "while consumers spend roughly the same amount of time at lifestyle centers as they do at regional malls—about an hour—and visit an average of three stores per visit in each place, the financial returns are very different. Lifestyle center shoppers spend 50 percent more per visit and return an average of five times per month, compared to just two times at regional malls."[17] For retailers, this also means greater sales per square foot. According to the ICSC, average sales in lifestyle centers are about $397 per square foot and can range up to $500—almost double that of the average regional mall.[18]

For some upscale retailers, the lifestyle center immediately seemed to be a natural fit. Polo Ralph Lauren, Talbots, and Banana Republic are among the handful of chains to successfully exploit the format from its earliest days. Junior retailers (those focused on teens) have been more cautious because of the lifestyle center's adult orientation, but McEwen explains, "The early [junior] entrants are finding that their sales in the lifestyle center format are just as good as those in traditional malls. Even though teenagers do not hang out and roam the center, they do come to shop, often with their parents."[19]

But mass retailers, department stores, and certain specialty shops are tending to sit on the sidelines. This is a missed opportunity. While not a replacement for other real estate formats, lifestyle centers are a powerful complement to them, filling the gap in traditional retailing's geographic coverage. Department stores can and should, therefore, play a role. Although they are unlikely to win the privileged real estate they are accustomed to elsewhere (lifestyle centers do not have anchor stores), they cannot afford to miss out on locations where a key customer segment shops. For instance, Saks has expressed interest in creating a new version of its stores for lifestyle centers that can fill geographic gaps in its coverage.[20] One can imagine Nordstrom following suit, with a scaled-down store (perhaps leaning heavily on its famous shoe department) aimed at the affluent in underserved markets such as New England.

What should marketers do to take make sure their companies take full advantage of the lifestyle center opportunity? First, they must forge stronger relationships with their own companies' executives whose areas of expertise are outside the typical purview of brand strategy—namely, their internal real estate and finance specialists. Today, these professionals are the drivers behind many lifestyle center locations. The goal of marketers should be to ensure that these executives' efforts are aligned with a broader strategy of positioning the brand properly for the site. The intended result is that when a retailer signs a lease on a lifestyle center location, marketing has already determined and is prepared to implement the changes in merchandising, marketing, and positioning required to make the lifestyle center store an immediate success. Participating retailers must anticipate the branding and financial implications of such moves outside their traditional business practices, and marketing needs to lead that charge.

What about the Mall of America, the Versailles of the palaces of consumption that are today's shopping centers? The developers that dreamed up the mall are now suing to gain control of the partnership that owns it. They intend to build an additional 5.7 million square feet of retail space on forty-two acres down the street, to be modeled on—what else?—the lifestyle center.[21]

Good Things in Small Boxes

Seeking more immediate access to locations in the heart of affluent consumer neighborhoods, many companies are experimenting with redesigning their formats to fit inside smaller boxes. While big boxes work well in suburban and even rural areas, building them in central cities—to capture the significant pockets of the moneyed masses that have always lived there, and those that are returning in droves—is difficult. Expensive and scarce land, strict zoning regulations, and demanding community groups are just three of the daunting obstacles. So daunting, in fact, that many national chains have avoided such areas altogether.

A few market leaders, however, are proving that a compromise in format—creating *small-box stores,* designed specifically for urban environments—can overcome these challenges and directly reach heavy concentrations of moneyed consumers. The earliest versions of small boxes are already elbowing their way into downtown residential areas. For example, electronics giant Best Buy recently ventured into Manhattan's affluent Chelsea neighborhood with a 35,000-square-foot, two-floor store (in contrast to the 100,000 to 200,000-square-feet of a typical big box store).[22] The company insists that such stores are an important complement to its fundamental big-box store strategy. One company source even speculated that the Chelsea location could become the retailer's first store to cross the threshold of $100 million per year in sales.[23]

Now, even Wal-Mart is looking for sites that can host a new urban version of its original store format. A prototype for downtown Dallas would include a two-level store with underground parking on a lot half the size usually allotted to its locations.[24] Such urban locations ensure that paying a visit to a mass retailer is no longer an occasional or special trip for affluent city dwellers, but instead a daily option. But Wal-Mart's experience here is instructive. Despite the store's novel design, concerns about the impact of such a store on the neighborhood, including increased traffic flow and insufficient parking, evoked a negative response from some residents. Resistance from the people whom developers refer to as the NIMBY (or Not In My Back Yard) crowd was so strong, in fact, that the Dallas planning commission was led to deny the zoning change required. Wal-Mart was thus forced to appeal the decision and consider additional modifications to the format. Clearly, care must be taken when facilitating shopping for the moneyed masses to avoid inconveniencing them in the course of bringing them greater convenience.

Combining the Brand and the Format

For some retailers, the changes to their merchandising model required to appeal directly to more affluent consumers are so onerous that the development of a separately branded, upscale spin-off chain becomes a more attractive option. The new units make the most sense when the target customers not only are more affluent, but also differ from the company's core customers in terms of what they want to see regarding product assortment, shopping experience, and service levels.

The Home Depot identified just such an opportunity when it made a bid for affluent home improvement customers with its Expo Design Center stores. The market opportunity the company was pursuing was clear: $480 million in annual spending on home remodeling and repair.[25] But, in The Home Depot's case, going upscale forced it to confront some fundamental differences in customer demographics and shopping patterns. For starters, The Home Depot, a company that still generates 30 percent of its revenues from mostly male contractors, needed to shift focus to the women, who today comprise 85 percent of Expo's customers.[26] Second, the customers being targeted didn't want to do home improvements themselves. They wanted to hire someone to do it for them. Finally, these customers wanted a different shopping experience, viewing upscale products such as $400 home patio heaters and $250 Kitchen Aid mixers in a design context, not stacked in boxes on warehouse shelves.

As a result, Expo Design Center stores feature an entirely new format comprising eight specialty showrooms under one roof, from lighting to baths. Although the stores sell products individually, they tout their custom design and installation services. A customer wanting an entirely remodeled kitchen need only walk through the showroom with a sales associate and point—designers and contractors take care of the rest. The fifty-two stores opened to date are deliberately located near a substantial number of households with annual incomes exceeding $100,000. While Expo's expansion plans have been scaled back amid the general economic uncertainty, the chain is now profitable, and Home Depot chairman and chief executive Robert Nardelli characterizes the absence of new store openings in 2004 as "a pause," allowing management to focus on having the merchandise mix and service performance levels the stores' more affluent customer base expects.[27] In addition, "Home Depot also plans to broaden its customer base by reducing the low end of the annual income threshold it targets to $50,000 from $75,000," aiming the store's positioning more directly at serving mass affluence.[28] By developing a separately branded format, The Home

Depot has created a compelling value proposition for affluent consumers, even those who have never shopped at its traditional stores.

Upgrading Product Assortment to Increase Transaction Size

"Whether you're rich or whether you're poor, everybody wants a bargain."[29] So says John R. McMillin, an analyst from Prudential Securities, in describing why affluent families have a tendency to buy household basics from mass retailers such as Wal-Mart. While these retailers do have nearly universal appeal for basic purchases, mass retailers that offer product assortments distinguished primarily by their low prices leave money on the table. They're failing to provide a value proposition for affluent consumers beyond the opportunity to stock up on basics, such as household cleaners or bulk cereal, during the occasional weekend run.

Instead, discount merchants need to offer high-income consumers a greater variety of better-quality, value-priced products across all of their departments, from apparel to toys to consumer electronics. Properly executed, improved merchandise selections attract more affluent customers, convince them to buy more products at higher price points, increase their satisfaction by the time they leave the store, and encourage them to return more frequently. Of course, "properly executed" is a loaded term. There's a fine line between offering a greater variety of high quality goods and drifting into the no-man's-land of retailers that end up heavily discounting their wares because they tried to be everything to everyone and ended up losing their identity. The experiences of a few leading retailers demonstrate how other merchants can realize the potential of this strategy while avoiding the pitfalls.

Improve the Mix

Perhaps no mass retailer has made a stronger bid for mass-affluent consumers than Target Stores, which has pioneered a focus the company itself characterizes as "upscale discount." Target's activities provide a blueprint that other merchants can follow to increase their appeal to upscale consumers. It has commissioned esteemed brands such as

Calphalon and Waverly to launch affordable lines of their kitchen and home products for its stores, while recruiting well-known figures in the design world—notably, Michael Graves and Philippe Starck—to create exclusive items with a European flavor for its home furnishings categories. Target then further tailors the product mix in its more upscale locations to showcase these exclusives. While the most expensive child car seat at most stores reaches $99, Target features a leather Eddie Bauer seat for $179 at its location in the upper-income North Side of Chicago.[30]

The company's diverse product selection coupled with upscale merchandising has made Target an everyday shopping phenomenon among well-heeled urbanites and prosperous professionals. The higher a consumer's income bracket, the more likely he or she is to prefer Target to competitors Wal-Mart and Kmart. According to a 2002 CNN/USA Today Gallup poll, only 16 percent of consumers earning $16,000 or less choose Target, but the percentage grows to 47 percent among those with annual incomes exceeding $75,000.[31] Such loyalty has paid off for the firm, which "has seen annualized growth of between 16 and 19 percent over the past five years, ten years and 15 years, respectively," and similar growth between 1998 and 2002 in profits and earnings per share, a very difficult period of economic downturn for the average retailer.[32] Target's success illustrates the potential benefits for retailers that work directly with recognized manufacturers and designers to elevate their stores' product assortments.

Have all of these initiatives clouded Target's brand or endangered the loyalty of its lower-income customers? Hardly. Target was named *Fortune* magazine's most admired American general merchandiser of 2002, edging out the much larger Wal-Mart. Not only was Target rated number one for innovativeness, but it also, only somewhat surprisingly, held the same leading rank for the quality of its products and services—placing well ahead of upscale retailers such as Saks, Federated Department Stores, and May Department Stores Company.[33]

Similarly, warehouse discounter Costco has successfully integrated higher-end product lines into the endless rows of bulk paper towels and industrial-sized cereal boxes that made the chain famous. Consider a location in Detroit's affluent Bloomfield suburbs. The three surrounding towns are solidly in blue-blood territory, with median per-capita incomes of $91,661 (West Bloomfield), $103,897 (Bloomfield Township), and $170,790 (Bloomfield Hills).[34] Costco's Bloomfield location offers exclusive specialty items not found at its other stores, such as $3,000 plasma television sets, expensive chandeliers, and baby grand pianos. Yet, it also provides upgrades of its core product lines, selling, for example, upscale beers such as Heineken and Tecate.[35] Costco's CEO, George Sinegal, told the *Chicago Tribune* that his company's upscale forays have been successful and will continue: "Because we've had success with high-end goods, we've had a tendency to keep moving up the scale and keep testing how far we go."[36] So far, Costco has gone far enough to become one of the leading distributors of Dom Perignon champagne.[37]

Wal-Mart, aware of such successes and facing the prospect of slowed growth as it saturates its traditional markets, has also begun to experiment with more upscale products. At its newer locations in the upscale suburbs of Plano, Texas, and Alpharetta, Georgia, Wal-Mart has added items such as fresh herbs and gourmet desserts to its food sections, digital cameras to its electronics department, and the more expensive fourteen-karat (rather than ten-karat) gold in its jewelry section.[38] Wal-Mart, however, remains publicly understated about the significance of such moves. As Wal-Mart president Thomas M. Coughlin recently told the *Washington Post*, "We are very committed to the customer that took us to the party."[39]

Coughlin's desire to move by degrees is prudent. As mass retailers seek partners to develop product assortments that will appeal to higher-income groups, they must tread carefully, ensuring that corporate and brand strategies of both parties remain fully aligned.

Sears's partnership with upscale Italian apparel designer Benetton in the late 1990s provides a cautionary tale. Coming off its highly successful "softer side of Sears" campaign, the retailer announced plans to expand its apparel lines through an exclusive collection of juniors', kids', and men's apparel called Benetton USA.[40] It seemed as though Sears faced just one enviable problem: keeping product on the shelves. Benetton USA sales were projected to hit $100 million in the first year of sales.[41]

What could have been a lucrative partnership was undermined, however, by a damaging brand conflict. Just a few months after its new clothing line hit Sears's shelves, Benetton, already known for its contro-versial ad campaigns, outdid itself with a campaign depicting death row inmates. The backlash heaped negative media coverage on both part-ners and sparked an outcry from activist groups. Outraged, Sears pulled the Benetton products off its shelves and terminated the relationship. As a result, Sears had to take what former CEO Arthur Martinez later char-acterized in his autobiography as "a $20 million bath."[42] When Sears made its next foray into upscale apparel, it maintained complete control over the initiative—completely acquiring catalog retailer Lands' End. Though Sears has owned the brand only a short time, analysts expect Lands' End to drive up Sears' store visits and grow its business.

Exploit Upscale Stores-in-Stores

We've shown that stocking more upscale products is an effective strategy for luring the fatter wallets into traditional mass-market retail establishments. But what environment will moneyed mass consumers find when they walk through the doors? Today, nearly all discount retailers have identical warehouse formats and cavernous aisles. The shopping experience is so uniform, one researcher found, 74 percent of consumers say all stores look alike.[43]

For disaffected, affluent consumers, this sameness can mean their discount retail experiences are uniformly bad. Sometimes, upscale products just don't fit into downscale formats. Current discount retail formats are mostly inhospitable to the presentation—and preserva-tion—of some higher-priced items. Upscale goods may either prove hard for consumers to find among countless bins and stacks of mer-chandise or may sit cheek by jowl with clearance items, an arrangement that detracts from their perceived value and sometimes even makes them look shopworn. For example, one customer at a home improve-ment store found a $50 set of backyard grill tools stocked beside a pile of $1 kabob skewers. A customer needs a high degree of confidence in the retailer to feel comfortable that he or she is getting the best deal to buy under such circumstances, and may be more comfortable putting off a tool purchase until the next trip to Williams-Sonoma.

Retailers should look to stores-in-stores as an effective vehicle for supporting the sale of merchandise with higher price points. How? They can gather quality items together in an environment that evokes the more upscale retailers the affluent might otherwise patronize. In this way, retailers can achieve three compulsory goals of marketing to the moneyed masses: Compete against upscale specialty stores, enable a low-risk entry into premium product categories, and assemble diverse offerings in a convenient format for affluent consumers' harried lifestyles.

Give the Good Stuff Some Space Supermarket chains, locked in a competitive battle with low-end mass merchandisers and higher-end specialty outlets, have realized that stores-in-stores can help retailers to successfully target higher-income households and differentiate their shops on attributes other than price. For example, some mass-market grocery store chains are leveraging store-in-store formats as they stake their claim to the fastest-growing segment of the American food industry: organic foods.

Once considered the domain of college-town farmers' markets, organically grown foods have entered the mainstream. They have become an $11 billion business that is forecast to grow at 20 percent annually, dwarfing the 5 percent increases that overall supermarket sales have experienced in the 1990s. Yet, the organic food category has a decidedly up-market appeal, with about 46 percent of customers placing in the top quartile of American household incomes.[44] No surprise, then, that the industry giant Whole Foods, which generates $2.6 billion in revenues on nearly 150 stores, has locations in such mass-affluent hubs as Palo Alto, California; Reston, Virginia; and Newton, Massachusetts.

To prevent these relative upstarts from dominating the organic market and to create environments attractive to more affluent customers, a number of mass supermarkets have launched store-in-store concepts that showcase their organic lines. From Shaw's in New England to New York–based Wegmans and Bashas' in Arizona, products such as soy milk, organic frozen meals, and all-natural hot dogs are increasingly gathered together in separate, distinctly branded areas. A few grocers even complement these offerings with lifestyle services. In North Carolina, Lowes Foods has allowed customers to e-mail their dietary questions to the chain's natural-foods specialist in order to promote its Lowes Naturally program.[45]

There is evidence that this approach is already helping mass-market grocers take control of the category as its popularity grows. Although more than half of organics were purchased at mainstream supermarkets in 2001, some observers placed this number at 70 percent by 2004.[46] The success of these organic stores-in-stores demonstrates that it is possible to convince the moneyed masses to make upscale purchases in a modified traditional mass-market environment, which should help other marketers defend their turf from similar threats.

Netherlands-based grocer giant Royal Ahold has also taken a page from this strategy in its bid for the health and beauty care category. The company's joint effort with Procter & Gamble to develop a health and beauty products store-in-a-store was so successful, Ahold slated it to launch in more than eighty locations.[47] Procter & Gamble, of course, has benefited as well. It has leveraged the relationship to better showcase its brands in select in-store locations, while gaining new insights into consumer shopping behaviors and preferences.[48]

Experiment with High-End Partnerships In some cases, retailers are linking with manufacturers on store-in-store concepts that provide them with low-risk, potentially high-reward entrees into new and more expensive product categories. For example, Sears has become the first retailer to work with computer maker Dell on an aggressive new deployment of store-in-store kiosks that allow consumers to try out and configure their own PCs and peripherals. Consumers can then order the machines immediately through an online connection, or later from home. The deal with Sears announced in January 2003 will eventually result in locations in ten stores.[49]

In this case, the store-in-store concept enables some important operational benefits, while minimizing the risks to both sides. First, the online ordering option means that neither party need worry about maintaining a sufficient stock of inventory—a problem when Dell initially experimented with selling through stores such as Wal-Mart and Staples in the early 1990s.[50] Consumers in that case would examine the products in the stores, then return home, call Dell, and negotiate better prices.[51] Retailers ended up holding surplus and quickly obsolete models. By keeping products out of stores, both sides also avoid losses related to shrinkage and shipping damage as well.

For retailers like Sears, agreements such as the one with Dell also provide a low-risk way to experiment with newer, premium product lines. If the offering fails to sell, correcting the problem is as straightforward as removing the displays and kiosks. If the offering sells beyond expectations, Sears is positioned to introduce a wider product assortment—potentially carrying inventory or accommodating other manufacturers.

Retailers, however, must be careful not to overreach with stores-in-stores dedicated to new product lines. If both partners stretch too far from their core constituencies, it might prove difficult to convince consumers to follow. Such has been the case with a partnership between JC Penney and Avon, which launched more than ninety stores-in-stores, showcasing the cosmetics company's new product line, beComing.

Items in the beComing line not only sell for up to 60 percent more than other comparable Avon products—think $40 for a jar of moisturizer—but are offered to a customer base more accustomed to purchasing JC Penney's stock of value-priced Iman and Color Me Beautiful lines. No wonder sales in the first year amounted to a disappointing $30 million, well below initial forecasts of $100 million.[52] Although JC Penney and Avon insist that they are on track to hit revised estimates moving forward, their partnership illustrates the perils of moving too upscale too fast in a bid for increased customer spending.

Create Convenient Bundles of Stores Retailers need not limit themselves to creating stores-in-stores that house products and services of just one brand. For example, marketers can seek to provide consumers with the convenience of several complementary brands all under one roof, assembling portfolios of partners operating in their own dedicated areas. Stop & Shop, one of the Northeast's largest supermarket chains, is taking this approach to the stores-in-stores idea, recruiting a portfolio of partners that, collectively, increase the merchant's appeal to more affluent consumers who are strapped for time and looking for convenience.

Stop & Shop is implementing its strategy under the banner of a next-generation store concept. The first location, in Walpole, Massachusetts, includes stores-in-stores operated by Toys "R" Us, Office Depot, and Boston Market.[53] The choice of Toys "R" Us as a partner is, in itself, a nod to a more upscale clientele—the toy seller has spent recent years redesigning product assortments and store environments to compete for the customer base typically attracted to the likes of FAO Schwartz.[54] But it is the juxtaposition of these stores-in-stores that will make a strong bid for higher-income groups, drawing customers who will pay extra for the increased convenience of several high-quality, branded product and service providers under one roof. This approach is also another way in which traditional big box retailers can create a small box solution positioned closer to their target customer base.

Better Retailing Through Technology

The moneyed masses can be tough customers to please, expecting retailers not only to sell them what they want, but to do so with immediate service, no stock-outs, convenient locations, and competitive prices. Satisfying these needs is a costly proposition in retailing, which is why a growing number of retailers are relying on technology to help them lower costs and make better decisions about the locations, layouts, and products mixes for their stores.

Retailers have used technology to select store locations for decades. What some retailers may not be aware of, however, is how affordable—and powerful—this technology has become. PC-based applications can now provide everything from customer travel-time modeling to competitor location analysis, to predefined, demographic-based consumer clusters like those defined by PRIZM and Microvision. Nationwide coverage is priced under $30,000, with prices considerably lower for individual regions and states. The ability to search for the optimal mix of population density and spending power, in other words, is at retailers' fingertips.

This is a good thing, but just a beginning. Though marketers have long used technology for site selection, they have often avoided using it to make differential decisions about store formats, building identical layouts on those sites. This consistency—in design elements, layout, and product assortment—while appearing to be the height of efficiency, can in fact be highly inefficient. By delivering the same product assortments, pricing, and promotions to nearly all of their locations, retailers are accounting for only the most basic variations in demand. Every retailer knows not to fill shelves with bikinis in Barrow, Alaska, and not to place snack foods adjacent to smelly lawn fertilizer. But truly optimizing store layout and assortment requires that far more knowledgeable decisions be made.

Yet, many retailers haven't used the available technology either at all or to its potential, frequently fearing the cost and the impact of change. As a result, inventory management suffers; stores are often left with too many of the wrong products and not enough of the right ones. One national retail chain, for example, suffered when it failed to deliver different assortments of clothing from its newly purchased subsidiary to its different stores. This oversight wound up costing them sales performance during their critical holiday season. While sales of the new line were generally brisk, the stock outs in some stores, coupled with leftover inventory in others, led to disappointing sales overall. (The company soon after committed to tailoring its clothing assortment for different ethnic, regional, and income groups.) On average, one-third of all retail items must eventually be sold at a markdown, while customers find that 8 percent of the items they've come into the store to purchase are out of stock.[55] When these stock-outs occur for the premium products most attractive to the moneyed masses, it can become very costly for the retailer, very quickly. Upscale electronics retailer Tweeter once had to tell analysts during an earnings call that it had run out of stock of its fastest-selling product, a $2,500 television set, for a period of nearly forty-five days.[56] Even a few hundred lost sales in this case could add up to a revenue hit of over $1 million—to say nothing of lost margin and the impact on customer goodwill.

Leading retailers are overcoming this and similar challenges by embracing and employing technologies deeper in their businesses. Doing so has helped them to make important, fact-based decisions about product selection, placement, and stocking levels at the individual store level. We expect that other retailers will soon follow suit. Scientific retailing, as it is called, can pay off in spades.

Let's delve a little deeper into the technology itself. Scientific retailing is enabled by software from companies like Retek and ProfitLogic. This software applies emerging analytical tools and other processes to optimize product assortments, pricing, promotions, and store layouts. To understand it in action, consider the experiences of pharmacy chain Walgreens. At one time, the company prescribed that all of its stores should adhere to a standard layout and product assortment, regardless of their location or the demographics they served, even though their stores ranged in location from inner-city neighborhoods to blue-blood suburbs.[57]

As a result, Walgreens, like many other retailers at the time, struggled to clearly identify and meet the needs of local customers, including those in affluent areas. The company realized that it needed to begin merchandising at the store level if it were going to significantly improve customer loyalty and inventory management. To start getting exactly the right products to the right customers, Walgreens developed new tools and an infrastructure for measuring individual store-level market needs.

The result was a system called Basic Department Management (BDM), which allows Walgreens to analyze demand for items in the context of local factors such as demographics, geography, seasonal changes, and store and shelf sizes. Walgreens corporate headquarters uses the system to produce merchandising blueprints for each store. For example, these plans enable the company to optimize assortments of high-margin general merchandise and seasonal items. They also helped guide the addition of entirely new items, such as expanded convenience food selections at locations in urban areas being underserved by supermarkets.[58]

The BDM system has driven improvements in sales, profitability, and differentiation across Walgreens' product assortment. In 2001, for example, the company grew market share in fifty-five out of its top sixty categories.[59] Importantly, the chain's streamlined inventory management capabilities free up capital for its aggressive expansion plan, which includes important upscale markets such as Orange County, California.[60] Walgreens has proven that, with a solid technology and process infrastructure, a mass retailer can successfully harness economies of scale while delivering greater variety to a more diverse, and increasingly affluent, customer base.

Fortunately, using scientific retailing to achieve such results does not require companies to roll out another expensive enterprisewide system or technology flavor of the month. Rather than implement new stand-alone systems, retailers should look to customer insight and merchandising software tools that sit directly atop existing applications, such as those from SAP and JDA, drawing out critical data. They can then direct these tools to apply complex algorithms that will model demand at the individual store and item level. Depending on their product mix, customer demographics, resources, and internal processes, merchants can implement scientific retail tools for a single, specific process, or across their entire merchandising cycle.

The experiences of other leading retailers also demonstrate the ability of scientific retailing tools to improve inventory management. Early users of scientific retail software—companies such as Gymboree and JC Penney—have observed gross margin increases between 5 and 10 percent.[61] U.K. grocer Sainsbury now uses actual customer demand patterns to optimize its product forecasting and replenishment for more than 60,000 items across 450 stores.[62] These pioneers also report increased customer satisfaction as a result of scientific retailing programs. As retailers create store clusters and distribute merchandise according to fact-based assessments of customer needs, their patrons are becoming more likely to find the products they want, where they expect them, and in stock.[63]

Scientific retailing does not just help retailers to grow incrementally through better-targeted merchandise. It can also lead to the transformation of a business. Best Buy, for example, used scientific retailing practices as part of a dramatic corporate turnaround. Following blistering growth in the mid-1990s (the business tripled in size to $8 billion in revenues in just three years), the company's operational practices became overextended, endangering shareholder value. Investors watched as within one year, the company's stock price deteriorated from $10 to $2, and earnings per share sank to just one cent.

Product assortment and pricing were two of Best Buy's most critical challenges. Its stores at the time carried more products than could be supported by sales associates, while a commitment to best-in-market pricing had eroded profits and forced the company to follow, not lead, competitive pricing strategies.

To turn the ship, Best Buy initiated a scientific retailing program. After conducting a fact-based analysis of customer purchases and other research directly with consumers, Best Buy came to some surprising conclusions. First, the company learned that the store's most profitable customers did not require such a broad product selection. Instead, these consumers wanted fewer, select items with better sales support and a greater focus on solutions, particularly for complex purchases such as home theater systems.

Second, research into price sensitivity revealed that customers did not expect Best Buy to maintain the lowest price point on every item in order to maintain its reputation as a value retailer. As a result, Best Buy focused discounting on a few critical items and was able to raise prices on others. This new pricing precision resulted in remarkable improvements in operational performance, including a 36 percent increase in key category revenues and profit improvement of $50 million. In addition, focusing price discounts where they would have the greatest impact helped Best Buy to improve consumer perception of their price competitiveness by an additional 18 percent.

How important is pricing management, particularly in light of today's moneyed masses? One consulting firm has found that companies that can raise prices by 1 percent can increase profits by up to four times as much as they could by making a 1 percent cut in overhead and fixed costs.[64]

Selling Mass Retailing to the Moneyed Masses

Aristide Boucicaut's place in retail history begins and ends, by most accounts, with his founding of the world's first department store. But Boucicaut generated a great many more retail innovations throughout his life, all to better serve the growing affluence of Parisians in the decades after the founding of The Bon Marché. These include the availability of home delivery by horse and coach, free delivery of all catalog purchases exceeding twenty-four francs, and the addition of clearly labeled bargain offers (or "sale" items). These amendments to his original design allowed The Bon Marché to prosper throughout years of change. By the time of Boucicaut's death in 1877, The Bon Marché boasted nearly 1,800 employees and 72 million francs in revenues, enormous amounts for the time.[65]

Today's retailers face a similar challenge to Boucicaut's in trying to determine how best to profit from a growing mass affluence. Retailers must deploy merchandising strategies, product assortments, and retail formats that award different customers, especially those of differing incomes, highly targeted offerings that appeal to their specific preferences, lifestyle needs, and buying behaviors. If retailers fail to do so, they risk becoming as irrelevant as an early 1900s specialty store.

Where are today's retailers headed? We predict that years from now, efforts to attract consumers across a broader range of incomes will result in a far more diverse industry landscape than we see today. Successful retailers will have followed affluent consumers into their communities and through their daily routines, even when it requires reorienting the stores' formats, rethinking product assortments, and dealing with new branding and competitive issues. Category killers will keep their suburban box stores, but will also operate in lifestyle centers, downtown neighborhoods, and perhaps even as stores-in-stores with select department and grocery store partners.

New diversity in product assortment and presentation does not necessarily lead to brand cacophony, however. The new focus required to please more affluent consumers will, if anything, compel retailers to hone their brand values more carefully than ever—driving them to define themselves around innovations in service, merchandising, and customer insight, rather than just prices and products stocked on shelves. Effectively serving the new mass market will also produce benefits that, in the spirit of Boucicaut, will accrue to every one of a retailer's customers.

Become Apropos of Everyone

Old Rule
Keep spending on promotion until the masses are
convinced they want your offering.

New Rule
Limit the need for spending on promotion by becoming highly relevant
to the masses, revealing to them the wisdom in choosing your offerings.

"Peaty!" shouts one man. Others shout, "Smoky!" and "Caramel!" A woman in the back of the room yells, "Cinnamon!" Everyone is laughing. They are in the middle of tasting single-malt Scotch whiskeys, and it is critical that they understand the individual flavor notes emanating from each of the four major production regions if they are to fully appreciate the benefits of a first-rate, blended Scotch whiskey like Johnnie Walker Black Label. Or so says the man with the thick Scottish accent at the microphone at the front table. Hence the yelling.

The man at the mike is leading this tasting, but he is not a company representative; rather, he is one of its brand ambassadors. And there are about sixty "students-for-a-night," sitting at tables arrayed with tasting-size glasses of spirits and pitchers of water. The students are mostly men and mostly middle-aged, but there are a few younger women and older gentlemen who keep the crowd from melting into uniformity. All are professional, or at least appear to be, and all have come to the event by invitation from friends or in response to a targeted mailing. They have been asked to enjoy appetizers and cocktails, perhaps to see a famous building (this particular event has been held at the Playboy Mansion), and to learn what Scotch drinking is all about.

Johnnie Walker sponsors these gatherings around the globe, from California to Australia. In 2001, the company even held a large event in Lagos, Nigeria. The Journey of Taste, as the events are called, mixes socializing and tasting to dispel insidious myths about blended Scotch and to bring new devotees into the fold. The campaign—for it is that— is all part of what makes Johnnie Walker Black Label the number-one-selling blended Scotch in the world. It is also part of a new way of selling to masses of upscale consumers. And the results are worth noting: Johnnie Walker Black Label sales were up 6.1 percent in 2001, the year the company started the Journey of Taste series, at a time when the total of the top ten leading scotch brands *declined* by 2.7 percent and when single malts grew only in the low single digits.[1]

Event marketing is, of course, not new, at least not in the business-to-business world. Sales teams have always wined, dined, and held lavish parties for important buyers, often tying their soirées to sporting and cultural events. But these new-style events are distinctly different; they aren't planned as one-off events designed to seal a particular deal. Instead, they are planned as a series, or as "sales parties" that are designed to beget more of the same. And although the marketers would be ecstatic if attendees purchased their products in droves after the event, that isn't the only goal. These sessions are also intended to seed the beliefs and experiences necessary for future sales, with a focus on emerging and potential customers. In other words, the marketers seek to influence the influencers of the ultimate consumer, by sowing ideas that break down barriers to buying, and dispelling negative myths that surround certain products. In the case of Johnny Walker, the company is hoping that attendees will help spread the word that blended Scotch is not inferior to single malts, but rather is an improvement on them, and that adding water to taste is more than just acceptable, it is the way real Scots drink their whiskey.[2]

Bagging a Moving Target

Johnnie Walker's success is all the more remarkable when marketers consider how hard it is to home in on the moneyed masses and their influencers. Many executives we've spoken to lamented the short supply of quality demographic and psychographic data available to help pinpoint the richest veins of mass-affluent consumers. For example, while government-supplied information is plentiful, it is often incomplete or misleading—omitting data about passive income, and obscuring pockets of more affluent consumers by reporting only average income in zip codes and towns.

And even when these target customers can be found, they must still be wooed successfully. Marketers still must get their attention amid the surfeit of advertising already out there. Worse, academic research has shown that educated consumers (which the more moneyed of the masses unquestionably are) are less tolerant of advertising and more sensitive to marketing clutter than other groups.[3] Their increased levels of skepticism often lead them to actively resist persuasion, and deliberately avoid advertisements.[4] Our own survey revealed that the affluent are significantly less likely than their lower-income peers are to use television and radio as a source of buying information. The likely effectiveness of these traditional mass-market media is therefore diminished for these customers. Not to mention that this group is busy and doesn't relish interruptions. Witness the recent passing of the federally mandated National Do Not Call Registry. Overt or undifferentiated promotions not only will fail to persuade these consumers, but also can unwittingly antagonize them.

Promoting the New Mass Market

All these challenges can lead businesses to forsake mass-marketing approaches to promotion, because marketers judge them either ineffectual by today's standards or too blunt an instrument to cost-effectively influence the well-heeled customers they seek. Marketers have instead focused on new, individualized direct marketing approaches, relying on expensive technologies to communicate one-to-one with customers.

But our research uncovered a number of developments that have allowed even the most traditional forms of mass-marketing promotion, advertising, and public relations to evolve into forms that compete effectively for the "mindshare" of today's moneyed masses. These new methods of reaching the intended market are distinct from direct marketing approaches because—while they are frequently somewhat targeted—they are designed to influence large numbers of anonymous potential customers. These methods succeed because they are highly relevant to many consumers or are made so by the companies using them. This heightened relevance is the key to obtaining new low- and even no-cost mass promotion, which spares companies the expense of individually identifying and targeting customers.

And no, we're not simply talking broadly about how technology has aided market research and how the Internet is a wonderful thing. Although books can be—and have been—written about the wealth of technology-enabled marketing techniques becoming available today, our discussion will concentrate on those approaches that are decidedly mass market *but have been adjusted to be in sync with today's more affluent masses.* Specifically, our discussion will focus on marketing techniques that have successfully overcome the challenges of (a) finding effective ways to access the affluent market, (b) competing with other marketers for these consumers' limited available time, and (c) overcoming the affluent market's instinctive distrust of overt marketing efforts.

Our research indicates three ways in which effective marketers have modified their approaches to traditional methods to get the job done:

Advertise in the bottlenecks. Even the busiest of affluent consumers are sometimes more reachable—at the times and places where life itself slows them down. These include time spent commuting to and from their desk or shop floor and the time spent enjoying one of today's upscale entertainment, social, or other leisure activities. The essential requirement is to step into recurrent moments of underutilized time, generating passive as well as active uptake of information.

Entice them with incentives other than money. Affluent
consumers, as we've said, are often admirers of knowledge
and education. Successful marketers are improving their
promotions by exploiting this interest, helping consumers to
become connoisseurs of their product category—teaching
them not just to be a Kendall-Jackson drinker, for example,
but how to be an armchair sommelier. Leading promoters
are also enticing the moneyed masses differently by making
greater use of upscale locations in their sales activities, from
country clubs to the very homes of the affluent—taking
advantage of in-home promotions styled for more than just
plastic storage items.

*Shift public relations focus from the "wow" factor to here-
and-now benefits.* The limited attention and increased
skepticism of those with greater affluence drives savvy
marketers to focus public relations efforts on communicating
immediately appreciable benefits. One way to do this is by
publicizing the specific areas of innovation that address long
held consumer desires, as JetBlue Airways did in promoting
its on-board satellite TV. Companies without novel here-
and-now benefits of their own to highlight for the media are
finding success creating unique brand associations that are
meaningful to the moneyed masses. When brands hook up,
as with celebrities and merger announcements, the media
become curious and want to learn more. Public relations
professionals are able to leverage such interest in partnerships to broaden the media appeal of a company's offerings,
gaining them exposure in new outlets seen by the affluent.

Wringing Out the Opportunity in the Bottlenecks

In the early 1900s, mass marketers often had the luxury of their audience's undivided attention—during radio programming and then television shows, for example. Today, the new mass market is far less

captive. Advertising strategies must focus sharply on the handful of places and advertising outlets where the affluent congregate and can spare some attention. A marketer can exploit two particular moments of opportunity to reach these consumers during their busy daily routines: on their way to and from work and within upscale leisure and entertainment activities. Not only do these targets of opportunity make the most of affluent consumers' limited time and attention, but they also have the important benefit of improving marketing's overall return on investment. Because these strategies venture away from the well-trodden times and places companies promote to consumers, these promotions are generally less expensive than conventional mass media promotions, and much less expensive than highly targeted, direct approaches.

It's Working

Targeting affluent consumers where they live is straightforward: Follow them to work. The correlation between income and hours labored is strong, suggesting companies should look to the time spent in and around offices and even certain shop floors for moments of consumer influence. A handful of entrepreneurial marketing firms are doing just that, opening new channels to reach upper-income consumers while they travel to and from, and *for* their jobs.

One such start-up is Massachusetts-based Captivate Network. The company helps its clients target affluent consumers by delivering programming and advertisements over flat panel TV screens installed in the elevators and lobbies of more than 400 office towers with more than 700 additional under contract. With this placement, Captivate accesses a consumer base of 1.4 million professionals a day, with an average household income of $105,000.[5] Alongside content provided by the likes of the *Wall Street Journal* and CNN, advertisers such as Volkswagen, British Airways, and Johnnie Walker have found that Captivate can deliver higher-than-average ad recalls.[6] After all, elevator riders have precious little else to compete for their attention and cannot readily tune out the content.

Why has the medium been so successful? Captivate's CEO and founder, Mike DiFranza, gave us his reasoning for launching the company: "Elevator behavior is dysfunctional. People head for the corners and try to avoid eye contact. They are hungry for distraction."[7] DiFranza recognized this peculiarity as a critical difference between his concept and ones that failed, noting that most failed grocery store attempts were based on ads that annoyed people who were busy trying to do something else, like shopping or paying at the checkout. On the other hand, Captivate "gives people on elevators a positive alternative for time they can't spend any other way," says DiFranza.

Captivate's model is distinctive in other ways as well. Its company executives recognized that failing models needed substantial amounts of human interaction and physical media to distribute their content across far-flung locations, all of which added tremendous cost. Captivate's approach uses economical, wireless distribution of content to displays near each other and captures additional benefits to its cost structure by sharing each display terminal with thousands of consumers, rather than just the scores that might see a screen attached to a grocery cart. "We realized that [to be attractive to advertisers,] you had to get a critical mass of consumers," says DiFranza. "The idea came to me in the elevator of a four-story building, but I realized that the market was for businesspeople in high-rise buildings, where each building can easily deliver 5,000 to 10,000 consumers . . . multiple times a day."

Elevator advertising has one particular benefit that DiFranza sees as most critical and the hardest for any other medium to compete with: "[With elevator advertising] the consumer is influenced much closer to the time of purchase decision, when their minds are on work. We have research that shows most business advertising is done during prime time, far from when most business people are thinking about buying." DiFranza emphasizes the importance of using this advantage of elevator and lobby advertising in combination with other advertising: "They see the commercial on TV the night before, say, for Oracle software, but then the messages are reinforced the next day in an environment where actual purchase decisions are being made."

Though Captivate has been approached about other ventures— including letting other businesses piggyback on its wireless network— DiFranza insists on remaining focused on the core elevator media business: "This is easily a $2 billion industry in the coming years, so I can't let us get distracted."

Another way to reach affluent commuters is in and around airline flights. The Airline Advertising Bureau has found that airline passengers have a medium annual income of $93,822—a number that can rise significantly on shuttle flights between major metropolitan areas or in business-class sections or frequent-flyer lounges (Delta Shuttle passengers, for example, have an annual income average of over $180,000).[8]

Marketers interested in targeting the airborne affluent should consider partnering with airlines for highly integrated advertising efforts. Belgian beer Stella Artois not only sponsors Virgin Atlantic's in-flight movie channel, but also ensures that its beer is served on-board. Sony's Vaio went a step further with a campaign on Delta Air Lines that included buying in-flight programming commercials, advertising in the in-flight magazine, e-mailing customers through Delta.com, and furnishing laptops to Crown Room Club lounges.[9]

The coffee run is also a good choice for marketers trying to reach affluent employees at work. Media-promotion companies like Encompass Media Group and PromoCup provide millions of disposable cups and lids free to thousands of bagel shops, delis, and coffee carts every month. The cups and lids are printed with ads from companies like Cingular Wireless and Lifetime television.[10] A sort of advertising Trojan horse, the cups are intended to be looked at by customers trying to ensure their coffee doesn't spill on the way back to the office, but then also later by the entire office staff as the cups sit on desks and conference room tables and function like mini-billboards. The ads can be further targeted for the affluent by limited distribution to, for example, the financial districts of major cities.

Even bathroom walls and pay stubs can make for good advertising platforms. A growing number of companies are selling ad space in their restrooms. And promotion company AdCheck has been offering employers the opportunity to sell ad space on their paychecks since 1999 and now does so for a host of large companies, including United Airlines and grocery chain Kroger. These ads reach more than a million employees each pay cycle.

Finally, marketers can benefit greatly by seeking out the less-than-well-known places where the affluent gather to work. In *Marketing to the Affluent,* Thomas J. Stanley notes that unglamorous industrial areas attract large concentrations of successful and wealthy entrepreneurs: "Often, the number of affluent prospects per acre, block, or zip code is higher in industrial areas than in Greenwich, Connecticut!"[11] If companies can identify these hot spots, then a well-chosen billboard in a city's industrial periphery could deliver better results—at a far cheaper cost—than the same dollars spent in a more visible, prestigious location.

The Right Place, and the Right Time

Ever since James Dean took an Ace comb to his famous locks in 1955's *Rebel Without a Cause,* product placements have become an increasingly important part of the marketing mix.[12] For companies targeting the moneyed masses, entertainment placements, or *advertainment,* as it is becoming known, can effectively drive associations between the quality or benefits of a product and the situations in which it is placed and the celebrities who use it.

What's more, these placements serve as an important hedge against the threat of technologies that enable people to escape traditional discreet advertising approaches. The affluent consumer can easily use video recorders that automatically delete commercials; they can also employ ad-scrubbing Web browsers. But they can't dodge or delete a product that is embedded in the content they want to see (though that day may one day come).

There's an added bonus as well: The trend of the moneyed masses to purchase more of their chosen content (versus renting it) means the returns on placement investments can last far longer than a brief commercial's life span—potentially the consumer's life span, or even longer.

In the film industry, few movies have provided a more effective vehicle for affluent product placements than the James Bond series. Sophisticated and debonair, Bond resonates with the moneyed masses. While they cannot live his dangerous lifestyle, they can afford to buy some of his equipage. That was what BMW counted on when it chose the film *GoldenEye* to provide consumers with a glimpse of its new Z3 coupe in the mid-1990s. The car made its movie debut three months prior to its market release. That appearance created such a sensation with consumers that the car won orders up to a year in advance and became recognized as one of the fastest creations of brand awareness in advertising history.[13] BMW's success motivated a flood of other products, such as Philips razors and Bollinger champagne, to demonstrate that they were the preferred choice of the suave secret agent.

Companies pursuing such placements often pay little or nothing out of pocket; they routinely bankroll the placements with cross-promotions or joint promotions instead. Some, like Kraft Foods Inc., General Motors Corp. and Microsoft Corp., enlist the aid of product placement shops to work with Hollywood prop masters, set designers and production studio executives to ensure their products are selected to be used, and therefore seen, on the silver screen and television.[14] Both approaches can be a small price to pay for an advertising vehicle that is likely to have a captive audience on DVD for years to come.

Of course, not every company will negotiate a Bond placement. But the field is wide open, and the world of Bond isn't the only silver-screen venue attractive to the affluent. And the advertainment arena isn't confined to single products. For example, retailers are getting into the act, with Saks Fifth Avenue commandeering the leading role (for a store) in the movie production of *Shopgirl,* a part originally written with the eponymous sales clerk working at a Neiman Marcus counter.[15] In addition to providing for the store's prominence in the film, the agreement calls for window displays in Saks stores touting the movie (allowing the company to monetize the value of its window-display asset, a marketing medium it values at over $350,000 a week based on estimated consumer impressions), premiere party events for reasons like those we mentioned earlier, and tie-ins with Saks's 600,000 circulation catalog. All this with no money changing hands: one of the key potential benefits of these kinds of arrangements.

Few placements can create the impact of an appearance in a major motion picture. But there are a host of other placement opportunities that can put a product in front of an affluent audience in a favorable way. Consider Baz Luhrmann, who adapted *Moulin Rouge* into an award-winning film. Luhrmann recently introduced a Broadway version of the Puccini opera *La Bohème.* Recognizing the opportunity to reach a large volume of cultured, affluent consumers, Piper-Heidsieck champagne and Montblanc pens entered an innovative partnership with the new Luhrmann production. In return for promotional assistance, billboards for the two brands appeared on stage as part of the set, with correct graphic design to ensure their logo's fit within the Parisian streetscape of 1957. Such opportunities enable offerings to literally become part of the drama, while reaching an upscale audience of theater fans.

Commissioning content is another approach (and one that virtually guarantees that the product will be given "star" treatment). Although the same motivation sparked the rise of mass-market infomercials, the concept of commissioning content has recently been updated and pushed upscale for a far higher tier of consumer. When is it worthwhile for a company to invest in the production of a compelling, credible piece of entertainment and to accept the risk that a substandard result will be easily dismissed as commercial? Such an effort is most likely to be successful when a brand has an impeccable reputation, an offering that generates strong consumer interest, and the need to show its product performing in a situation beyond the realm of a consumer's daily experience.

BMW, mentioned earlier for its presence on the big screen, is also a pioneer in this area. The company has succeeded creating star vehicles for its own products by recruiting famous directors and actors to create its own series of five short films, titled "The Heist." One executive discusses the motivation for this series: "Right from the beginning, we knew BMWs came alive when doing 125 miles per hour on a racetrack. That's when you understand how well they perform. We wanted to convey that."[16]

"The Heist," made available online, received nearly 15 million viewings within its first months of release and was so well produced that it won an award at Cannes. And while BMW won't disclose numbers, the results it enjoyed likely exceeded the investment. "The Heist" was credited with helping BMW to increase its 2001 sales by over 12 percent and won the company an estimated $20 million in free media.[17]

Companies without the resources to commission their own films should consider a related opportunity—creating placements that become part of the scenery in the consumer's daily life. In Los Angeles and Houston, for example, Italian company Piaggio hired models to ride around on its new line of Vespa scooters, not to act as salespeople, but rather to be seen (and envied) by affluent target customers going about their daily routines.[18] Why wait for trendsetters or early adopters to be seen using a product, when a company can hire the trendsetters and accelerate the market's movement toward the "tipping point" of product adoption? Beware a different sort of tipping point, if you take that approach, however. The target market just might find the tactic deceptive or intrusive if the company goes too far. Consumers widely criticized Sony Ericsson, for example, for one staged promotion, in which actors roamed the streets of New York posing as tourists and asking passersby to take their pictures (with the camera being marketed). After unsuspecting consumers acquiesced, the actors would then try to discuss the camera and its features. The promotion backfired when critics, including many in the media, expressed their opinion that the campaign crossed a line of decorum by preying on the goodwill of unsuspecting strangers.

Marketers must also take care not to appear too brash or transparent. So many consumers now recognize placements as another form of advertising that movies like the Austin Powers series, a parody of the James Bond series, can now poke fun at the product placements in both the Bond films and their own, to great comic effect. Marketers must think through the possible negative consequences of participation as well. All the lasting benefits that are so attractive in successful movies can be lasting detriments if the product ends up being closely linked with a flop, and the product may even hasten a movie toward that fate by having too dominant a presence in the content. But the risks are probably smaller than the possible returns. Bad content tends to quickly disappear from theaters and consumers' consciousness, allowing advertainment, like surgery, to bury its mistakes.

Must-Be-Seen TV

Traditional media aimed at the mass market (like television) have suffered as an advertising vehicle for years, but television and radio are by no means a lost cause for companies trying to reach the moneyed masses. Though the concentrated audience once delivered by the three national networks has fragmented since the 1980s across hundreds of new channels, the moneyed masses can still be found here, tuned in to the channels that are committed to programming that reflects uniquely affluent lifestyles, needs, and personal interests. While the fortunes of individual programs wax and wane quickly, some networks are finding consistent success with marketers by keeping the moneyed masses in the fore of their programming strategies.

Among the major networks in the early 2000s, NBC has done the best job of creating a successful a connection with the moneyed masses. The network has developed a string of hit programs, often featuring white-collar characters and intelligent story lines, that have made it not only the nation's most popular network, but, more importantly, the preferred choice of the mass affluent. According to Nielsen Media Research, NBC runs thirteen of the twenty most popular shows among adults under fifty with household incomes exceeding $75,000.[19]

NBC manages its content in a way that positions it to be a useful partner for firms seeking to reach the affluent consumers for years to come. For example, while ABC has recently moved down-market in its quest to improve disappointing ratings, NBC has proven willing to retain programming popular with the affluent that might otherwise be marked for cancellation—such as a decision in May 2002 to retain the shows *Providence* and *Ed*.[20]

Nor has NBC been afraid to fine-tune the content of its most successful shows to connect even more closely with targeted affluent consumers. For example, the network replaced the street thugs on its popular drama series *Law & Order* with upper-class criminals who engage affluent viewers more directly.[21] NBC has also been willing to link its advertainment opportunities to its more affluent audience. While CBS scored audience points with the reality television show *Survivor*, NBC successfully countered with an upscale version called *The Apprentice*, which pits MBA-types against each other to win a job running one of Donald Trump's companies. The show is driven by shameless promotion—from the contestants' constant self-promotion to avoid being fired from the show, to the not-so-subtle selling of the show's featured upscale offerings, which range from Marquis Jet to Todd English's Olive's restaurants to Trump's own National Golf Club.

Yet the show managed to become NBC's top rated program in 2004, and a favorite of television viewers with an income over $100,000—second only to NBC's own *West Wing.*[22] Companies should expect to pay a premium for such access, however. NBC has been able to charge higher rates for commercials than competitors can, because of its dominance of upscale audiences.[23]

While NBC embodies the affluent-focused, mass-media format, companies should also look to more specialized media outlets. Increases in affluence drive consumers more toward news, arts and entertainment, and education, and to cable television channels and magazine subscriptions, where consumption among the affluent is growing. In radio, the highbrow news and lifestyle features of public radio programming, such as Minnesota Public Radio's *Marketplace,* attract listeners who are 117 percent more likely than the general population to have an income exceeding $100,000.[24]

More-than-Money Promotions

While advertising provides consumers with a *reason* to buy an offering, sales promotions furnish the *incentive* to complete their purchase.[25] For traditional mass marketing, those incentives have often been monetary discounts. Couponing, limited-time offers, and product rebates became the staples of promotional strategies in recent decades. These were delivered in low-cost, undifferentiated ways, either through shelf display units, advertisements, or company-representative-staffed promotional events. Promoting to the mass market this way tends to increase sales and market share as desired when applied, but at the cost of driving the prices realized in the market downward.

Although this approach served the mass market reliably (if not always cost-effectively) in the past, and continues to be effective for lower-income consumers, our research finds that it does not result in compelling incentives for more affluent consumers. To motivate these consumers, companies must instead focus on promotions that consider their distinct values, preferences, and behaviors. We believe that marketers will enjoy much greater success by changing the what, who, and where that textbook sales promotions are designed to deliver, to better target the new mass market.

Marketers should employ promotions that promise knowledge and connoisseurship, not just discounts; deliver the promotion through influencers such as friends and peers, not solely company representatives; and shift the locations of promotion from points of sale to neutral venues that the moneyed masses patronize and admire, such as country clubs and upscale sporting events. The common theme unifying these strategies is the use of promotion to reinforce a company's position as a trusted adviser—an agent that helps the moneyed masses make purchases that best meet their needs—not as opportunistic marketer.

Make Every Customer a Connoisseur

By virtue of their higher income, the moneyed masses tend to be less swayed by cents-off discounts or monetary rewards than are lower-income customers. Promotions that involve coupons and extensive rules and expiration dates are not complementary to a time-strapped, affluent lifestyle. Few moneyed consumers can easily find or make the time to search for, clip, collect, and redeem discount offers. Forrester Research found that affluent consumers ranked discounts and coupons fourteenth out of a possible sixteen factors motivating their purchases of luxury goods online—even less important than mere tactical issues such as shipping and delivery options.[26] And although over $10 billion in rebates was given back to consumers in 2002 and almost three-quarters of consumer electronics were sold with a rebate, affluent consumers find them as frustrating and unappealing as intended, leaving these discounts primarily a tool of the bargain shopper.[27]

Instead, companies should offer this group of shoppers another, more motivating take-away from their sales promotions: knowledge. We have already established that affluent consumers are enthusiastic about investing in products with educational value. We find that this enthusiasm also makes them willing to invest time and attention in promotions that will convey useful knowledge, particularly if it makes them *connoisseurs* of the entire category. In other words, consumers value being able to discuss items such as category history; distinctive

product characteristics, including places of origin, interesting manufacturing techniques, and artisans' traditions; and differences from competing offerings.

Companies should not confuse the desire for connoisseurship with
an ivory-tower scholarly interest. According to researchers, the up-
wardly mobile enjoy the prestige and cachet of knowing a little about a
lot of subjects, particularly those that are important to their affluent
lifestyle. This recalls what French sociologist Pierre Bourdieu has
described as the desire to acquire *cultural capital*—or, in very simple
terms, those pieces of knowledge that create the good taste that helps
one belong to, and advance within, a desired peer group. Companies
should direct connoisseurship, then, toward helping customers accumulate cultural capital, with the added benefit of seeming to help them
make purchases based on informed consideration, not marketing
manipulation.

This approach is not unprecedented. It's exactly what Stanley Marcus did to help grow his famous store, Neiman Marcus. Maria Halkias of
the *Dallas Morning News* describes how the approach succeeded: "He
learned the business quickly, and soon he was promoting The Store as
the center of fashion for nouveau riche Texas oil barons and their families, even as the Great Depression gripped the nation's psyche and pock-
etbook. By 1937 . . . *Fortune* magazine was commenting that 'Dallas
women came to look on Neiman Marcus not simply as a place where
they bought dresses, but as a place where they were educated about
clothes.'"[28]

More recently, automaker Lexus has successfully ingrained connoisseurship as a theme in its promotions. One way has been by hosting a
series of events that educate customers about the performance and han-
dling of not just its own luxury cars, but a broad range of them. In the
late 1990s, it launched an innovative twist on the classic ride-and-drive
event format as part of an eight-city tour called Taste of Lexus. Faced
with the launch of two strong, new competitor vehicles—an updated
BMW 3 Series and Mercedes S-Class—Lexus decided to educate consumers about the entire luxury category and allow them to make
informed, head-to-head comparisons. Taste of Lexus attendees were
invited to test eighteen of the competition's cars, in addition to the

entire Lexus lineup, on five separate, closed courses. Live music and catering from local celebrity chefs ensured an appropriately refined environment.

While Lexus representatives were available at the events to answer questions and provide information, the company refrained from direct sales pitches. It felt that fostering connoisseurship was enough to enable consumers to understand for themselves the superior performance and value of a Lexus. Furthermore, it believed that attendees, having reached their own conclusions about the product through firsthand experience and comparisons with many other models, would be more likely to promote the Lexus among friends, family, and associates.

Lexus's approach paid off. The Taste of Lexus series attracted twenty-three thousand attendees, 70 percent of whom were owners of competitors' vehicles.[29] These consumers stayed at the event for an average of four hours, a remarkable amount of time, considering their undoubtedly busy schedules. And though it can be challenging to measure the goodwill generated by the promotion, the events certainly provided many attendees with the incentive they needed to take action. A full 2,700 guests requested immediate follow-up from a Lexus dealer.[30]

Not every offering lends itself to a gala event. Yet, companies can also increase the effectiveness of more traditional types of promotions by reorienting them to create customer connoisseurship. Wine maker Kendall-Jackson has embraced this approach with its point-of-purchase displays, which educate consumers about how to choose and match wines. Recognizing that even affluent consumers (in particular the newly affluent) can still find wine selection intimidating, Kendall-Jackson takes the pressure off making the right choice. Its in-store promotions help customers understand the wine-making issues that should guide them to one of its bottles, such as how its approach to barrel aging improves wine quality.[31] Such general wine knowledge ensures that consumers sound intelligent when explaining their wine choice, rather than revealing less credible reasons (and who among us *hasn't*, on at least one occasion, chosen a bottle of wine by the attractiveness of the label?).

In addition, Kendall-Jackson has transformed the downscale practice of couponing to help instruct consumers on matching its wines with appropriate food. John Maxwell, a brand director at Kendall-Jackson, told *Point of Purchase* magazine that the company would not offer dollar-off coupons on its own bottles, because "once you go cheap in the sense of how you market, it's hard to rebuild and reinforce that [high-quality] imagery."[32] Instead, when the company offers instant coupons, it is often for complementary foods such as gourmet crackers or other complementary upscale items. Again, the promotions make customers look like heroes, providing both an incentive to buy and an educational benefit that enables them to demonstrate an ability to match wines with appropriate food.

Using the Promotion Power of the Masses

Some companies have found that in promotions, to paraphrase Marshall McLuhan, the messenger is often the message. So rather than rely on their own employees to distribute and manage promotions, these companies' marketers are turning to consumers' friends, neighbors, and peers to win higher levels of credibility. Their sales promotions present affluent consumers two added incentives to make a purchase: the implied endorsement of a respected personal acquaintance and, frequently, the perceived obligation to at least buy *something*.

Siccing consumers on themselves is as old as mass-marketing itself. Though many know the name of Earl Silas Tupper from his now famous Tupperware, it was Brownie Wise, a "single, middle-age mother from Detroit" who taught him how to sell it to homemakers in the early 1950s.[33] Though Tupper questioned how Tupperware parties could help him reach the mass-marketer status he desired, he pulled his product from retail shelves in 1951 (a peak time for traditional in-store mass-market retailing). And the merchandise has been off shelves ever since, with the exception of a too-successful experiment with Target between 2001 and 2003 (selling through staffed displays in Target Superstores was so successful it began to threaten the core party business) and the introduction of online selling, which the company began in 1999.[34] The company now has over a billion dollars in sales and hosts a Tupperware party every 2.5 seconds.

A new generation of entrepreneurs has successfully latched on to this direct sales approach, ratcheting up both the offerings and the experience for the more affluent households of the moneyed masses. One of these entrepreneurs is the Longaberger Company, which sells baskets in thousands of specialized shapes and sizes, and other home accessories. Handmade by American artisans, Longaberger baskets are priced at a premium. Items range from a $50 bagel basket to a $160 laundry basket (plan to spend an extra $100 for the lid and liner). From modest beginnings, the company has grown into a highly successful business with annual revenues of about $1 billion (yes, that's billion).[35]

While the company's story is well reported, few may realize that when founder Dave Longaberger established the company in the 1970s, he initially experimented with selling the baskets through his own store, malls, and other retail outlets, just as Tupper had initially done. But Longaberger felt that traditional retail channels were not conducive to successful promotions, which he believed were critical for accessing his target market. Consumers were most interested in the pricey baskets when they understood the basket-making craft, the high-quality materials he used, and the specialized capabilities of each piece (underscoring the importance of connoisseurship, as mentioned earlier). So Longaberger went with a direct sales event model, oriented around instruction, which would enable consumers to learn about his products. Yet, rather than conduct seminars, he too appreciated the value of an in-home event where hosts could gather friends and family to enjoy an informative and entertaining presentation from one of his representatives.

Consistent with affluent consumers seeking more than monetary rewards, the Longaberger's independent sales consultants are rewarded with access to their own exclusive line of products, in return for their hosting a successful event. Attendees, for their part, enjoy the relaxed, informal, and intimate environment of a friend's home, albeit with a risk of social embarrassment if they walk away without making at least one small purchase. The catch, of course, is that given the premium selling prices of the goods being promoted this way today, the guests often end up making a fairly substantial outlay.

The Pampered Chef is another company that has enjoyed great success with upscale direct sales, selling premium cookware and kitchen accessories. The company conducted over a million home shows in

2002, generating more than $740 million in revenues. And SheBeads is now on a roll. Started by an entrepreneur in the affluent North Shore suburbs of Chicago, the jewelry company distributes through home parties, rewarding hosts with credit toward purchases. One host recognized that she was going to spend far more on refreshments than she was likely to make in commission (a deal vaguely reminiscent of the one for the island of Manhattan), but she was unconcerned. Her attitude demonstrates how companies that use this approach can benefit from having a sales force that unwittingly or uncaringly subsidizes the company's promotion costs. With in-home sales becoming increasingly upscale, established companies with successful brands are beginning to join in, too. Time Inc., with its subsidiary business Southern Living At HOME, has managed to create "the fastest-growing party plan company in the history of direct sales," selling "home and garden décor that reflects the style of *Southern Living* magazine."[36] And Bill Blass has joined the like of Carlisle Collection and Worth Collection in bringing a line of expensive designer apparel to the home.[37] It may not be long before even higher-priced items—everything from floor coverings to living room furniture—are sold by inventive companies this way.

While companies can increase the effectiveness of sales promotions by delivering them through peers, they should also direct them through influencers whom the affluent would like to emulate. Cadillac leveraged this strategy in the successful launch of its Escalade EXT, a pickup-truck version of its sport utility vehicle. A day before the EXT's introduction at a Los Angeles car show, Cadillac provided a sneak preview at an exclusive promotional party that attracted local celebrities and taste makers—the younger, affluent demographic the company hoped would eventually buy the new trucks.

Before leaving the party, guests received simple black T-shirts featuring the famous Cadillac logo. Although free T-shirts abound at many promotional events, these were distributed in limited numbers and intended to serve as proof of the owner's presence at such an exclusive party. Within weeks, attendees were seen wearing the shirts in fashionable Los Angeles venues and health clubs—providing a remarkably targeted endorsement for a brand traditionally associated with a far older demographic.

Involving the right influencers helped create a chain reaction that made the Escalade something of a pop-culture phenomenon. The

'Slade quickly began appearing in the lyrics of chart-topping songs by Jennifer Lopez and a slew of rap stars, and became a must-have vehicle for actors in high-profile TV shows and movies. All this publicity was extremely valuable product placement at virtually zero cost.

As a result, Cadillac's targeted sales promotions created a double incentive for those affluent enough to purchase the car. Not only did consumers now want to emulate the bearers of the promotional messages, they could also count on the recognition and envy of other consumers who had been made fully aware of the Escalade's cachet. For Cadillac, the strategy helped to reinvigorate the brand by attracting younger buyers and increasing the average income for a particular model, reinforcing its exclusivity and cachet. Although the average Cadillac buyer was sixty-one years old at the time, with an average income of around $100,000, the average Escalade buyer has been only forty-eight years old, with an average income of $171,000.[38]

Events at Trusted Locales

Traditionally, promotions were offered and redeemed through stores or other points of sale. However, some companies are finding that promotions in general, and events in particular, are far more likely to win consumer trust when located in places the moneyed masses already are—or would like to be—on a regular basis. To make this a reality, these firms are supplementing broad, retailer-based strategies with promotions conducted in posh locations such as country clubs, lifestyle centers, and upscale sporting events, such as tennis matches and golf and polo tournaments.

For Edward Goldman, cofounder of MDVIP, country club locations have enhanced the company's efforts to educate target affluent consumers about his firm's concierge medical practices: "Country clubs provide one of the best environments for educating consumers about our service and promoting its benefits. For many of the attendees, it is a familiar environment where they enjoy spending time. For others, the curiosity about driving through the gates adds to the interest generated by the event."[39]

No doubt the use of a country club for a promotional event also provides a stamp of endorsement. Consumers can assume that if such a venue approves of such a promotional event, the service has been screened and found appropriately upscale and of potential interest to the club's members.

Lifestyle centers—the smaller, upscale malls discussed earlier in the book—provide another emerging venue for establishing the trust of the new mass market. These locations provide the added advantage of being a regular stop on the daily routines of the affluent, particularly women. Terry McEwen, cofounder of lifestyle center developer Poag & McEwen, told us that retailers believe the venues attract the affluent to promotional events more effectively than their regional mall or strip mall counterparts ever could: "We host a series of luncheon fashion shows, as well as many other community and charitable events at the centers. Upscale shoppers feel more comfortable attending events here than they do at mass retail outlets. Because of the smaller-scale, high-end retail mix, and local orientation, promotions conducted at lifestyle centers feel more like community events than sales events."[40]

Upscale leisure settings, such as select sporting events, provide another effective channel for reaching affluent consumers with sales promotions. Since 1991, for example, Heineken has used its sponsorship of the US Open to promote its beer to both attendees and viewers of the tennis matches.[41] Held in the Arthur Ashe Stadium in storied Flushing, New York, the US Open delivers a remarkably affluent base of fans. Indeed, 75 percent of US Open viewers are college-educated, while more than half have annual earnings in excess of $75,000.[42] This audience is a core market for Heineken, as the brand seeks to grow by capturing the middle ground of affluent consumers who can afford to drink imported beer regularly, but who may currently associate it with special occasions.[43]

However, companies selecting sporting events for sales promotions must ensure they can achieve enough visibility, through the clutter of competing advertisers, to make a meaningful connection with attendees. Heineken confronted this issue in its decision to favor tennis matches over golf tournaments. Steve Davis, the brand's senior vice president of marketing, told *Brandweek* that with tennis, Heineken would "have an opportunity to own the sport. Golf is clearly hot as hell, but there are 555 PGA events, and consumers can't remember who sponsors them."[44]

To reach the necessary threshold of sufficient visibility, Heineken created a number of on-site sales promotions. These were aimed at encouraging attendee interaction with both its brand—through extensive on- and off-court signage—and particularly its products. The beer company achieved this product interaction by operating a Red Star Café on the premises. The café allows the open's attendees to nurse (what else?) a Heineken or an Amstel Light while they watch the matches on closed-circuit television. In addition to other promotions such as the Heineken Star Award for the most exciting moments of the tournament, the company also sells limited-edition Heineken T-shirts at the event. Designed by tennis bad boy John McEnroe, the T-shirts are a status symbol that the company makes a point of connecting to its other promotion campaigns conducted via television, radio, and the Internet.[45]

Moving from "Wow" to the Here and Now

Ever since General Electric Company created a publicity department in 1897, a cornerstone of the public relations industry has been making offerings newsworthy by illustrating their unique characteristics in a dramatic fashion. Many marketers, borrowing from management writer Tom Peters, came to term this practice the *wow factor*.[46] This fundamental approach has served PR professionals well over the years and has been used quite successfully to influence the affluent since its earliest days. In one case, legendary PR guru Edward Bernays employed the wow factor to reposition radios for a wealthier audience for his client Philco Radio back in 1939. (The devices were associated with the lower classes at the time.) He rented out the Grand Ballroom of New York's Waldorf-Astoria Hotel and transmitted to the audience the voice of a famous opera star through a high-fidelity radio. Bernays's bravado worked. The attending press raved about the sound quality, helping to establish the radio as a product befitting an affluent home.

But today's time-strapped moneyed masses are a more jaded audience, regularly confronted with would-be wow factors and acutely aware of the potential for corporate spin. Marketing executives seeking a step change in the effectiveness of their corporate PR efforts should instead focus on conveying messages that illustrate here-and-now benefits, which are compelling to affluent consumers because they represent immediate, substantive improvements to the consumer's busy daily life.

Our research reveals two successful approaches marketing executives can use to equip PR staff and agencies with the bases for such messaging:

> *Connect benefits delivered to recognized consumer annoyances,* and communicate these benefits in easily digestible sound bites.

> *Create a step-change improvement through someone else's product,* through partnerships that broaden the consumer *and news* appeal of the combined offering.

The Solutions to Life's Problems

One way for marketers to communicate meaningful here-and-now solutions is to focus on the immediate improvements an offering can make to the annoyances of everyday life. For example, start-up airline JetBlue Airways has built its brand identity by taking aim at the negative feelings that many consumers have about air travel. Long realizing that many consumers found flying inconvenient and uncomfortable—e.g., crowded check-in lines, surly staff, cramped in-flight quarters, and limited entertainment options—the company was designed to address these problems. But many in the company saw its primary value proposition as being that of a low-cost carrier. A modest advertising launch budget of just $12.8 million ensured that PR would have to be a primary vehicle for getting its messages out to the market.[47]

The key for marketers looking to connect with the media and new mass-market consumers is to avoid launch messages that will be regarded as incremental improvements for secondary problems. Meeting this challenge can require executives to put aside preconceived notions about what makes their offering truly distinctive. For JetBlue, that meant choosing not to make too much of its status as a low-cost airline and recognizing that it could only be considered one of many. While CEO David Neeleman was initially tempted to promote JetBlue's pricing, PR executives pushed back, citing the limited opportunity to differentiate on fares alone. As Gareth Edmonson-Jones, JetBlue's vice president of corporate communications, recalled to *Advertising Age,* "David felt bargain hunters were our calling. We were saying, 'We should set our sights higher.' That first year felt subversive because we were saying, 'This is about bringing the humanity back to air travel,' and everyone else was saying, 'Aren't we just low fares?' And we were like, 'No! If you just pick it on price, you'll be destroyed.' It took a while, but finally everyone agreed we had to think and talk product, too."[48]

Working with management, JetBlue's in-house staff launched a series of targeted PR efforts that touted its instantly recognizable, substantive improvements to the air travel experience. These included spanking new Airbus planes, comfortable all-leather seats, premium service, and free live satellite television broadcasts to every seat. The PR team was proven right. By focusing on how JetBlue improved the "humanity" of air travel with premium perks, the airline won a flood of free publicity in lifestyle, business, and news outlets—ones that might not otherwise cover news of a new airline launch. Such success led one industry publication to name the airline Marketer of the Year.[49]

Marketers seeking to emulate JetBlue's approach may find the wind at their backs. Many media gatekeepers, such as the managing editors of leading publications and senior-level producers from radio and television, are themselves members of a relatively affluent crowd. Being part of the target audience, they are well positioned to see the benefits being touted quickly. And, like most of us, once they are convinced of the product's usefulness, they become eager to tell their friends (in this case, potentially millions of viewers and listeners) about the great new product or services they have discovered.

JetBlue earned some of its best coverage after winning over influential media figures. The television news program *Sixty Minutes* approached the airline for a profile after the positive firsthand experiences of its producer. And even a *New York Times* restaurant critic praised the airline in print after a staff member was unusually helpful in returning a laptop that he had forgotten on the plane.

By demonstrating how the airline solved the discomfort of air travel, JetBlue's PR strategy is helping to attract mass affluents in droves. A recent analysis of JetBlue customers revealed that the number one zip code of origin for its passengers is 10021, on New York City's well-heeled

Upper East Side. As the company's vice president of marketing told *Advertising Age,* "Grandma was always going to find us, but we've converted the travel snob."[50] In 2002, those travel snobs awarded JetBlue the Best Domestic Airline distinction in the upscale magazine *Condé Nast Traveler.*[51]

Sometimes, the problem can be solved by the promotion itself, as well as the product. Recognizing how much event-goers dislike using typical portable toilets, Procter & Gamble created Potty Palooza (their name, not ours), a semitrailer hauling twenty-seven individual bathrooms. Each air-conditioned unit comes complete not only with flowers, aromatherapy, and a TV, but also with Charmin Ultra toilet paper, Safeguard soap, and Bounty paper towels. Servicing over sixty events annually, ranging from the NFL Super Bowl to the Annual Bean Fest and Outhouse Race in Mountain View, Arkansas, the company expects more than a million visitors a year.[52] But a major benefit of the promotion goes beyond these consumers' goodwill. It is the vast amount of free media coverage P&G has obtained from scores of media outlets, including *USA Today* and CNN, which are fascinated by this unusual promotion to which every one of its viewers, readers, and listeners can relate.

Becoming a Vast Improvement

Not every offering can hope to capture the media's and the moneyed masses' attention by solving problems. But many companies have offerings with qualities that make them particularly valuable as part of *another* company's offerings. Public relations departments can use these qualities—and ensuing partnerships—as fodder for their pitches to the media, which, it seems, are intrigued by the notion of brands from different companies working as a team. American Airlines, for example, made forays into the news and lifestyle press in 1999 by entering into a partnership with audio-component maker Bose. The company agreed to provide American's first- and business-class passengers what was then an exclusive new product: high-tech Noise Cancellation Headsets that eliminated airplane noise with highly targeted sound waves.

The airline's PR efforts profited from the new brand association in two ways. First, its campaign was able to capitalize on the momentum of

Bose's new product introduction, because American offered the headsets months before they became publicly available. But American was also able to stress that its premium flyers would be the first to enjoy the innovation, positioning the airline as a leader in understanding affluent travelers' needs. The partnership with a major air carrier was also good for Bose. It allowed the company to win widespread coverage in major metropolitan dailies and trade publications—coverage that it might not have received if it had announced the offering on its own. And approval from the partner's customers can help sustain media interest well after the initial launch. Lynn Knight, an American Airlines product manager for cabin amenities, told *Air Transport World* that by offering and communicating the Bose ingredient, "our survey numbers have skyrocketed."[53]

Some partnership opportunities are so compelling once identified that cobranding the entire offering is appropriate; the combination itself becomes a key selling point. For example, a partnership between Lexus and Coach in the late 1990s generated substantial press coverage and helped win the attention of the affluent beyond traditional automotive media audiences. The automaker introduced a limited Coach Edition of its ES300 sedan. The cars included leather interiors and center consoles made by Coach, with the brand's logo appearing on the carpeted floor mats. Owners also received a Coach-made cabin bag and a leather portfolio to hold their car manual.

When Lexus extended the partnership to its LS400 sedan, its PR efforts concentrated on reaching up-market consumers through media outlets it might otherwise find challenging to pitch to without a tremendous wow story. In the weeks leading up to the launch, the press team sent influential editors at nonautomotive publications a Coach classic key fob with the message "It takes two to build a masterpiece," promising more details at a later date. The enticement garnered so much attention that the launch won coverage in major metropolitan markets such as New York and Chicago, beyond the scope of Lexus's typical press outlets in those areas. Such awareness enhanced the company's advertising efforts and helped support a healthy premium for the Coach Edition cars—which cost $3,000 extra on the ES300 version alone—while protecting margins during the last sales period of a three-year model cycle.[54]

Give Me the Sound Bite

Companies that develop compelling offerings for the new mass market have conquered only the first challenge. The subsequent challenges are finding the affluent, gaining their attention, and convincing them to buy. As the promotional successes of a few pioneering firms have demonstrated, these later challenges can be met with great success, though not by traditional mass-market or direct-marketing approaches alone. The new mass market is more demanding than before, expecting precise, meaningful messages about how an offering will improve their everyday lives. Yet, companies cannot afford to wine and dine these consumers on a one-to-one basis to deliver such messages, as has traditionally been done for the champagne-and-caviar wealthy and has been recreated to some extent in certain lavish one-to-one marketing approaches. The advertising, sales promotion, and PR strategies we have highlighted address this challenge head-on.

Though these strategies are powerful, they have so far been largely applied only to a single brand introduction, product improvement, or messaging challenge. How should companies evolve these strategies in the future to achieve the maximum impact for every brand and offering? We believe that future initiatives should resemble the integrated promotional efforts of Samsung, which has fired on every one of these promotional cylinders in an effort to bring its brand up-market. Lee Ki Tae, the chief executive of Samsung Electronics Telecommunications Network, reflected this drive when he told *BusinessWeek,* "What I want to see is Samsung becoming a BMW or Mercedes of handsets."[55]

Following a successful branding campaign in 2001, Samsung invested $200 million in a far-reaching global advertising effort entitled "DigitAll Experience." While media buys blanketed most outlets, Samsung designed the campaign's print ads to resemble pages from a fashion magazine, and made a particular effort to advertise the DigitAll message in upscale lifestyle publications. Samsung also entered the world of entertainment marketing by placing its products in the film *The Matrix Reloaded.* The movie, along with its associated print campaign, increased both brand and product awareness and their connection to high tech imagery. Also included were sales promotion events, through a so-called world tour that included presenting the company's latest product innovations in the halls of New York's Guggenheim Museum. In addition, a PR campaign was aimed at promoting awareness of Samsung's futuristic DigitAll products by aggressively publicizing the numerous design awards and product accolades that the company had received.

Collectively, this integrated neo-mass-marketing effort reflects the messages and media preferred by the new mass market, and it has already helped to fuel sharp growth in Samsung's brand value. According to a study conducted by *BusinessWeek* and consultancy INTER-BRAND, the company's brand value rose by an estimated 30 percent, to $8.3 billion in 2002.[56] By 2003 it had grown to $10.9 billion, a total of 61 percent growth in just two years. As other companies hone their focus on the moneyed masses, they too must unify their disparate promotional efforts in order to present a persuasive, unified face across brands and products. The result will be a leap forward in awareness, consideration, price realization, and, most importantly, sales.

PART FOUR

What Next?

Tomorrow's Mass Market

A reasonable concern for all marketers looking to make a shift toward selling to the moneyed masses is whether the current trend in income distribution is likely to last. Not to worry. The U.S. Bureau of Labor statistics projects a 70 percent growth in personal income between 2000 and 2010 (to $14 trillion in 2010). This is an amount so large that even if the current distribution changes somewhat, the moneyed masses will almost certainly receive the lion's share of this tremendous influx of cash. Personal consumption expenditure is also projected to grow by approximately 75 percent between the years 2000 and 2010, boding well for business so long as the growth occurs mostly among those who can afford it. For marketers, the important question about the future of income is whose incomes will grow, as well as by how much.

Of course, different economists slice the pie in different ways and also calculate different total figures. Regardless, there is certainly a high degree of income mobility in the United States, meaning that a great many of those in lower income households today are likely to find themselves in a higher bracket in years to come. One study, conducted by the U.S. Department of the Treasury, showed that 86 percent of the earners in the bottom 20 percent of incomes in 1979 were no longer there a decade later, with 66 percent of them making it at least to the middle 20 percent.[1] Nearly 15 percent had made it all the way to the top quintile of earners, and there was a similar level of upward mobility for those who started out in the middle quintile. Greater still than this mobility is the belief in it. A recent Gallup poll found that only 2 percent of Americans consider themselves rich, but 31 percent expect to be so one day. And this number jumps to 51 percent for those ages eighteen to twenty-nine.[2]

This hope for a more prosperous future, especially among the young, is supported by an equally important trend: the increasingly steeper curve of lifetime earnings. This trend is tied to the shift in the work force from blue-collar work toward knowledge work, where experience draws a premium. The old mass-market consumers could not expect to be earning much more later in life than they were shortly after joining the work force. In 1950, earnings peaked between the ages of 35 and 44, at roughly one and a half times that of 20- to 24-year-olds (a relatively meager 50 percent increase). In 1997, the peak earning years had shifted to between 45 and 54 years of age, with these earners garnering an average wage over three times that of 18- to 24-year-olds.[3] As economist Michael Cox and coauthor Richard Alm point out in describing this change in the pattern of American income, "The center of income distribution isn't a destination. It's just one step on the ladder of upward income mobility. Forty years ago, with a flatter earnings profile, families spent most of their working lives in the middle income brackets. Today's more rapid rise in incomes means they move to the top faster, spending less time defined as 'middle class.'"[4]

You Can't Take It with You

Another significant source of income to be considered when marketers are pondering the future of income and spending in U.S. households is inheritance. Researchers John Havens and Paul Schervish of Boston College's Social Welfare Research Institute predict that even by the most conservative of estimates, $41 trillion will pass from the U.S. baby boomers in the years between 1998 and 2052. The total could be as high as $136 trillion.[5] To understand the magnitude of this transfer, consider that total household wealth in the United States in 2003 was between $32 trillion and $36 trillion (the amount fluctuates with the market).

While only $25 trillion of the $41 trillion is expected to go to pure inheritance (the rest going to taxes, gifts, and endowments), this monumental transfer still represents an extraordinary event in the movement of intergenerational wealth.

And not just the wealthy will benefit. Two-thirds of the amount is expected to go to the heirs of the richest 7 percent, but these recipients will not necessarily be wealthy themselves. Inheritance tends to diffuse rather than concentrate wealth these days, unlike in more feudal times. And the remaining $14 trillion is not insignificant in light of the existing lower income and wealth levels of these remaining households. These calculations account for, in great detail, probable longer life spans, unpredictable market returns, increasing annuity participation, and a host of other factors, making this transfer of wealth a reliable windfall in the years ahead for a great many consumers. It should also help marketers breathe just a little easier.

Plus Ça Change...

Up to this point, our analysis has been decidedly ethnocentric, with examples drawn almost exclusively from the United States. But our U.S. focus has been more a matter of convenience than necessity. The world's free-market economies are all beginning to show signs of an emerging moneyed mass market. There are countless reasons that one can't make easy comparisons about incomes across countries (even the best economists have yet to build a data set with consistent measures), and some analysts argue that top income earners obfuscate their real earnings in all countries. But it is clear that something has happened to the average household incomes in many countries, and marketers would be well advised to know what it is. Even if the increase in wealth is not as pervasive or as nominally enriching as the one in the United States, we expect that marketers in every country will find a growing mass of consumers not among the superrich, but with enough new buying power to constitute an important market force of their own. In other words, marketers in every country will find a new, attractive mass market of their own today.

While we expect that the rules will remain in effect, we recognize that the ideas we put forth in this book must be tailored to each country's context. One major difference non-U.S. marketers will face in serving their own moneyed masses will be in their compatriot's attitudes toward affluence. Three highly regarded economists recently revealed that income inequality affects U.S. and European consumers differently.[6] While income inequality often had a negative effect on happiness in Europe in the study, it was almost neutral in the United States. The study also found Europeans to be more sensitive in general to social inequality. (This finding was supported by our international research on consumer receptivity toward differentiated offerings covered in chapter 2, which revealed European consumers are generally less receptive to offering differentiation across all product and service categories.) Executives should note who among their consumers is being affected, and not presume that attitudes regarding differentiated consumer treatment will be similar across countries.

For example, the same research suggested that in the United States, the rich lose sleep over income inequality, but the economically challenged appear to be less bothered by it. In Europe it was the reverse. This is likely due, at least in part, to differences in attitudes toward income mobility, belief in which has been shown to be significantly higher in the United States than in Europe. In his 2002 book, *The Elephant and the Flea: Reflections of a Reluctant Capitalist,* Charles Handy reflects that while envy is corrosive in some countries, in others like the United States, it seems "to fuel ambition and hope."[7]

Becoming a Trickle-Up and Trickle-Down Economy

Some of this hope is probably being generated by the real consumption gains that consumers have been experiencing—and are continuing to experience—over time. For example, it is well known that increasing demand for a product or service lowers its price, largely because greater demand encourages competition and allows companies to operate at a more efficient scale. The lower prices then increase demand and the cycle continues, a progression referred to by economists as the trickle-down process.[8] A DVD player that entered the market in 1997 at a price of roughly $800, for example, could be had in 2003 for under $60, and DVD penetration, as mentioned earlier, is growing by leaps and bounds. As far back as the turn of the nineteenth century, author and commentator G. K. Chesterton lamented this inevitable truth in his own curmudgeonly way: "Comforts that were rare among our forefathers are now multiplied in factories and handed out wholesale; and indeed, nobody nowadays, so long as he is content to go without air, space, quiet, decency and good manners, need be without anything whatever that he wants; or at least a reasonably cheap imitation of it."[9]

However, some economists today are more intrigued by the complementary reverse effect—the trickle-up process. Lower prices generated by growing mass-market demand have the effect of lowering expenses in high-income households, enabling these consumers to buy other, additional items on their wish lists. Kiminori Matsuyama, a professor of economics at Northwestern University, explains why this is so important: "Through this *trickle-up process* productivity gains in one industry lead to productivity gains in the next."[10]

Matsuyama has built a model of the trickle-down and trickle-up process. The results from the model help put the chart of household income distribution we presented in chapter 1 into a broader context; his model explains how different shapes of income distribution affect levels of purchasing and overall economic growth. He likens the process to dominoes: "[I]n order to trigger the process, the economy needs a critical mass of the rich households, which can afford to buy some goods, even when they are still expensive. With too much inequality, on the other hand, the process stops prematurely. This is because neither trickle-down nor trickle-up mechanisms would work if [income gaps are too great]. To put it another way, the rise of mass consumption [in a] society requires income to be distributed in certain ways."[11]

While the model is quite complex, its results support the intuitive conclusion that a more level and smoother distribution of income, as we see in figure 1-1 for the year 2000, can spur growth and actually increase access to goods for consumers at lower levels of income. Income growth at the top end is needed to drive the model, but the rest must keep up as well: The dominoes can't keep falling if they are spaced too far apart. The evolving shape of today's mass market should therefore be very encouraging to marketers who fear that consumers have become too saturated or jaded to increase their spending in the years ahead.

When they take this view (now that income distribution has done its part), marketers may recognize they have a responsibility to fill in the gaps that lead to an efficient flow of consumer offerings and that spur greater economic growth. These are the offerings consumers felt were missing when they said they must often choose between too good and not good enough. Bridging the gap is a heavy burden, to be sure, but one we are confident marketers will soon gladly accept.

Finale

Even if the rightward shift of income should dissipate some, the fundamental new shape of the income distribution curve is certain to remain. With expectations of real economic growth, companies can expect the moneyed masses to be the vanguard of new earning and spending, both in the United States and abroad.

Executives should find their newfound awareness of the moneyed masses exhilarating—so large a segment with so much money to spend represents a tremendous opportunity. What's more, the opportunity, in large part, has yet to be tapped. It is clear from the growing percentage of their income affluent consumers are dedicating to savings that no competitor, or set of competitors, has completely won the battle for share of income.

These untapped funds offer opportunity for marketers everywhere to profitably innovate. The goal is to find superior margins in offerings expensive enough to have superior margins, and to sell these offerings to those who can justly afford them. Herein lays the wealth for business in the phenomenon of mass affluence.

Reenvisioning an Industry

Throughout the book, we've described and illustrated the seven new rules of mass marketing. We've covered how to position offerings for today's moneyed masses; how to develop new offerings with new views about usage context, ownership, and return on investment; and how to bring these offering to today's mass market by getting closer to who and where these consumers are.

Perhaps the best way to drive the lessons home, though, is to apply the rules to an example product segment, in this case, the jewelry and watch business. The idea behind this exercise is to bring together all of the ideas presented, put them into sharper focus, and give readers some additional insight into how they might assess their own offerings' market situation and formulate a host of new ideas about how to grow their business. We selected jewelry and watches because it is a consumption category that has an aura of luxury and wealth, but is also one in which nearly every consumer participates. It is also a category one might assume performed fairly well in the enriching economic run-up of the 1990s.

First, we considered historic spending in the category. We looked at both groups in which jewelry and watch spending was measured in the U.S. Bureau of Statistics Consumer Expenditure Data. In these two groups—Other Apparel and the Jewelry and Watches subcategory of the Gifts group—consumer spending failed to grow with income. As part of the Other Apparel group, expenditures on jewelry and watches were classed in a subcategory with belts and dry-cleaning expenditures. Spending in the subcategory declined by 9 percent in 2000 dollars in the 1990s and did not increase proportionally with average income by quintile. As a subcategory of the Gifts group, Jewelry and Watches expenditures remained constant in real dollars relative to 1984, and spending as a percentage of income declined dramatically.[1] The jewelry and watches industry was evidently more challenged than one might initially suspect.

A Diamond in the Rough

Since 50 percent of consumer spending in the jewelry category is on diamonds, our next move was to look at the average selling price of diamonds over time to see if a change in diamond prices could be the cause of the decline. Wholesale diamond prices have risen steadily since at least the 1970s, as a result of the highly coordinated nature of their market. Though retail prices are not perfectly correlated with wholesale prices, the stagnation in this portion of jewelry sales has more likely been caused by price competition and commoditization of the offering. While the diamond jewelry industry recognizes that differentiation is a must, the latest ongoing trend in diamonds is branding (emphasizing a guarantee of cut quality), which is costing the industry millions of dollars in marketing expenditures and is resulting in what many industry analysts regard as minimal consumer impact. (Did you even know that diamonds were now being branded?)

Gold prices might likewise have been a factor in some portion of the relative spending decline. A 1997 survey, however, found that "85 percent of U.S. customers have no knowledge of the price of gold, and half of the 15 percent who claim to know the price are wrong."[2]

Although jewelry and watches clearly exist at every price point, it was apparent to us at this point that the moneyed masses do not recognize sufficient must-have pieces that would drive up their spending. Here's where the fun began. We started speculating about how the seven new rules of mass marketing might play out.

For example, although there is an astonishing array of watch brands on the market (eighteen in the Swatch group alone, from "soup" to "caviar"), it seems companies still have a way to go in establishing dominant new-middle-ground brands (though watches over $2,000 have been growing by a healthy 13 percent a year).[3] How challenging has it been to get consumers to move up in price for a product that performs extremely well at even the lowest price points? President Bill Clinton chose to wear a Timex Ironman Triathlon during his term in office, presumably because he considered it the right watch for him. Yet the watch retails for only $40; far less than watchmakers must hope someone of his stature would spend on a watch. And he was certainly not alone. Within a year of its introduction in 1986, the Ironman Triathlon became America's best-selling sports watch, and future lines for men and women made it the *world's* best-selling sports watch, a distinction it held through the 1990s.[4]

While it did not capture the new middle ground in terms of an elevated price point, the watch achieved its level of success using another of our rules. Like the wet suit and bicycle-parts examples in chapter 4, the Ironman was designed for a particular *use*, in partnership with serious athletes and industrial designers. With USA Triathlon (the sport's governing body) estimating only 90,000 Americans participating in the sport, the watch has clearly been appreciated by a great many consumers more for its authenticity and fashion statement than for its actual use.[5]

We realize that the Triathlon watch is not alone. Timex and other watchmakers have made many additional efforts at design for occasion (e.g., the dive, sport, and dress watches, which are all fairly distinct, and which many companies have specialized in providing). But there is ample opportunity remaining. For example, Tag Heuer has had startling success introducing a watch specifically for golf. In late 2002 the company partnered with Tiger Woods to create the Tiger Woods Link Calibre 36 model. While demand has been tremendous, what is surprising about the timepiece's success is that Woods has long preferred to play the sport without wearing a watch. This now irrelevant detail did not keep the company from targeting what has been for them a clearly attractive market. The company reports that 90 percent of golfers (which we numbered at over 26 million in chapter 2) do not wear watches when they play![6] That Tag Heuer was able to identify the opportunity in golf usage should come as no surprise. The company was the first to introduce pocket chronographs in 1882 for use in horseracing, which the company followed up with a patented waterproof watch in 1895 and a string of auto racing and other sports related watches throughout the 1900s.[7]

The jewelry market has seen similar opportunities, and occasional successes. Tiffany & Co. has captured at least a portion of the new middle ground for jewelery by successfully introducing expanded lines of sterling silver pieces. These items are much more affordable than gold, yet retain the aura of quality and affluence consumers desire. Although jewelry marketers have made limited forays into the occasional-use and special-use arena, there remains a great deal of opportunity. Consider the tennis bracelet. Although this piece created an entire fashion trend, that was some years ago. Where is travel jewelry, for example, distinguished by stronger clasps and other appreciable design features that make it perfect for active travelers roaming in rougher ports of call?

Diamond marketers have done a phenomenal job of creating the compulsory diamond engagement ring and the ten-year anniversary band. (The diamond engagement ring is a fashion created in the United States only in the late 1930s and was not introduced into Japan—where a quarter of all diamonds are now sold—until the early 1960s.) So where is the sapphire sweet-sixteen ring or other pieces of jewelry dedicated to honoring important milestones in the lives of millions of adults, including those unlikely to ever marry?

There are signs of movement in this arena, however. The DeBeers Group has recently gone after the other hand of women—the right one—with a collection of sixteen rings, hoping for multiple purchases. The group aims to grow demand for their smaller diamonds, and it is targeting women between the ages of thirty and fifty-four with household incomes over $100,000.[8] We are curious to see where DeBeers goes next.

Still, there are many marketing strategies yet to be mined. For example, though a diamond may be forever, must its ownership be? Jewelry and watches are still primarily purchased as lifetime investments. Why?

New York jeweler Tourneau has garnered success by creating a guaranteed-price return policy for the watches it sells and has created an active resale market in its retail stores and online, but others have been slow to follow. Why can't a person easily lease a $4,000 watch or necklace, say, at $40 a month, with the option to purchase later based on residual value? Or better yet, time-share a $50,000 one. Deploying this strategy successfully might take a considerable reframing of consumer attitudes about jewelry ownership (similar to the one taken on by IKEA in furniture), but surely, there is a value proposition to being a part owner (not renter) of a $250,000 or $500,000 collection of jewelry.

For example, a jeweler could sell shares in a $250,000 collection for an affordable $5,000. The company would then insure and maintain the collection, giving owners access to all the pieces for all their special occasions and even daily wear. Owners would impress their friends (and rivals) with jewelry far more expensive than they could otherwise afford, in addition to having a variety that implies much broader wealth and ownership. The jeweler could continue to refresh the collection, selling off and replacing worn pieces or those that the owners have become bored with, and could take a service fee in the process.

The best-case result of such an offering could be a sea change in the demand for high-end jewelry. The worst case might still be OK, a model not unlike the modern health club, where hundreds of consumers share a valuable set of resources. Most members would use the service only occasionally, while still being committed to it and happily paying the service fees.

Is there a return on consumption for jewelry ownership? What about small dividends recognizing watch or jewelry wearers? For example, there could be complimentary drinks on certain nights at sporting events or social events for Rolex wearers. And what is the jewelry industry doing to ensure the investment properties of its offerings? Patek-Philippe is highlighting the heirloom quality of its watches, but what about necklaces? Can the industry do a better job of guaranteeing residual values, creating increasingly liquid markets that would lessen consumers' apprehension about jewelry's being a sunk cost?

Many jewelers that serve the luxury market are well known, even to those who can only dream. Recall the movie *Breakfast at Tiffany's*. And every mall has its requisite branded chain purveyor. But where is the national brand that is dedicated to the service of the moneyed masses, but not superrich? Where is the brand that has just the right balance of assortment, location, and personal service that makes its customers feel a cut above, yet not apprehensive about not measuring up to the jeweler's standards?

Wrapping It Up

How good are jewelers at knowing their customers and communicating their knowledge and respect for the buyer-seller relationship? Certainly the 26,000 independently owned jewelry stores work on this every day with customers in their communities. But the experience of one watch owner demonstrates that some firms have a long way to go in effectively communicating with the moneyed masses. Though this customer has purchased three watches from a certain top luxury brand, he has never been personally contacted or invited back to the store. Instead, the company regularly mails him a slick (and clearly expensive) in-house marketing publication built around hip topics like the modern art scene, something he cares nothing for. Even making an allowance for its auto-personalized letter, these mass mailings are so badly matched to his expectations that he is unsure he will ever be as interested in the company's products the same way again.

We've raised a host of questions for the jewelers and watchmakers of the world—and they're not likely to be solved quickly or easily. (And we recognize that being an armchair marketer, when you have our research on hand, is not unlike being an armchair football coach.) Nonetheless, these are the questions that the moneyed masses will soon be asking—if they are not already. And the consumers will be followed only shortly thereafter by shareholders. Successful executives will, we hope, be well on their way to having answers by the time the questions are fully vetted in the marketplace. We believe that the strategies, data, and examples presented throughout this book will help them prepare.

Notes

Preface

1. For a more detailed discussion of balancing customer relationship investments with return, see Robert E. Wollan and Paul F. Nunes, "Toward a Customer Meritocracy," *Outlook* (published by Accenture) 14, no. 2 (July 2002).

Chapter 1

1. We recognize income is only one of the three standard economic measures of affluence. The other two are earnings (from employment, generally) and wealth, or accumulated assets. We elected to focus on income because of its very high correlation with wealth and especially with household expenditure. Income has also become more highly correlated with earnings as capital gains have become a smaller portion of total income for the affluent since the early 1900s.

2. According to Steve Cocheo, executive editor of the *ABA Banking Journal*, Sutton attributed the quote to a fabrication by a reporter on deadline. Being enterprising, however, Sutton did use the quote in the title of his second book, *Where the Money Was: The Memoirs of a Bank Robber* (New York: Viking Press, 1976), sealing the connection forever <http://www.banking.com/aba/profile_0397.htm> (accessed 5 November 2003).

3. Ibid.

4. The shape is actually well known to economists and statisticians as a lognormal curve. And ironically, although income is often used as the prime example of this type of distribution, managers are rarely able to make the reverse connection.

5. In year 2001 CPI-U-RS adjusted dollars, as reported in DeNavas-Walt, Carmen and Robert Cleveland, U.S. Census Bureau, Current Population Reports, P60-218, Money Income in the United States: 2001, U.S. Government Printing Office, Washington, DC, 2002.

6. "What the Boss Makes," *Forbes* Web page, <http://www.forbes.com/2003/04/23/ceoland.html> (accessed 30 October 2003).

7. Though the shift is largely uncontested, its underlying cause is the center of fierce ongoing debate, with little consensus emerging from leading economists. Definite influences include the rise in dual-income households, the growing wage disparity among male earners, winner-take-all compensation levels for top-performing employees in many

industries, and the premium for knowledge work coupled with the loss of manufacturing work to open borders. There is almost no agreement, however, on the relative impact of these and other factors, nor is there agreement on their desirability, or lack thereof. Therefore, we leave these questions to the reader for further investigation.

8. U.S. Internal Revenue Service, "[Individual Income Tax] Returns with Positive Adjusted Gross Income (AGI): Number of Returns, Shares of AGI and Total Income Tax, AGI Floor on Percentiles in Current and Constant Dollars, and Average Tax Rates, by Selected Descending Cumulative Percentiles of Returns Based on Income Size Using the Definition of AGI for Each Year, Tax Years 1986–2001," Internal Revenue Service Web page, <http://www.irs.gov/pub/irs-soi/01in01ts.xls> (accessed 15 November 2003).

9. Elizabeth Shove and Alan Ward of Lancaster University have identified six "mechanisms of consumption," each of which is clearly altered by increased affluence. Marketers must understand how prosperity changes the way we buy things to generate social comparison; create self-identity; find mental stimulation (novelty); build consistency across our possessions (usually of quality, the so-called Diderot effect); increase the specialization of what we own to improve its suitability and performance; and better leverage new infrastructures of consumption, like electricity and computing power. See Elizabeth Shove and Alan Ward, "Inconspicuous Consumption: The Sociology of Consumption and the Environment," <http://www.comp.lancs.ac.uk/sociology/soc001aw.html> (accessed 5 November 2003).

10. Pete Engardio, Aaron Bernstein, and Manjeet Kripalani, "The New Global Job Shift," *BusinessWeek,* 3 February 2003, <http://businessweek.com/magazine/content/03_05/b3818001.htm> (accessed 30 October 2003).

11. Christine Spivey, "U.S. Outsourcing Decelerates," March 2002, <http://www.forrester.com/ER/Research/Report/Summary/0,1338,13161,00.html> (accessed 30 October 2003).

12. See W. Michael Cox and Richard Alm, *Myths of the Rich and Poor* (New York: Basic Books, 1999), for a highly detailed discussion.

13. Robert H. Frank, *Luxury Fever: Money and Happiness in an Era of Excess* (New York: Free Press, 1999), 15.

14. U.S. Bureau of Labor Statistics, "Consumer Expenditure Survey 1984 to 2001," <http://www.bls.gov/cex/csxstnd.htm> (accessed 5 November 2003). We report numbers based on before-tax income because detailed analysis of the Consumer Expenditure Survey data revealed errors in the reported after-tax earnings, errors acknowledged by the U.S. Bureau of Labor Statistics. We therefore also ran the regression using proxies for after-tax income based on applying weighted tax averages. In all cases, however, the results are similar and the differences do not materially affect the results of the findings.

15. The three-year averages are somewhat arbitrary, but they help the reader to better see what is evident in the graph, particularly the impact of this shift on spending.

16. K. Dynan, J. Skinner, and S. Zeldes, "Do the Rich Save More?" working paper 7906, National Bureau of Economic Research, Cambridge, 2000. Available at <http://www.nber.org/papers/w7906>.

17. Christopher D. Carroll, "Why Do the Rich Save So Much?" working paper 6549, National Bureau of Economic Research, Cambridge, May 1998. Available at <http://www.nber.org/papers/w6549>.

18. For a more detailed discussion of how media portrayals of affluent lifestyles affect consumption, see Juliet Schor, *The Overspent American* (New York: Basic Books, 1998), 80.

19. For detailed results of this study, see Paul F. Nunes and Brian A. Johnson, "Where the Money Is," 2002, Accenture Web page, <http://www.accenture.com/xd/xd.asp?it= enweb&xd=_ins/insresearchreportabstract_150.xml> (accessed 12 February 2004).

20. For detailed results of this study, see Paul F. Nunes and Brian A. Johnson, "Mind the Gap: Consumer Attitudes to Innovation," 29 October 2002, Accenture Web page, <http://www.accenture.com/xd/xd.asp?it=enweb&xd=services\sba\sba_ideas_innovation. xml> (accessed 21 January 2004).

21. Thomas Stanley and William Danko, *The Millionaire Next Door* (New York: Pocket Star Books, 1996), 37.

22. Bernard Dubois and Patrick Duquesne, "The Market for Luxury Goods: Income versus Culture," *European Journal of Marketing* 27, no. 1 (1993): 35–44.

23. Lauren Weber, "The Diamond Game: Shedding Its Mystery," *New York Times,* 8 April 2001.

24. Gian Luigi Longinotti-Buitoni, *Selling Dreams: How to Make Any Product Irresistible* (Collingdale, PA: Diane Publishing Company, 1999).

25. Richard S. Tedlow, *New and Improved: The Story of Mass Marketing in America* (New York: Basic Books, 1990), 4.

26. Daniel Akst, "Where Those Paychecks Come From," *Wall Street Journal,* 7 May 2003.

Chapter 2

1. Gerry Dulac, "Missing the Green," *Pittsburgh Post-Gazette,* 7 April 2002.

2. Robert G. Gowland, "Early Golf Clubs and Balls," *The Magazine Antiques,* 1 August 2001, 184.

3. Wal-Mart Web page, <http://www.walmart.com/catalog/product_listing.gsp?cat= 5208&path=0%3A4125%3A4152%3A5208> (thirty-pack of Top-Flite XL 3000 balls for $35.76), (accessed 5 November 2003).

4. Mike Stachura, "The Best Buy in Golf? It's the Low-Price Balls. Here's Why," *Golf Digest,* 1 July 2002, 59.

5. Adam Gorlick, "Top-Flite Golf Co. Files for Bankruptcy," AP press release, 30 June 2003.

6. For industry-specific details, see Paul F. Nunes and Brian A. Johnson, "Mind the Gap: Consumer Attitudes to Innovation," 29 October 2002, Accenture Web page, <http://www. accenture.com/xd/xd.asp?it=enweb&xd=services\sba\sba_ideas_innovation.xml> (accessed 21 January 2004).

7. Fred Cooper, telephone interview by author, tape recording, 21 March 2003.

8. Kira McCarron, telephone interview by author, tape recording, 21 March 2003.

9. Andrew Bary, "Gimme Shelter," *Barron's,* 10 February 2003, 18–19.

10. Cooper interview, 21 March 2003.

11. McCarron interview, 21 March 2003.

12. Ibid.

13. "What Makes Coach a Winner? A Sharply Focused Game Plan," *Home Furnishing News,* 13 January 2003, 20.

14. Julia Boorstin, "How Coach Got Hot," *Fortune,* 28 October 2002, 131.

15. Coach, Annual Report 2002.

16. Boorstin, "How Coach Got Hot."

17. Leigh Gallagher, "Endangered Species," *Forbes,* 31 May 1999, 105.

18. Sandra Dolbow, "Strategy: Lacoste Looks to Take Its Crocodile Upstream," *Brandweek,* 3 June 2002.

19. Jeremy Kahn, "Gillette Loses Face," *Fortune,* 8 November 1999, 147.

20. Paula Hendrickson, "Groomed for Success," *Point of Purchase,* April 2002, 35.

21. Ibid.

22. Naomi Aoki, "Gillette Creates a Little Buzz with its New Razor," *Boston Globe,* 16 January 2004.

23. Naomi Aoki, "The War of the Razors: Gillette–Schick Fight over Patent Shows the Cutthroat World of Consumer Products," *Boston Globe,* 31 August 2003.

24. "P&G's Crest Brand Continues to Gain Momentum," *Chain Drug Review,* 24 June 2002, 86.

25. Neil Buckley, "The E-Route to a Whiter Smile," *Financial Times,* 26 August 2002, 8.

26. A. G. Lafley, Event Brief of Q4 2003 Procter & Gamble Company Earnings Conference Call, 31 July 2003 (FDCH e-Media, Inc., 2003).

27. Melinda Fulmer, "Growing Bags of Green," *Los Angeles Times,* 21 August 2002.

28. Jill Duman, "Dole Fresh Vegetables Launches Museum of Salad in New York City," *Monterey County Herald,* 13 May 2002.

29. Matt Nauman, "Volvo SUV Goes Against the Mainstream," *San Jose Mercury-News,* 14 December 2002.

30. Gregory J. White and Joseph B. White, "Luxury Lite," *Wall Street Journal,* 7 February 2003.

31. Terry Box, "Entry-Level Luxury Cars Drive Up Dealer's Profit," *Dallas Morning News,* 21 September 2002.

32. Neal E. Boudette and Jeffrey Ball, "Europe's Luxury Cars Show Some Vulnerability," *Wall Street Journal,* 12 November 2002.

33. Gail Edmondson, Christine Tierney, and Chris Palmeri, "Classy Cars," *BusinessWeek,* 24 March 2003, 62.

34. Kathleen Kerwin, "Ford: Luxury Is Job One," *BusinessWeek,* 11 November 2002, 116.

35. Mark Rechtin, "Mass Luxury: Folly or Savvy Business?" *Automotive News,* 24 June 2002, 1.

36. Jim DuPlessis, "BMW Plant Will Gear Up Slowly," *(Columbia, S.C.) State,* 16 November 2002.

37. Eileen Daspin, "The T-Shirt You Can't Get," *Wall Street Journal,* 10 October 2003.

38. Sabrina Jones, "Wait of Success," *Washington Post,* 4 August 2002.

39. Bob Sperber, "Fast Casual Dining Ahead," *Brandweek,* 2 September 2002.

40. W. Michael Cox and Richard Alm, *Myths of the Rich and Poor* (New York: Basic Books, 1999), 39–45.

41. Christopher C. Muller, "Redefining Value: The Hamburger Price War," *Cornell Hotel and Restaurant Administration Quarterly,* June 1997, 62–73.

42. Sperber, "Fast Casual Dining Ahead."

43. Tiffany Montgomery, "Taco Bell's New Product Aims to Draw More Upscale Customers," *Orange County Register,* 19 June 2002.

44. Bob Sperber "Taco Bell Builds Beyond Border Bowls," *Brandweek,* 4 November 2002.

45. Irene B. Rosenfeld, "Brand Management in a Marketplace War Zone," *Journal of Advertising Research,* September/October 1997, 85–89.

46. Stephanie Thompson, "*Brandweek*'s Marketers of the Year: Mary Kay Haben, Kraft Pizza Co.," *Mediaweek,* 20 October 1997.

47. Stephanie Thompson, "Kraft's DiGiorno Pizza Links to Golf in Drive to Reach Upscale Families," *Brandweek,* 23 March 1998.

48. Michael Hartnett, "It's a Bird, It's a Plane: It's Superpremium Pizza," *Frozen Food Age,* May 2001, 28.

49. Neal E. Boudette, "VW's $100,000 Phaeton Is Slow Out of the Gate," *Wall Street Journal,* 12 February 2003.

Chapter 3

1. Deborah Ball and Shirley Leung, "Latte Versus Latte," *Wall Street Journal,* 10 February 2004.

2. "Leading Online Directory Assistance Provider Announces New Name and URL," *PR Newswire,* 13 March 2003.

3. Jeff Gelles, "World-Class Customer Experience at Dell Now Costs Extra," *Philadelphia Inquirer,* 7 July 2002.

4. Robert E. Wollan and Paul F. Nunes, "Creating a Customer Service Meritocracy," *Outlook* (published by Accenture), no. 2 (July 2002).

5. Sam I. Hill, Jack McGrath, and Sandeep Dayal, "How to Brand Sand," *Strategy and Business,* April 1998, 22–34.

6. Daniel S. Hamermesh and Jungmin Lee, "Stressed Out on Four Continents: Time Crunch or Yuppie Kvetch?" working paper 10186, National Bureau of Economic Research, Cambridge, December 2002. Available at <http://papers.nber.org/papers/W10186>.

7. Edward Baig, "Platinum Cards: Move Over, Amex," *BusinessWeek,* 14 June 1997, <http://www.businessweek.com/1996/34/b3489117.htm> (accessed 30 October 2003).

8. Readers interested in further discussion of pricing strategies and tactics have at their disposal a wide variety of resources, including the seminal article by Gerard J. Tellis, "Beyond the Many Faces of Price: An Integration of Pricing Strategies," *Journal of Marketing* 50, no. 4 (October 1986): 146–160.

9. Erik Brynjolfsson and Michael D. Smith, "Frictionless Commerce? A Comparison of Internet and Conventional Retailers," *Management Science* 46, no. 4 (2000): 563–585.

10. Julia Angwin and Motoko Rich, "Big Hotel Chains Are Striking Back Against Web Sites," *Wall Street Journal,* 14 March 2003.

11. For more on the dynamics of this ironic pricing situation, see "Full Price: A Young Woman, an Appendectomy, and a $19,000 Debt—Ms. Nix Confronts Harsh Fact of Health-Care Economics: Uninsured Are Billed More—Moving in with Mom at Age 25," *Wall Street Journal,* 17 March 2003.

12. David Ulph and Nir Vulkan, "Electronic Commerce and Competitive First-Degree Price Discrimination," December 2000, <http://else.econ.ucl.ac.uk/papers/vulkan.pdf> (accessed 29 October 2003).

13. And there is, of course, no substitute for sound ethical decision making. Here we point our readers to the work of Joseph Badaracco, especially *Defining Moments: When Managers Must Choose Between Right and Right* (Boston: Harvard Business School Press, 1997).

14. Marcia Stepanek, "Weblining: Companies Are Using Your Personal Data to Limit Your Choices—And Force You to Pay More for Products" *BusinessWeek,* 3 April 2000, <http://www.businessweek.com/2000/00_14/b3675027.htm> (accessed 29 October 2003).

15. Gary H. Anthes, "Picking Winners and Losers," *Computerworld,* 18 February 2002, 34.

16. David Streitfeld, "On the Web, Price Tags Blur: What You Pay Could Depend on Who You Are," *Washington Post,* 27 September 2000.

17. Anthony Danna and Oscar H. Gandy Jr., "All That Glitters Is Not Gold: Digging Beneath the Surface of Data Mining," *Journal of Business Ethics* 40, no. 4, (November 2002): 373–386.

18. Donna L. Goodison, "Kozmo.com Wraps Up Food Deal, and Faces Redlining Rap," *Boston Business Journal,* 28 April 2000.

19. Daniel Kahneman, Jack Knetsch, and Richard Thaler, "Fairness as Constraint on Profit Seeking," *American Economic Review* 76, no. 4, (1986): 728–741.

20. More than just a matter of sulking, backlash can result in a loss of customer goodwill or even loss of brand equity. Kahneman, Knetsch, and Thaler, "Fairness as Constraint," describe three possible enforcement actions available to customers for expressing their displeasure with a company's unfair actions. First, customers can abandon the company, or threaten to do so, when competitors finally enter the market. Second, they can refuse to purchase from a company because of the loss of the firm's reputation from the offending, unfair act. (This response is often made out of simple spite and even at a cost to the customers themselves.) Third, they can avoid the companies' offerings because of a desire to act fairly and to feel good about their actions and to possibly bring the company in line. With these in mind, marketing executives should look to avert consumers who desire enforcement, rather then trying to overcome this customer behavior later.

21. Barbara Kingsley, "Theme Is Status," *Orange County Register*, 29 October 1999.

22. Ibid.

23. Universal Studios Web page, <http://www.usoinfo.com/Parkinfo/tickets.html# UniversalStudiosVIPTour> (accessed 2 November 2003).

24. Christine Blank, "Parking It for Fun," *American Demographics,* 1 April 1998, 6.

25. "Nowhere Else on Earth," *Maclean's* (advertising supplement), 11 November 2002, 8.

26. Edward Goldman, telephone interview by author, tape recording, 19 March 2003.

27. Alexander Laback, telephone interview by author, tape recording, 10 September 2001.

28. Stephen Wood, "Winter Pursuits: It's A Rich Man's Game," *Independent* (London), 8 February 2003.

29. Ibid.

Chapter 4

1. D. Marie Victoriana, Victorian Gallery Web page, <http://www.geocities.com/ Wellesley/Gazebo/9456/VLady/dinner/dinner.html> (accessed 10 September 2002).

2. Gaye Bland, Rogers Historical Museum Web page, <http://www.rogersarkansas. com/museum/donationOfTheMonth/02-02.asp> (accessed 12 February 2004).

3. Pilar Guzman, "Hey, Man, What's for Dinner?" *New York Times,* 28 August 2002.

4. In describing specialization as an important mechanism that drives consumption, Elizabeth Shove and Alan Warde of Lancaster University point out: "The paraphernalia required to be a successful social participant at Ascot, Henley, the White City, the opera and the rock concert, as well as to be an employee, a supporter of a football team and a dabbler in d-i-y [do-it-yourself, or home repair] is enormously varied and costly, often requiring a gallery of items that are largely or potentially alike in terms of function but which are in fact quite precisely specialised, so much so that they are no longer interchangeable. It is probably true that informalisation has relaxed rules about what it [*sic*] is

appropriate to wear on what occasions, thereby moderating the effect to some degree. But the constant invention of new activities, or more often the separation of once similar activities into demarcated and specialized fields, each requiring singular accoutrements, is a powerful social and commercial impetus to expanded consumption." Elizabeth Shove and Alan Warde, "Inconspicuous Consumption: The Sociology of Consumption and the Environment," Department of Sociology, Lancaster University, revised October 1998, <http://www.comp.lancs.ac.uk/sociology/soc001aw.html> (accessed 29 October 2003).

5. Grant McCracken, *Culture and Consumption* (Bloomington, IN: Indiana University Press), 19.

6. Linda O'Keeffe, *Shoes: A Celebration of Pumps, Sandals, Slippers and More* (New York: Workman Publishing, 1996), as reported in Beverly Hall Lawrence, "Polishing the Shoe's Image," *Newsday* (New York), 3 April 1997.

7. Shove and Warde, "Inconspicuous Consumption: The Sociology of Consumption and the Environment."

8. William A. Rossi, "The Shoe Industry's Twenty-Year Snooze: Sales Trends in the Footwear Industry," *Footwear News*, 22 June 1998, 12.

9. Louis Ripple, telephone interview by author, tape recording, 19 February 2003.

10. Stuart B. Chirls, "Americans Head for the Water: In, On, and Under," *Daily News Record*, 31 July 1989, 18.

11. Alan Cooperman, "Imelda Marcos Had 2,000 Pairs, But Did She Have One of These?" Associated Press, 11 July 1989, published in "Water Shoe Is a Runaway Hit," San Francisco Chronicle, 7 August 1989.

12. Bob Ford, "Other Shoe Drops: Converse Seeks Bankruptcy Protection," *Philadelphia Inquirer*, 23 January 2001.

13. John Kenneth Galbraith, *The Affluent Society* (Boston: Houghton Mifflin, 1998), 120–121.

14. U.S. Census Bureau, "Statistical Abstract of the United States: 2000," <http://www.census.gov/prod/www/statistical-abstract-us.html> (accessed 29 October 2003).

15. David Kiley, "Baby Boomers Splurge on 'Road Candy,' Just for Fun; Buyers Make Room for Third—Even Fourth—Cars in the Driveway," *USA Today*, 21 June 2002.

16. Ibid.

17. "New Single-Family Home Characteristics," *Housing Economics* 50, no. 7, (July 2002). 13–18.

18. Patrick O'Driscoll, "Only Ashes Left of 'Dream Place,'" *USA Today*, 1 July 2002, <http:www.usatoday.com/news/nation/2002/07/02/rebuild.htm> (accessed 29 October 2003).

19. Soap and Detergent Association Web page, <http://inventors.about.com/gi/dynamic/offsite.htm?site=http://www.sdahq.org/sdalatest/html/soaphistory1.htm> (accessed 29 October 2003).

20. Dial Corporation Web page, <http://www.dialcorp.com/index.cfm?page_id=15> (accessed 29 October 2003).

21. For the frequency of shampooing, see Leigh Grogan, "Heads Above the Rest?" <http://www.bonitabanner.com/02/08/neapolitan/d659157a.htm> (accessed 29 October 2003).

22. Johnson & Johnson and its subsidiaries own T-Gel and Nizoral A-D, two of the ten best-selling of any shampoos by dollar sales.

23. Euromonitor Web page, <http://www.euromonitor.com/results.asp?orderby=full textsearch&company=&username=&password=&search=Johnson+and+Johnson+baby +care&x=0&y=0> (accessed 29 October 2003).

24. Grogan, "Heads Above the Rest?"

25. In-Cosmetics Web page, <http://www.in-cosmetics.com/page.cfm/Link=49> (accessed 29 October 2002).

26. Williams-Sonoma Web page, <http://ww1.williams-sonoma.com/cat/pip.cfm? src=srki1%7Cwasparagus%2Fsrki1%7Cwasparagas%2Fhme%2Fhme&skus=4547964& pkey=sa0s10asparagus&cmsrc=sch> (accessed 5 November 2003).

27. Walter Mossberg, "The Mossberg Solution: Is That an iPod in Your Pocket? More Clothing Makers Target Gadget Users; a Ski-Jacket with a Remote Sewn In," *Wall Street Journal,* 15 January 2003.

28. According to the NPD Group (Florence, Italy), a market information company.

29. Betsy McKay, "Thinking Inside the Box Helps Soda Makers Boost Sales," *Wall Street Journal,* 2 August 2002.

30. Erin Brennan, quoted in Mekeisha Madden, "Mints Go Mod; Designer Tins, New Flavors Are the Latest Trends in the Billion Dollar Business of Freshening Breath," *News Tribune* (Tacoma, WA), 27 February 2002.

31. PR Newswire, "Starbucks Customers Have Enjoyed 1.7 Billion After Coffee Mints . . . So Cool," press release, 25 September 2002.

32. Body Glove Web page, <http://www.bodyglove.com/company/company.php> (accessed 29 October 2003).

33. Schwinn's assets were acquired by Pacific Cycle LLC in 2001, which continues to sell Schwinn branded products.

34. Mike Larsen, telephone interview by author, tape recording, 12 August 2002.

35. Ibid.

36. Ibid.

37. J. Peterman Web page, <http://www.jpeterman.com/default.htm> (accessed 5 November 2003).

38. U.S. Census Bureau, "Statistical Abstract of the United States: 2001."

39. Troung Phouc Khanh, "Atherton, California, Wins Honor of State's Car Capital," *San Jose Mercury News,* 21 May 2002.

40. Ray A. Smith, "A Crypt to Die For," *Wall Street Journal,* 24 September 2003.

41. Thorstein Veblen, *The Theory of the Leisure Class* (1899; reprint, New York: Penguin Books, 1994), 100.

42. H. L. Mencken, "Professor Veblen" (1919), reprinted in "Thorstein's Endless Train of Thought: Where's the Caboose?" <http://www.blancmange.net/tmh/articles/hlm_veblen.html>, (accessed 29 October 2003).

43. Veblen, *Theory of the Leisure Class,* 101.

Chapter 5

1. Starkey Institute Web page, <http://www.starkeyintl.com/placement_terms.html> (accessed 29 October 2003).

2. Chana R. Schoenberger, "Ask Jeeves," *Forbes,* 13 November 2000, 304.

3. Steve Jordon, "Hours Add Up for Americans," *Omaha World-Herald,* 9 September 2002.

4. Mimi Avins, "Tranquility the House a Haven on the Home Front; Some Scale Back Design Plans, While Others Splurge in a Live-for-Now Attitude," *Los Angeles Times,* 18 October 2001.

5. U.S. Census Bureau, <http://www.census.gov/const/C25Ann/sftotalmedavgsqft.pdf> (accessed 12 February 2004).

6. L. Z. Granderson, "Searching for Space," *Atlanta Journal-Constitution,* 13 June 2002.

7. FirstService Corporation, Annual Report 2003.

8. Tammy Stables Battaglia, "Home Buyers Set Store by the Pantry as a Top Amenity," *Cleveland Plain Dealer,* 26 January 2002.

9. Thomas C. Boyd and Diane M. McConocha, "Consumer Household Materials and Logistics Management," *Journal of Consumer Affairs* 30, (summer 1996): 218.

10. Association of Home Appliance Manufacturers Web page, 2001 <http://www. aham.org/News/newslist.cfm> (accessed 29 October 2003).

11. For prices of entry-level dishwashers, see Best Buy Web page, <http://www.Best-buy.com> (accessed 29 October 2003).

12. "Appliances Triples Profit," *Christchurch Press,* New Zealand, 9 November 2002.

13. An English gentleman visiting India at the turn of the century recalled in his memoirs, "[An elephant] takes a great deal of feeding with expensive fodder. When he gets a sore back it is an enormous thing to deal with; and when he dies, he is an awful clog on the sanitary arrangements." Sir Robert Baden-Powell, "Memories of India," <www.pinetreeweb. com/bp-memories14.htm> (accessed 29 October 2003).

14. "Fractional Jet Ownership," <http://www.fractionaljetownership.com/content/ history.html> (accessed 29 October 2003).

15. George Kiebala, telephone interview by author, tape recording, 19 February 2003.

16. Exotic Car Share Web page, <http://www.exoticcarshare.com> (accessed 29 October 2003).

17. Kiebala interview, 19 February 2003.

18. Ibid.

19. Vicki Parker, "Floating an Idea," *News and Observer* (Raleigh), 23 April 2002. Similarly, an Australian venture named Peter Hansen Yacht Brokers offers a 7.1 percent holding in a boat for about U.S. $24,000, which entitles buyers to twenty-one days of use annually. "A Piece of the Boating Action for a Fraction of the Cost," *Gold Coast Bulletin* (Queensland, Australia), 20 September 2002.

20. Jonathan Heller, "Ticket Plan Set for New Ballpark," *San Diego Union-Tribune,* 23 June 2002.

21. Elizabeth Razzi, "Prime Time," *Kiplinger's Personal Finance,* August 2002.

22. Private Retreats Web page, <http://www.private-retreats.com/locations/tortola. htm> (accessed 29 October 2003).

23. Exclusive Resorts advertisement copy, *Wall Street Journal,* 30 January 2004, W13.

24. Razzi, "Prime Time."

25. Todd Pack, "Affluent Baby Boomers Buy Time," *Sun-Sentinel* (Florida), 25 February 2002.

26. "Sales for the Phillips Club Reach $35 Million in Two Years," *Real Estate Weekly,* 18 September 2002.

27. Benjamin Franklin, in his 1758 best-seller *The Way to Wealth,* summed up the social mores of his time, admonishing, "Many a one, for the Sake of Finery on the Back, have gone with a hungry Belly, and half starved their Families . . . 'tis as truly Folly for the Poor to ape the Rich, as for the Frog to swell, in order to equal the Ox."

28. John Gallagher, "Consumers Are Carrying $1.6 Trillion in Credit," *Detroit Free Press,* 26 December 2001.

29. Naedine Joy Hazell, "Diners Club Gets Its Due Credit," *Hartford Courant,* 25 July 2000.

30. Zipcar Web page, <http://www.zipcar.com/press/> (accessed 29 October 2003).

31. Marcia Myers, "Wheels at Will," *Baltimore Sun,* 28 May 2002.

32. Zipcar, "Zipping Away from the Heat of Another Summer in the City Is Now Fast, Easy, and Affordable," press release, 23 May 2002.

33. Nancy Rosenzweig, telephone interview by author, tape recording, 4 March 2003. Subsequent quotations in this section were from the same interview.

34. Rob Turner, "Luxury to Let," *Money Magazine,* July 2002, 114.

35. *Wall Street Journal,* advertisement, 24 January 2003.

36. Virginia Center for the Creative Arts Web page, <http://www.vcca.com/artleasing.html> (accessed 5 November 2003).

37. Richard Craver, "Furniture Industry Contemplates Retail Leasing," *High Point Enterprise* (N.C.), 15 December 2001.

38. Jane Spencer, "How Much Is Your Time Worth?" *Wall Street Journal,* 28 February 2003.

39. Wendy Cole Columbus, "Personal Chefs: Busy Households Are Hiring Pros to Cook for Them at Home," *Time,* 8 April 2002, 15; and Personal Chefs Network Web page, <http://www.personalchefsnetwork.com/index.html> (accessed 29 October 2003).

40. Jane Boaz, "Personal Chef Services: A Personal Career Choice for Entrepreneurial Chefs," *Global Chefs,* May 2002, <http://www.globalchefs.com/career/current/coj013per.htm> (accessed 13 February 2004).

41. Lew Sichelman, "FHFB Says Average Home Price Approaching 300K in Top Markets," *National Mortgage News,* 21 October 2002.

42. Ibid.

43. John Gourville and Dilip Soman, "Pricing and the Psychology of Consumption," *Harvard Business Review* (September 2002): 90.

44. Christian Mathieu, telephone interview by author, tape recording, 28 March 2003.

45. Linda Hales, "Jeepers Keepers," *Washington Post,* 21 September 2002.

46. Susan B. Garland, "Making Social Security More Women-Friendly," *Business-Week,* 22 May 2000, 103.

47. Mathieu interview, 28 March 2003.

48. This recalls the importance of the Diderot effect on consumption, whereby consumers seek uniformity in the quality and value of their possessions.

49. Sarah Robertson, "Out with the New," *Wall Street Journal,* 6 June 2003.

50. Rachel Emma Silverstein, "Nu 5BR/4BA Home, Perfect to Tear Down," *Wall Street Journal,* 20 August 2003.

51. Stuart Elliott, "IKEA Challenges Attachment to Old Stuff," *New York Times,* 16 September 2002.

52. Mathieu interview, 28 March 2003.

53. Elliott, "IKEA Challenges."

54. Mathieu interview, 28 March 2003. Subsequent quotations in this section were from the same interview.

55. Jack Wayman, "From '22 to '02," *Dealerscope* 44 (October 2002): 10.

56. Steve Caulk, "Gearing Up for Gadgets," *Rocky Mountain News,* 6 January 2003.

57. Ibid.

58. Wayman, "From '22 to '02."

59. Betsy Spethmann, "Shutter Shudder," *Promo,* January 2002, 2.

60. Randolph Picht, "Kodak Introduces Two Disposable Cameras, New Film," Associates Press, 18 April 1989; and Dorothy Leonard-Barton, et al., "How to Integrate Work and Deepen Expertise," *Harvard Business Review* (September–October 1994): 121.

61. Picht, "Kodak Introduces."

62. David Gussow, "2002 Holiday Gadget Guide," *St. Petersburg Times*, 2 December 2002.

63. Borja de la Cierva Alvarez de Sotomayor, interview in Madrid by Luk van Wassenhove, Daniel Guide, and Vadim Gritsay, 12 March 2002.

64. Ibid.

65. Tracy Mullin, quoted in Miguel Helft, "Fashion Fast Forward," *Business 2.0*, May 2002, 60–66.

66. De la Cierva interview, 12 March 2002.

67. Helft, "Fashion Fast Forward."

68. Robert Murphy, "The Far Reaches of Fast Fashion," *Women's Wear Daily*, 4 February 2003.

69. Ibid.

70. De la Cierva interview, 12 March 2002.

71. Helft, "Fashion Fast Forward."

72. Verne Kopytoff, "The eBay Logic," *San Francisco Chronicle*, 1 December 2002.

73. Richard Rayner, "An Actual Internet Success Story," *New York Times*, 9 June 2002.

74. Ibid.

75. Mark O'Keefe, "Donating Car No Smooth Ride," *New Orleans Times-Picayune*, 8 September 2002.

76. Eric Auchard, "Dell Faces Tough Market for Recycling," Reuters, 19 January 2003.

77. For more detail on how increasing the effectiveness of resale can speed sales and accelerate markets, see Paul Nunes and Julia Kirby, "What Goes Around Comes Around," *Outlook* (published by Accenture), no. 1 (January 2000): 37–41.

78. Deborah Snow Humiston, "A New Breed of Butler," *Chicago Tribune*, 12 April 2002.

Chapter 6

1. Amazon Web page, <http://www.amazon.com/exec/obidos/tg/detail/-/0253213495/qid=1046889919/sr=1-1/ref=sr_1_1/103-0933758-5970219?v=glance&s=books> (accessed 29 October 2003).

2. Rotten Tomatoes Web page, <http://rottentomatoes.com> (accessed 29 October 2003).

3. Christopher D. Carroll, "Why Do the Rich Save So Much?" working paper 6549, National Bureau of Economic Research, Cambridge, May 1998, <http://papers.nber.org/papers/W6549> (accessed 12 February 2004).

4. Karen E. Dynan, Jonathan Skinner, and Stephen P. Zeldes, "Do the Rich Save More?" working paper 7906, National Bureau of Economic Research, Cambridge, September 2000. Available at <http://papers.nber.org/papers/w7906> (accessed 13 February 2004).

5. Carroll, "Why Do the Rich Save So Much?"

6. Robert H. Frank, "Does Growing Inequality Harm the Middle Class?" *Eastern Economic Journal* 26, no. 3 (summer 2000): 251–264.

7. Chris O'Malley, "Dividend Stocks Return to Favor," *Indianapolis Star*, 17 January 2003.

8. *American Heritage Dictionary of the English Language*, 4th ed., s.v. "dividend." (New York: Houghton Mifflin Company, 2000).

9. Margery Myers, interview by author at Talbots headquarters, Hingham, MA, 28 March 2003.

10. Ibid.

11. Ibid.

12. The Robinson-Patman Act, for example, prohibits deep price discounts that would give larger firms an unfair advantage over smaller competitors and inhibit "free enterprise," since small companies may lack the economics of scale to buy in bulk and match such levels. For example, Wanda Borges, "Antitrust in the Internet Era," *Business Credit,* 1 November 2002, explains: "Section 3 of the Robinson-Patman Act (15 U.S.C. [section] 13[a]) provides criminal liability for any person who discriminates through the use of discounts, rebates, allowances or advertising service charges, or by selling at unreasonably low prices to destroy competition or a competitor. This section, technically, is not an 'antitrust' law."

13. Mike Fine, "NE Ski Areas Put Jeep Owners in Driver's Seat," *Patriot-Ledger* (Quincy, MA), 17 January 2002.

14. Peter Francese, "The College-Cash Connection," *American Demographics,* 1 March 2002, 42–43.

15. U.S. Bureau of Labor Statistics, "Consumer Expenditure Survey 1984 to 2001," <http://www.bls.gov/cex/csxstnd.htm> (accessed 5 November 2003).

16. Daniel Golden, "For Supreme Court, Affirmative Action Isn't Just Academic: Five Justices or Their Kids Are College 'Legacies'; Another Admissions Aid," *Wall Street Journal,* 14 May 2003.

17. U.S. Department of Education, National Center for Education Statistics, *Digest of Education Statistics,* Table 359 "Participation in Adult Education During the Previous 12 Months by Adults 17 Years Old and Older, by Selected Characteristics of Participants," 2001, 404–405.

18. Skip Barber Racing School Web page, <http://www.skipbarber.com/drivingschool/default.asp?sel=> (accessed 7 February 2004).

19. Mary K. Nolan, "Take a Frying Saucier and Head to the Big Leagues," *Hamilton Spectator* (Ontario), 23 March 2002.

20. JoAnna Daemmrich, "Gourmet Getaways," *Baltimore Sun,* 26 June 2002.

21. Tony Ku, "Cooking School, Resorts Offer a Lesson on Cooking," *Business Journal* 23 (17 January 2003): 23.

22. Ibid.

23. U.S. Department of Education, National Center for Education Statistics, "Education Directory, Colleges and Universities" Web page, <http://nces.ed.gov/pubs2002/digest2001/tables/dt244.asp> (accessed 29 October 2003).

24. Daniel Golden and Matthew Rose, "Kaplan Transforms into Big Operator of Trade Schools," *Wall Street Journal,* 7 November 2003.

25. David Brooks, "The Organization Kid," *Atlantic Monthly,* 1 April 2001, 40.

26. Ibid.

27. Peter Van Sant, "Time Out," *CBS Sunday Morning,* CBS Broadcasting, Inc., 12 May 2002.

28. Liz Seymour, "Seeking Tutors to Get Ahead and Not Just to Catch Up," *Newsbytes,* 29 November 2002.

29. Robert King, "New Centers Tutor Kids for a Price," *St. Petersburg Times,* 22 July 2002.

30. Lisa Gubernick, "This Camp Sure Grades Tough," *Wall Street Journal,* 21 February 2003.

31. Ibid.

32. EPM Communications, "Consumers Pamper Themselves in Small Ways," EPM Communications Research Alert press release, 20 December 2002.

33. Nick Sortal, "Ahead of the Game: Parents Are Taking Young, Focused Athletes to Private Tutors," *Fort Lauderdale Sun-Sentinel*, 29 September 2002.

34. Clint Williams, "Business Niche in Athletic Edge," *Atlanta Journal-Constitution*, 29 November 2002.

35. Sortal, "Ahead of the Game."

36. Gary Becker, *Accounting for Tastes* (Boston: Harvard University Press, 1998), 153–154.

37. Readers who feel that this analysis reduces too many family emotions to economic terms will take heart that Becker admits his research has some limitations—for example, not taking into account "the behavior of children—such as crying and acting 'cute'—that tries, in turn, to influence the attitudes of parents."

38. Bartleby Web page, <http://www.bartleby.com/66/55/20755.html> (accessed 29 October 2003).

39. U.S. Bureau of Labor Statistics, "Consumer Expenditure Survey."

40. Mayrav Saar and Debbie Talanian, "More Check Out Nouveau Checkups," *Orange County Register*, 12 January 2003.

41. Lewis Braham, "Laser Eye Surgery: Take a Second Look," *BusinessWeek*, 20 May 2002, 140.

42. Trebor Banstetter, "Vanity Medicine Lags as Economy Sags," *Fort-Worth Star Telegram*, 11 February 2001.

43. Linda Jenkins, "Fitness Gets Personal," *Atlanta Journal-Constitution*, 3 January 2002.

44. Nancy Ann Jeffrey, "The Bionic Boomer," *Wall Street Journal*, 22 August 2003.

45. Saar and Talanian, "More Check Out Nouveau Check Ups."

46. Patricia Callahan, "Scaning for Trouble," *Wall Street Journal*, 10 September 2003.

47. Gail Edmondson, et al. "Classy Cars: Why Everyone Wants to Make Luxury Autos," *BusinessWeek*, 24 March 2003, 62.

48. Roberta Bernstein, "Navigating the Attitudes of Luxury," *Brandweek*, 19 April 1999.

49. Patek-Philippe, "The Inauguration of the Patek-Philippe Museum," press release, November 2001.

50. Neal McChristy, "The Ultimate Writing Experience," *Office Solutions*, 1 November 2001, 31.

51. Ibid.

52. Terence A. Shimp and William O. Bearden, "Warranty and Other Extrinsic Cue Effects on Consumers' Risk Perceptions," *Journal of Consumer Research* 9 (June 1982): 38.

53. Allen-Edmonds Web page, <https://www.allenedmonds.com/webapp/wcs/stores/servlet/AEOnLineStore?langId=-1&krypto=09xWFXbsP4zz%2BkM8qdKxnk128vwvw5QDx6FjZlJedWVhY7em6YWC2ID6bNGJKszi%0A> (accessed 30 October 2003).

54. Louis Ripple, telephone interview by author, tape recording, 19 February 2003. Subsequent quotes are from this interview.

55. Philip Siekman, "The Last of the Big Shoemakers," *Fortune*, 30 April 2001, 154.

56. Porsche Web page, <http://www3.us.porsche.com/english/usa/preownedcars/default.htm> (accessed 12 November 2003).

Chapter 7

1. Walter Goodman, "Nonfiction in Brief," review of *The Bon Marché: Bourgeois Culture and the Department Store*, by Michael B. Miller, *New York Times*, 17 May 1981.

2. Ibid.

3. University of Virginia, American Studies Program, "Pre-Department Stores," hypertext link, <http://xroads.virginia.edu/~HYPER/INCORP/stores/PartonePredeptstore. html> (accessed 30 October 2003).

4. The lavish window displays of the time reminded passersby of the luxuries that remained just out of their reach and gave rise to the expression "window shoppers," from the more vivid French original *leche vitrine,* or "window lickers." This term today seems equally evocative of the behavior of affluent consumers as they drool over granite counter tops and plasma-screen TVs.

5. Robert Tamilia, quoted in Goodman, "Nonfiction in Brief."

6. According to the National Retail Federation, conventional department stores and discount department stores had equal market share in 1992. But conventional stores' share has since fallen to just over 39 percent, whereas discount stores rose to nearly 61 percent in 2001. To better understand the dominance of discount stores, consider that Wal-Mart alone now accounts for 60 percent of American retail sales and nearly 8 percent of overall national consumer spending, excluding cars and white goods. See "Wal Around the World," *The Economist,* 8 December 2001; and Brenda Lloyd, "Majors Seek Alternative Retail Formats," *Daily News Record* (New York), 26 August 2002.

7. Clearly, the lower and middle classes are the primary customers for discount retailers. Of Wal-Mart's 110 million weekly customers, for example, 70 million earn between $25,000 and $50,000 a year (Constance L. Hays, "Enriched by Working Class, Wal-Mart Eyes BMW Crowd," *New York Times,* 24 February 2002). Few low-end customers now shop anywhere else. According to Levi Strauss, more than 160 million people in the United States shop in mass-merchandise stores, but fewer than 10 percent of these consumers also shop in higher-end stores (Sally Beatty, "Wal-Mart to Neiman Marcus Is Jeans Maker's New Goal," *Wall Street Journal,* 31 October 2002).

8. Our belief is that, although retailers have struggled with multiple approaches to selling since the time of Boucicaut, today's channels must become a seamless flow of value-added activities designed to serve the behavior of customers, not demographic segments. In this way marketers best serve the moneyed masses, by identifying them not by their pocketbooks, but by shopping behaviors distinct to them. See Paul Nunes and Frank Cespedes, "The Customer Has Escaped," *Harvard Business Review* (November 2003): 31, for more on multichannel selling.

9. "Cheers to One Hundred Years: Twentieth Century Timeline," *Shopping Center World,* December 1999.

10. Terry McEwen, telephone interview by author, tape recording, 18 February 2003.

11. Ibid.

12. Ibid.

13. Eddie Baeb, "Upstart Mall Holds Its Own," *Crain's Chicago Business,* 8 July 2002, 3.

14. McEwen interview, 18 February 2003.

15. Ibid.

16. Susan Reda, "Lifestyle Centers Emerge as Solution to Monotony of Traditional Malls," *Stores Magazine,* August 2002, <https://www.stores.org/archives/aug02edit.asp> (accessed 16 February 2004).

17. McEwen interview, 18 February 2003.

18. Reda, "Lifestyle Centers."

19. McEwen interview, 18 February 2003.

20. "Saks Looks Outside the Mall, Plans Lifestyle Center Stores," *Home Furnishings News,* 6 January 2003, 10.

21. Daniel Henninger, "Mall of America Still Home for Shop till You Drop," *Wall Street Journal,* 3 October 2003.

22. Laura Heller, "Best Buy Enters Manhattan, Tests New Store Initiatives," *DSN Retailing Today,* 24 June 2002.

23. Jim Ostroff, "Saturated Markets Force a Retail Scramble," *Kiplinger Business Forecasts,* 1 May 2002.

24. ASD/AMD merchandise Group Web site, <http://www.merchandisegroup.com/password/archive/050602.shtml> (accesed 2 November 2003).

25. Gary Dymski, "Home Work," *New York Newsday,* 25 July 2002.

26. The Home Depot Web page, <http://ir.homedepot.com/reports.cfm> (accessed 30 October 2003).

27. Mary Ellen Lloyd, "Home Depot CEO: Store Modernization Will Double In '04," *Dow Jones Business News,* 16 January 2004.

28. Tony Wilbert, "Home Depot's Expo Centers to Get Overhaul," *Atlanta Journal-Constitution,* 22 January 2003.

29. John R. McMillin, quoted in Constance L. Hays, "Enriched by Working Class, Wal-Mart Eyes BMW Crowd," *New York Times,* 24 February 2002.

30. Laura Heller, "Wal-Mart, Target Open 95 in October," *DSN Retailing Today,* 28 October 2002.

31. Matthew Grimm, "Target Hits Its Mark," *American Demographics,* 1 November 2002, 10.

32. Target, Annual Report 2002.

33. "2002 America's Most Admired Companies," *Fortune,* 3 March 2003, 81.

34. L. L. Braser, "A Warehouse Store of Their Own," *Detroit Free Press,* 21 December 2002.

35. Ibid.

36. George Sinegal, quoted in Judy Hevrdejs, "Theater of the Absurdly Large," *Chicago Tribune,* 16 February 2003.

37. Ibid.

38. Hays, "Enriched By Working Class."

39. Thomas M. Coughlin, quoted in Margaret Webb Pressler, "Discount Nation," *Washington Post,* 23 December 2001.

40. Terry Savage, "Terry Savage Talks Money with Arthur Martinez," *Chicago Sun-Times,* 29 April 2001.

41. Alice Z. Cuneo, "Sears Accentuates Its Harder Side," *Advertising Age,* 21 February 2000, 62.

42. Arthur Martinez, *The Hard Road to the Softer Side: Lessons from the Transformation of Sears* (New York: Crown Business, 2001); quoted in Susan Chandler, "Designers Finding Their Target," *Chicago Tribune,* 19 August 2001.

43. Tracie Rozhon, "A Bored Shopper's Lament: Seen a Store, Seen Them All," *New York Times,* 4 January 2003.

44. Somlynn Rorie, "Organics Reach New Heights with Mainstream and Natural Retailers," *Organic & Natural News,* November 2000.

45. "Organic Growth," *Chain Store Age Executive* 77 (May 2001): 70.

46. Barry Janoff, "Food Marketing," *Brandweek,* 30 April 2001.

47. Luisa Kroll, "A Fresh Face," *Forbes,* 8 July 2002, 48.

48. Ibid.

49. Gary McWilliams and Ann Zimmerman, "Dell Plans to Peddle PCs Inside Sears, Other Large Chains," *Wall Street Journal,* 30 January 2003.

50. Ibid.

51. Ibid.

52. Katarzyna Moreno, "Unbecoming," *Forbes,* 10 June 2002, 46.

53. Chris Reidy, "Stop & Shop's Next Generation," *Boston Globe,* 7 November 2002.

54. Elizabeth Sanger, "Toy Sellers Play for Sales," *Chicago Tribune,* 19 December 2001.

55. Scott C. Friend and Patricia Walker, "Welcome to the New World of Merchandising," *Harvard Business Review* (November 2001): 3.

56. Tweeter, third-quarter earnings call, Fair Disclosure Wire, 25 July 2002.

57. Accenture, "Understanding Customers Leads to Store Innovation," case study of Walgreens, <http://www.accenture.com/xd/xd.asp?it=enweb&xd=industries%5Cproducts %5Cretail%5Ccase%5Creta_walgreens.xml> (accessed 30 October 2003).

58. Rob Eder, "Out-Foxing the Hedgehog's Rivals," *Drug Store News,* 25 March 2002, 24.

59. Ibid.

60. Accenture, "Understanding Customers"; and Doug Desjardins, "New Players May Shift Balance of Power Out West," *Drug Store News,* 16 December 2002, 21.

61. Friend and Walker, "Welcome to the New World."

62. Accenture, "Scientific Retailing: Bringing Science to the Art of Retail," white paper, <http://www.accenture.com/xd/xd.asp?it=enweb&xd=industries%5Cproducts%5C retail%5Creta_science.xml> (accessed 30 October 2003).

63. Friend and Walker, "Welcome to the New World."

64. D. C. Denison, "Tweeter Center's 'Reserved Lawn' a Sign of the Times," *Boston Globe,* 30 June 2002.

65. Carol Mongo, "France's Oldest Shopping Paradise," *Paris Voice Magazine,* May 2002, <http://parisvoice.com/02/may/html/art1.cfm> (accessed 16 February 2004).

Chapter 8

1. Howard Reill, "The Appeal of Scotch: Blending Tradition with New Product Variations, Scotch Suppliers Try to Bring New Customers to the Category," *Beverage Dynamics* 114 (1 March 2002): 30.

2. Research by Roper ASW finds word of mouth increasingly important to consumer decision making. More information about this trend and how influencers affect consumer decision making can be found in Jon Berry and Ed Keller, *The Influentials* (New York: Free Press, 2003); Emanuel Rosen, *The Anatomy of Buzz* (New York: Random House, 2002); and Malcolm Gladwell, *The Tipping Point* (Boston: Back Bay Books, 2002).

3. Michael T. Elliott and Paul Surgi Speck, "Consumer Perceptions of Advertising Clutter and Its Impact Across Various Media," *Journal of Advertising Research* 38, no.1 (1998): 29.

4. For a more complete discussion, see ibid.

5. Captivate Network, "Major Corporate Advertisers Choose Captivate Network"; and "Nielsen Study Shows Captivate Network Delivers 45% Average Ad Recall," press releases, 23 September 2002 and 27 May 2002.

6. Captivate has a 45 percent recall rate, according to Nielsen Media Research, "Pilot Intercept Study," January/February 2002. Captivate Network press release, 27 May 2002, <http://www.captivatenetwork.com/news/news.asp?ID=210> (accessed 16 February 2004).

7. Michael DiFranza, telephone interview by author, tape recording, 4 November 2003. Subsequent quotes are from this interview.

8. Pamela Paul, "Advertisers Climb on Board," *American Demographics*, 27 September 2002, 9.

9. Ibid.

10. Robert Gutsche Jr., "(Work)Space Available—for a Price: From Coffee Cups to Desktop Mouse Pads to Bathroom Stalls, Advertisements Are Showing Up More Frequently in the Office," *Chicago Tribune*, 14 September 2003.

11. Thomas J. Stanley, *Marketing to the Affluent* (New York: McGraw Hill, 1998), 186.

12. Suzanne Carbone, "Using the Hard Sell, with a View to Make a Killing," *Melbourne Age* (Melbourne, Australia), 12 December 2002.

13. Allyson Stewart-Allen, "Product Placement Helps Sell Brand," *Marketing News*, 15 February 1999.

14. Brian Steinberg and Suzanne Vranica, "Prime-Time TV's New Guest Stars: Products," *Wall Street Journal*, 12 January 2004.

15. Shelley Branch, "Saks Steal Scene from Neiman's in Movie," *Wall Street Journal*, 26 September 2003.

16. Trista Vincent, "The Fast and the Frivolous," *Boards*, 1 November 2002.

17. Ibid.

18. Alyson Ward, "Underhanded Pitches," *Fort Worth Star Telegram*, 8 September 2002.

19. Stephen Battaglio, "Top Earner$ Bolster NBC," *New York Daily News*, 20 November 2002.

20. For ABC's move down-market, see Emily Nelson and Bruce Orwall, "Change of Season," *Wall Street Journal*, 13 September 2002. For NBC's decisions, see Joe Flint, "Prime Time: How NBC Defies Network Norms—to Its Advantage," *Wall Street Journal*, 20 May 2002.

21. Flint, "Prime Time."

22. "In Praise of the Donald," *Economist*, 14 February 2004, <http://www.economist.com/people/displayStory.cfm?story_id=2424133> (accessed 16 March 2004).

23. Flint, "Prime Time."

24. Pat Nason, "Marketplace Has Fun with Money," United Press International, 1 November 2002.

25. Philip Kotler, *Marketing Management* (New York: Prentice Hall, 1997), 645.

26. Ekaterina O. Walsh, "Selling Luxury to the Affluent Online," *Forrester Research*, March 2001.

27. Howard Millman, "Customers Tire of Excuses for Rebates That Never Arrive," *New York Times*, 17 April 2003.

28. Maria Halkias, "Merchant Prince Made Neiman's 'The Store,'" *Dallas Morning News*, 23 January 2002.

29. Jenny King, "Goodwill Hunting," *Chicago Tribune*, 9 December 1999.

30. AMCI Web page, <http://www.amcitesting.com/taste.htm> (accessed 30 October 2003).

31. Jeffrey Steele, "Kendall-Jackson: In a Glass by Itself," *Point of Purchase* 7 (July 2001): 12.

32. Ibid.

33. Paul Lukas, "Party Like It's 1951," *Fortune Small Business*, 23 June 2003, 118.

34. Ibid. Tupper also made Wise his vice president in charge of in-home sales that year, and she went on to become the first woman to appear on the cover of *BusinessWeek*.

35. Longaberger Web page, <http://www.longaberger.com/cgi-bin/bv/ourStory/our_story.jsp?BV_SessionID=@@@@0623929403.1076430492@@@@&BV_EngineID=ccchad ckjdihmmhcfngcfkmdgfhdgfi.0&datetime=02%2f10%2f04+11%3a28%3a47+AM&chan nelID=-536879785> (accessed 10 February 2004).

36. Southern Living At HOME, "Fall 2003 Catalog Unveiled," press release, 24 July 2003.

37. Shelly Branch, "Catwalk to Coffee Table," *Wall Street Journal*, 7 November 2003.

38. Terrill Yue Jones, "Cadillac Propelled by 'slade Star Power," *Los Angeles Times*, 24 November 2002.

39. Edward Goldman, telephone interview by author, tape recording, 19 March 2003.

40. Terry McEwen, telephone interview by author, tape recording, 18 February 2003.

41. US Open Web page, <http://www.usopen.org/en_US/about/sponsors_heineken. html> (accessed 5 November 2003).

42. Rich Thomaselli, "Open Season," *Advertising Age*, 27 August 2001.

43. "Marketers of the Year: It's All About the Beer Ads," *Brandweek*, 16 October 2000.

44. Ibid.

45. US Open Web page, <http://www.usopen.org/about/sponsors_heineken.html> (accessed 9 April 2003).

46. A term that gained momentum with Thomas J. Peters's book *The Pursuit of Wow!* (New York: Vintage Books, 1994).

47. Jonah Bloom, "Upstart JetBlue Marketer of the Year," *Advertising Age*, 9 December 2002, S2.

48. Gareth Edmonson-Jones, quoted in ibid.

49. Ibid.

50. Ibid.

51. JetBlue, "JetBlue Is Best US Airline Say *Condé Nast Traveler* Readers," press release, 4 November 2002.

52. Procter & Gamble Web page, <http://charmin.com/en_us/pages/whatsnew.shtml> (accessed 7 November 2003).

53. Lynn Knight, quoted in Bill Sweetman, "And Then There Were Three," *Air Transport World*, 1 February 2001.

54. For the added cost of Coach detailing, see "Coach and Lexus Renew Partnership to Produce Coach Edition ES 300; 2001 Model to Be Unveiled At Detroit Auto Show," *PR Newswire*, 4 January 2001. For an overview of the joint venture, see Incentive Performance Center Web page, <http://incentivecentral.org/IPC/frames.asp?page=/IPC/casestudies.asp> (accessed 30 October 2003).

55. Ki Ho Park, "Making Handsets Do Handsprings," *BusinessWeek*, 8 July 2002, 50.

56. Gerry Khermouch, "The Best Global Brands," *BusinessWeek*, 5 August 2002, 92.

Chapter 9

1. "No Need to Envy the Upper-Crusters When You Expect to Be One of Them," *Adweek* 44, no. 13 (March 31, 2003): 31.

2. Earnings are of men by age, adjusted for educational level where possible: U.S. Bureau of the Census Current Population Reports Consumer Income P60-009, Distribution of Persons 14 Years of Age and Over By Total Money Income, By Age, Sex, and Veteran Status, for the United States, Urban and Rural: 1950 Table 18, p. 25, <http://www2.census. gov/prod2/popscan/P60-009.pdf> (accessed 8 March 2004) and U.S. Bureau of the Cen-

sus Current Population Reports Consumer Income P60-200, Money Income in the United States: 1997 (With Separate Data on Valuation of Noncash Benefits), Educational Attainment—Total Money Earnings in 1997 of People 18 Years Old and Over by Age, Work Experience in 1997, and Gender Table 9, p. 54, <http://www.census.gov/prod/3/98pubs/p60-200.pdf> (accessed 8 March 2004).

3. U.S. Census Bureau and University of Michigan data reported on by W. Michael Cox and Richard Alm, *Myths of Rich and Poor* (New York: Basic Books, 1999) 76–77.

4. Ibid., 85.

5. John J. Havens and Paul G. Schervish, "Why the $41 Trillion Wealth Transfer Estimate Is Still Valid: A Review of Challenges and Questions," *Journal of Gift Planning* 7, no. 1 (2003): 11–15, 47–50.

6. Alberto Alesina, Rafael DiTella, and Robert MacCulloch, "Inequality and Happiness: Are Europeans and Americans Different?" working paper 02-084, Harvard Business School, Boston, revised June 2002.

7. Charles Handy, *The Elephant and the Flea: Reflections of a Reluctant Capitalist* (Boston: Harvard Business School Press, 2002), 133.

8. Some offerings move even more quickly to the masses because they must be delivered on a considerable scale if they are to be worthwhile, yet they are only truly profitable on the margins from the highest-spending customers (who are not always, but often the most affluent). Airlines, retail banking, and telecommunications are just some examples of offerings that depend on scale. Home grocery delivery is one example of such a service that may come around again, with benefits to countless marginally profitable customers, once a model is devised that rapidly achieves scale and drives sufficient margin from the biggest spenders.

9. G. K. Chesterton, *Commonwealth*, 1933, The American Chesterton Society Web site <http://www.chesterton.org/acs/quotes.htm> (accessed March 19, 2004).

10. Kimmori Matsuyama, "The Rise of Mass Consumption Societies," *Journal of Political Economy* 110 (October 2002): 1035–1070.

11. Ibid.

Epilogue

1. U.S. Bureau of Labor Statistics, "Consumer Expenditure Survey 1984 to 2001," <http://www.bls.gov/cex/csxstnd.htm> (accessed 5 November 2003).

2. Bellman's Jewelers, "Gold Notes," *Bellman's Jewelry News* (citing Research International, *Gold Acquisition Study 1997*, conducted exclusively for the World Gold Council), summer 1998, <http://bellmans.com/summer98.htm> (accessed 30 October 2003).

3. Robert H. Frank, "Does Growing Inequality Harm the Middle Class?" *Eastern Economic Journal* 26 (summer 2000): 251–264.

4. Timex Web page, <http://www.timexpo.com/timeline10.html> (accessed 12 February 2004).

5. Slow Twitch Web page, <http://www.slowtwitch.com/mainheadings/features/state.html> (accessed 30 October 2003).

6. Tracie Rozhon, "It's Comeback Time For Luxury Watches," *New York Times*, 6 January 2004.

7. Emiko Terazono, "The Value of Quality Time with the Family," *Financial Times* (London), 13 January 2004.

8. Blythe Yee, "Ads Remind Women They Have Two Hands," *Wall Street Journal*, 14 August 2003.

Index

About the Authors

PAUL NUNES is an executive research fellow in Accenture's Institute for High Performance Business, where he directs research on marketing strategy. His research focuses on the impact of technology on marketing practice and consumer behavior. His research results and frameworks have been used extensively in Accenture's strategy work and service offerings. During his eighteen years at Accenture, Nunes has served as a consultant to clients and as a founding member of both the company's Institute for High Performance Business and its Technology Assessment Group. He earned his M.A. in Management from the Kellogg School of Management at Northwestern University, and a B.S. in Computer Science from Northwestern University. A trustee of the Marketing Science Institute, Mr. Nunes has authored several book chapters on CRM. He is also the author of numerous articles in the *Harvard Business Review* and other leading management publications.

BRIAN JOHNSON is a senior research analyst at Sanford C. Bernstein in New York City, covering the automobile industry. Prior to his tenure on Wall Street, he spent twenty years in strategy consulting. At Accenture, he led the marketing strategy practice, helping major clients in a wide range of industries improve business performance. Before joining Accenture, he was a partner at McKinsey & Company. Mr. Johnson has also been an Adjunct Professor of Marketing at Northwestern University's Kellogg School of Management, where he developed the first course on CRM ever offered at a major business school. He received a B.S. from Stanford University and a J.D. from Harvard Law School, where he was a member of the *Harvard Law Review*.